Data-Intensive Workflow Management

For Clouds and Data-Intensive and Scalable Computing Environments

Synthesis Lectures on Data Management

Editor
H.V. Jagadish, *University of Michigan*

Founding Editor
M. Tamer Özsu, *University of Waterloo*

Synthesis Lectures on Data Management is edited by H.V. Jagadish of the University of Michigan. The series publishes 80–150 page publications on topics pertaining to data management. Topics include query languages, database system architectures, transaction management, data warehousing, XML and databases, data stream systems, wide scale data distribution, multimedia data management, data mining, and related subjects.

Data-Intensive Workflow Management: For Clouds and Data-Intensive and Scalable Computing Environments
Daniel C. M. de Oliveira, Ji Liu, and Esther Pacitti
2019

Transaction Processing on Modern Hardware
Mohammad Sadoghi and Spyros Blanas
2019

Data Management in Machine Learning Systems
Matthias Boehm, Arun Kumar, and Jun Yang
2019

Non-Volatile Memory Database Management Systems
Joy Arulraj and Andrew Pavlo
2019

Scalable Processing of Spatial-Keyword Queries
Ahmed R. Mahmood and Walid G. Aref
2019

Data Exploration Using Example-Based Methods
Matteo Lissandrini, Davide Mottin, Themis Palpanas, and Yannis Velegrakis
2018

Data-Intensive Workflow Management:
For Clouds and Data-Intensive and Scalable Computing Environments
Daniel C. M. de Oliveira, Ji Liu, and Esther Pacitti

ISBN: 978-3-031-00744-6   paperback
ISBN: 978-3-031-01872-5   ebook
ISBN: 978-3-031-00099-7   hardcover

DOI 10.1007/978-3-031-01872-5

A Publication in the Springer series
SYNTHESIS LECTURES ON DATA MANAGEMENT

Lecture #60
Series Editor: H.V. Jagadish, *University of Michigan*
Founding Editor: M. Tamer Özsu, *University of Waterloo*
Series ISSN
Print 2153-5418   Electronic 2153-5426

Data-Intensive Workflow Management

For Clouds and Data-Intensive and Scalable Computing Environments

Daniel C. M. de Oliveira
Universidade Federal Fluminense

Ji Liu
University of Montpellier, Inria & CNRS

Esther Pacitti
University of Montpellier, Inria & CNRS

SYNTHESIS LECTURES ON DATA MANAGEMENT #60

ABSTRACT

Workflows may be defined as abstractions used to model the coherent flow of activities in the context of an *in silico* scientific experiment. They are employed in many domains of science such as bioinformatics, astronomy, and engineering. Such workflows usually present a considerable number of activities and activations (i.e., tasks associated with activities) and may need a long time for execution. Due to the continuous need to store and process data efficiently (making them data-intensive workflows), high-performance computing environments allied to parallelization techniques are used to run these workflows. At the beginning of the 2010s, cloud technologies emerged as a promising environment to run scientific workflows. By using clouds, scientists have expanded beyond single parallel computers to hundreds or even thousands of virtual machines.

More recently, Data-Intensive Scalable Computing (DISC) frameworks (e.g., Apache Spark and Hadoop) and environments emerged and are being used to execute data-intensive workflows. DISC environments are composed of processors and disks in large-commodity computing clusters connected using high-speed communications switches and networks. The main advantage of DISC frameworks is that they support and grant efficient in-memory data management for large-scale applications, such as data-intensive workflows. However, the execution of workflows in cloud and DISC environments raise many challenges such as scheduling workflow activities and activations, managing produced data, collecting provenance data, etc.

Several existing approaches deal with the challenges mentioned earlier. This way, there is a real need for understanding how to manage these workflows and various big data platforms that have been developed and introduced. As such, this book can help researchers understand how linking workflow management with Data-Intensive Scalable Computing can help in understanding and analyzing scientific big data.

In this book, we aim to identify and distill the body of work on workflow management in clouds and DISC environments. We start by discussing the basic principles of data-intensive scientific workflows. Next, we present two workflows that are executed in a single site and multi-site clouds taking advantage of provenance. Afterward, we go towards workflow management in DISC environments, and we present, in detail, solutions that enable the optimized execution of the workflow using frameworks such as Apache Spark and its extensions.

KEYWORDS

scientific workflows, cloud computing, Data-Intensive Scalable Computing, data provenance, Apache Spark

Contents

Preface

Many large-scale scientific experiments take advantage of scientific workflows to model data operations such as loading input data, data processing, data analysis, and aggregating output data. Scientific workflows allow for scientists to easily model and express the entire data processing steps and their dependencies, typically as a Directed Acyclic Graph (i.e., DAG).

As more and more data is consumed and produced in modern scientific experiments, scientific workflows become data-intensive, i.e., each execution of a workflow can generate many gigabytes (or even terabytes) of data. To process large-scale data within a reasonable time, workflows need to be executed with parallel processing techniques in distributed environments such as clouds [Vaquero et al., 2008] and DISC [Bryant, 2011] environments. This book aims at presenting a broad view of data-intensive workflow management systems in these different environments.

A Scientific Workflow Management System (SWfMS), is a complex tool to execute workflows and manage datasets in a plethora of computing environments. Several SWfMSs, e.g., Pegasus [Deelman et al., 2007], Swift/T [Wozniak et al., 2013], Kepler [Altintas et al., 2004], Sci-Cumulus [de Oliveira et al., 2010, 2012a], eScience Central [Watson, 2012], VisTrails [Callahan et al., 2006], Taverna [Wolstencroft et al., 2013], Chiron [Ogasawara et al., 2013] and SWfMS gateway frameworks such as WS-PGRADE/gUSE [Kacsuk et al., 2012] and BioinfoPortal [Ocaña et al., 2019] are now intensively used by various research communities, e.g., astronomy, biology, and computational engineering. Although there are many SWfMSs, the architecture of SWfMSs presents common features, in particular, the capability to produce a Workflow Execution Plan (WEP) from a high-level workflow specification. Most SWfMSs are composed of five layers, e.g., presentation layer, user services layer, WEP generation layer, WEP execution layer, and infrastructure layer. These five layers enable SWfMS users to design, execute, and analyze data-intensive scientific workflows throughout the workflow life cycle. Chapter 1 presents two use cases coming from different application domains (i.e., astronomy and bioinformatics) to illustrate the main motivations and identify the challenges.

Since the sequential execution of data-intensive scientific workflows may take much time, SWfMSs should enable the parallel execution of data-intensive scientific workflows and exploit vast amounts of distributed resources. Executable activations can be generated based on several types of parallelism and submitted to the execution environment according to different scheduling approaches. Chapter 2 provides the main background necessary to understand the distributed and parallel execution of data-intensive scientific workflows.

Clusters, grids, and clouds provide the ability to exploit large amounts of computing and storage resources for scientific workflow execution. These resources are owned and managed by the institutions involved in a virtual organization. Cloud computing is a trend in distributed computing and has been the subject of much hype. The vision encompasses on-demand, reliable services provided over the Internet (typically represented as a cloud) with easy access to virtually infinite computing, storage, and networking resources. Through straightforward web interfaces and at small incremental cost, users can outsource complex tasks, such as data storage, system administration, or application deployment, to huge data centers operated by cloud providers. Chapter 3 presents the fundamental concepts and solutions to execute data-intensive workflows in a single-site cloud. Here we are faced with solutions involving static and dynamic scheduling to handle data and activation scheduling and virtual machines allocation.

However, most clouds are not single-site ones. Typically, a cloud is made of several sites (or data centers), each with its resources and data. Thus, to use more resources than available at a single-site cloud or to access data at different sites, workflows could also be executed in a distributed manner at different sites. Chapter 4 presents the fundamental concepts and solutions to deploy data-intensive SWfMSs in a distributed multi-site cloud architecture. Here we are faced with more complex scheduling challenges that also takes into account data transfer among the sites.

More recently, Data-Intensive Scalable Computing (DISC) frameworks (e.g., Apache Spark and Hadoop) have emerged and are being used to execute data-intensive scientific workflows. DISC environments are composed of processors and disks in large-commodity computing clusters connected using high-speed communications switches and networks. The main advantage of DISC frameworks is that they support and grant efficient in-memory data management for data-intensive workflows. Chapter 5 illustrates interesting approaches of data-intensive SWfMSs in DISC environments. Finally, Chapter 6 concludes this book by providing interesting research perspectives.

In all chapters, we provide a general problem definition and a global view of existing solutions. We choose some relevant solutions to ensure more profound comprehension and to be able to show how performance evaluation is made in each context. The book is intended for researchers, either in eScience or not, or as a textbook for master and doctorate students.

Daniel C. M. de Oliveira, Ji Liu, and Esther Pacitti
April 2019

Acknowledgments

First, we would like to thank our series editor H. V. Jagadish, who gave us the opportunity to write this book. We would also like to thank (a lot) Diane Cerra, who provided us the necessary administrative support from our publisher, Morgan & Claypool.

We would like to acknowledge many collaborators and friends who, through their discussions with us and comments, have influenced this book: Marcos Bedo, Cristina Boeres, Vanessa Braganholo, Jose Camata, Alvaro Coutinho, Rafaelli Coutinho, Lucia Drummond, Yuri Frota, Daniel Gaspar, Thaylon Guedes, Marta Mattoso, Eduardo Ogasawara, Douglas Oliveira, Aline Paes, Fabio Porto, Vitor Silva, Renan Souza, and Patrick Valduriez. We are also profoundly apologetic to anyone we may have forgotten.

We would also like to acknowledge Universidade Federal Fluminense, Zenith team from Inria and CNRS, and the University of Montpellier for all the support they provided in doing research and writing this book.

Much of the material in this book has been presented at several conferences and events across the world. During these presentations, we have received feedback from many attendees that helped us to improve the presentations and the material in this book. We are incredibly thankful to all who have provided this generous feedback.

Finally, we would like to thank our beloved families for their love and support during the time spent writing this book.

Daniel C. M. de Oliveira, Ji Liu, and Esther Pacitti
April 2019

CHAPTER 1

Overview

The term *in silico* is used in the computational science domain to refer to something occurring "in or through a computational simulation." It was coined from the *in vivo* and *in vitro* Latin expressions as highlighted by Travassos and de Oliveira Barros [2003]. This term is used to characterize a class of scientific experiments [Deelman et al., 2009, Hey et al., 2009, 2012, Mattoso et al., 2010]: experiments that are based on complex computer simulations that perform a series of data transformations, i.e., *in silico* experiments.

Several existing large-scale scientific experiments based on simulations (henceforth named only as *experiments*) produce very large files and datasets and require huge amounts of computing resources [Francisco et al., 2017, Jacob et al., 2009, Kanzki et al., 2016, Malik and Sharma, 2014, Mushtaq et al., 2017, Ocaña et al., 2011b, Zainon and Calder, 2006] in order to produce results in a feasible time. Many of these experiments are complex (e.g., involve the exploration of thousands of parameters and in many cases use repetition structures over dozens of complex data transformations) and running such simulations becomes an open, yet important, problem. To help scientists in managing resources involved in such experiments, data-centric scientific workflows (henceforth named as *workflow*) have gained much interest over the last decade [de Oliveira et al., 2018, Raicu et al., 2008].

A workflow can be defined as an abstraction that models a process, which consists of a series of activities and its data dependencies. Workflows can be represented as a graph of activities, in which nodes correspond to data transformation activities, and arcs represent the dataflow between them. Activities are commonly associated with programs, services, and scripts that prepare, process, and analyze data.

Although workflows can be manually executed or through using scripts [Pimentel et al., 2017], they are commonly modeled, executed, monitored, and analyzed using complex software engines named Scientific Workflow Management Systems (SWfMS). SWfMSs are able to produce a Workflow Execution Plan (WEP) based on a high-level specification of the workflow. There are many available SWfMSs, as discussed by de Oliveira et al. [2018], such as Vis-Trails [Callahan et al., 2006], Kepler [Altintas et al., 2004], Taverna [Missier et al., 2010, Wolstencroft et al., 2013], Pegasus [Deelman et al., 2007, 2014, 2016], Swift/T [Wozniak et al., 2012, 2013], SciCumulus [de Oliveira et al., 2010, 2012a], Chiron [Ogasawara et al., 2013], eScience Central [Watson et al., 2010], ASKALON [Fahringer et al., 2005, 2007], Galaxy [Afgan et al., 2018], Tavaxy [Abouelhoda et al., 2012], OpenMOLE [Reuillon et al., 2015], VIEW [Lin et al., 2009], OpenAlea [Long et al., 2018, Pradal et al., 2015], and Triana [Harrison et al., 2008]).

Each SWfMS presents specific features, such as parallel execution support, semantic support, provenance management [Freire et al., 2008b], visualization mechanisms, data versioning techniques, and so on.

It is possible to find several examples of experiments in the literature that can benefit from the workflow concept such as Montage, a workflow for astronomical analysis [Jacob et al., 2009], EdgeCFD, a computational fluid dynamics experiment [de C. Coutinho et al., 2014], X-Ray crystallography analysis [Ocaña et al., 2011b], phylogenomic analysis [Ocaña et al., 2011a], evolutionary analysis [Ocaña et al., 2012b], DNA analysis at scale [Mushtaq et al., 2017], genomic analysis [Kanzki et al., 2016], pharmacophylogenomic analysis [Ocaña et al., 2012a], cancer prediction [Tan et al., 2010], phylogenetic analysis [Malik and Sharma, 2014, Ocaña et al., 2011b], physics analysis [Smith et al., 2018], and chemical analysis [Kalos and Rey, 2005, Kwon and Yoon, 2017].

Many of these workflows process and store large amounts of data; thus they require parallel execution allied to High-Performance Computing (HPC) capabilities. Clusters, grids [Foster and Kesselman, 2000] and supercomputers have been traditionally used as HPC environments to execute workflows over the last decades. However, at the beginning of the 2010s, cloud computing [Gonzalez et al., 2009, Hey, 2010, Larus, 2011, Rad et al., 2017] technologies emerged as a promising environment to execute workflows. By using clouds, scientists have expanded beyond single parallel computers to hundreds or even thousands of virtual machines and scalable storage.

Although clouds represent a step forward, more recently, Data-Intensive Scalable Computing (DISC) frameworks [Bryant, 2011] (e.g., Apache Spark[1] and Hadoop [Dean and Ghemawat, 2008] and their variations such as Twister [Ekanayake et al., 2010], Storm (stream processing framework),[2] Samza (stream processing framework),[3] and Flink (stream processing framework that can also handle batch tasks)[4] and environments have emerged and are being used to execute workflows [Mushtaq et al., 2017, Zhang et al., 2018]. DISC environments are composed of processors and disks in large-commodity computing clusters connected using high-speed communications switches and networks. The main advantage of DISC frameworks is that they support and grant efficient in-memory data management for large-scale applications, such as data-intensive workflows. However, the execution of workflows in clouds and DISC environments raise many challenges such as scheduling activities, managing produced data, collecting provenance data, and many others.

This book aims at discussing the main challenges in managing workflows in clouds— single and multi-site ones—and DISC environments. The book is written in survey style. For the three main areas that are discussed in this book, we comprehensively outline the state of the art. In all chapters, we provide a general problem definition and a global view of existing

---

[1]https://spark.apache.org/
[2]http://storm.apache.org/
[3]http://samza.apache.org/
[4]https://flink.apache.org/

solutions. We choose some relevant solutions to detail. Although there are other survey-style books that discuss workflow management, e.g., the well-known *Workflows for e-Science* [Taylor et al., 2007b] and *Scientific Data Management: Challenges, Technology, and Deployment* [Shoshani and Rotem, 2009], this book considers novel topics such as using multi-site clouds and DISC environments for executing workflows.

Following, we illustrate some of the existing challenges with two fictional examples based on real astronomy and bioinformatics workflows. We will use these examples consistently in the rest of the book.

1.1 MOTIVATING EXAMPLES

1.1.1 MONTAGE

In the astronomy domain, Montage[5] is a computing and data-intensive toolkit that can be used to model a workflow. This workflow is the result of a national virtual observatory project that stitches tiles of images of the sky from various sky surveys into a photorealistic single image [Deelman et al., 2008, Jacob et al., 2009]. The structure of a small Montage workflow (at activation level) is presented in Figure 1.1, where each node represents the execution of a scientific application. The number within a node represents the name of activation in the workflow. The activations at the same line are associated with the same activity.

The first activity (activations 1–6) has no parent activities. Each of them invokes the *mProject* program to project a single image to the scale defined in a pseudo-FITS header template file. The second activity (activations 7–14) uses an *mDiffFit* program to create a table of image-to-image difference parameters. The third activity (activation 15) takes advantage of a *mFitplane* program to fit the images generated by past activities (7–14) to an image. The fourth activity (activation 16) uses an *mBgModel* program to interactively determine a set of corrections to apply to each image to achieve a "best" global fit according to the image-to-image difference parameter table. The fifth activity (activations 17–22) removes a background from a single image through an *mBackground* program. The sixth activity (activation 23) employs a *mImgtbl* program to extract the FITS header information (information about one or more scientific coordinate systems that are overlaid on the image itself) from a set of files and to create an ASCII image metadata table. Finally, the seventh activity (activation 24) pieces together the projected images using the uniform FITS header template and the information from the same metadata table generated by activation 23. This activity invokes a *mAdd* program.

Let us assume that an astronomer, Bob, needs to execute Montage workflow in his laboratory using Apache Spark framework. Bob has a few commodity machines in his laboratory, with heterogeneous hardware. Montage has several activations that can be executed in parallel (e.g., activations (1–6), (7–14), and (17–22)), since they are embarrassingly parallel activations. Each activation presents different CPU, disk, and memory requirements. Thus, Spark has

---

[5]Montage project: http://montage.ipac.caltech.edu/.

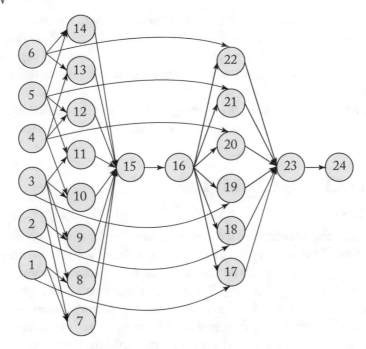

Figure 1.1: The structure of a small Montage workflow, adapted from Singh et al. [2008].

to define which activations will execute in which machines. Activation (Task) scheduling is a well-known non-deterministic polynomial-time (NP) complete problem even in simple scenarios [Al-Azzoni and Down, 2008, Pinedo, 2008]. The scheduling in Apache Spark is static and does not consider the performance estimation of each activation or the computing power of each machine. This type of scheduling can produce WEPs that are not optimized since an activation that demands high processing power can be scheduled to a machine that is not able to provide such processing power.

In terms of volume of data, a small instance of Montage workflow consumes and produces several gigabytes of data and Montage requires that all of the input images are on a local disk and writes the output mosaic to the local disk. It means that although Spark provides in-memory processing, all data must be flushed to disk since the workflow invokes black-box applications that cannot benefit from in-memory mechanisms of Spark. Also, although workflows modeled in Spark can be executed faster even when using default configuration parameters, a fine tuning of Spark configuration parameters can considerably improve performance, and even in some cases make the execution viable. The problem is that Spark has more than 100 configuration parameters that Bob has to fine tune to provide an optimized WEP. Thus, although Spark represents a step forward, there are many gaps to be bridged in order to support large-scale scientific workflows fully.

Bob also has to be able to perform runtime monitoring of the workflow since Montage can execute for many hours even when running in parallel. Besides, Bob has to analyze the results and provenance data of the workflow to foster reproducibility. Native Apache Spark requires programmers to collect historical data from log files and perform trial and error debugging. Ideally, provenance should be collected in order to help scientists monitor, debug, and analyze their workflows.

1.1.2   SCIEVOL

In the bioinformatics domain, SciEvol [Ocaña et al., 2012b] is a scientific workflow designed to perform molecular evolution reconstruction. It aims at inferring evolutionary relationships on genomic data. SciEvol consists of 12 activities as presented in Figure 1.2. The first activity (pre-processing FASTA file) is a Python script that formats the multi-fasta input file. FASTA file is a textual presenting format for nucleotide or peptide sequences. The second activity (MSA construction) constructs a Multiple Sequence Alignment (MSA) using a MAFFT program (or other MSA programs). A MAFFT program is generally for generating the alignment of three or more biological sequences (protein or nucleic acids) of similar length. The third activity (MSA conversion) executes ReadSeq to convert the MSA in FASTA format to in PHYLIP format, which is used in the phylogenetic tree construction activity.

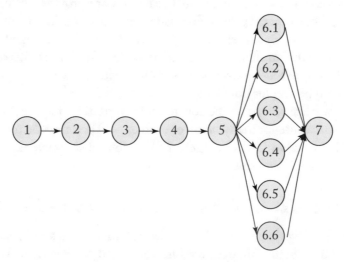

Figure 1.2: SciEvol workflow, based on Ocaña et al. [2012b].

The fourth activity (pre-processing PHYLIP file) formats the input file (referenced as "phylip-file-one") according to the format definition and generates a second file (referenced as "phylip-file-two"). The fifth activity (tree construction) receives the "phylip-file-one" as input and produces a phylogenetic tree [Felsenstein, 1989] as output. The sixth activities (evolutionary analysis from 6.1–6.6) analyze the phylogenetic tree with corresponding parameters and generate a set of files containing evolutionary information as output. Each of the activities (evolutionary phases) is related to one of six codon substitution models, which are used to verify if the groups of genes are under positive Darwinian selection. These activities exploit the same program using different parameters. The last activity (data analysis) automatically processes the output files obtained from the previous activities.

Let us assume that a bioinformatician, Alice, needs to execute SciEvol workflow in a public cloud (e.g., Amazon AWS, Microsoft Azure, Google Cloud, etc.) using an existing SWfMS. Similar to the aforementioned example in the astronomy domain, the SWfMS chosen by Alice has to produce a WEP to be executed in the cloud. However, scheduling and executing parallel workflows in clouds is a challenge for several reasons. First, clouds present different pricing models that have to be considered to fit in the budget informed by Alice. Cloud providers allow for users to acquire resources on demand, based on the pay-per-use pricing model, e.g., users pay per quantum of time used (e.g., minutes, hours, days, etc.).

Second, clouds are changing environments, and they may be susceptible to performance fluctuations during the execution of the workflow, thus requiring adaptive scheduling solutions. Ideally, SWfMS should benefit from cloud elasticity, i.e., depending on the demand of the workflow, resources can be deployed or undeployed at runtime. Third, in clouds, virtual machine failures are no longer an exception but rather a characteristic of these environments. Although the cloud provider guarantees that new virtual machines are provided in case of failure, the workflow scheduling has to consider reliability issues when distributing parallel tasks to execute on several distributed VMs. Finally, since resources are deployed on demand, Alice also has to define which types of virtual machines she has to deploy for a specific SciEvol execution. Here arises another problem on executing workflows in clouds: what is the number of virtual machines to instantiate of each type and for how long?

Similar to Bob, Alice also has to be able to perform runtime monitoring of the workflow since SciPhy can also execute for many hours or even days. Alice also has to analyze the results and provenance data of SciEvol. Although most SWfMSs collect provenance data, only a few allow for querying and analyzing this data at runtime.

1.2   THE LIFE CYCLE OF CLOUD AND DISC WORKFLOWS

One of the challenges of workflows is to allow scientists to manage several scientific computational resources (data, programs, models, etc.) in distributed environments such as clouds and DISC. As stated in the aforementioned examples, the effective management of such workflows requires a set of facilities, such as scheduling mechanisms, data movement techniques, provenance management components, and so on.

Scientists commonly rely on complex systems and frameworks such as existing SWfMSs and big data frameworks (e.g., Apache Spark and Hadoop) to provide such facilities. However, there are several gaps still to be bridged until these systems support the workflow execution in these environments fully.

Therefore, the organization of a cloud and DISC workflow life cycle poses an interesting idea. In this book we advocate a novel view of a large-scale cloud and DISC workflow life cycle based on provenance gathering during all phases. Each phase is discussed and solutions to support them are presented throughout Chapters 3, 4, and 5 as well as some open research questions to motivate future research. In this book, we define the life cycle of a workflow executed in clouds or DISC environments as being composed of seven main steps as presented in Figure 1.3.

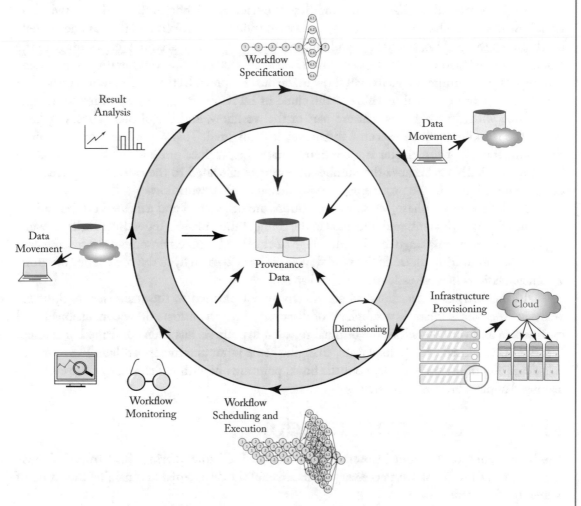

Figure 1.3: The Cloud and DISC workflow life cycle, based on Mattoso et al. [2010].

The life cycle of a workflow executed in the cloud or DISC environments describes the phases through which the workflow passes from its specification to the publication of the results. In addition to the composition, execution, and analysis phases already present in the traditional life cycle of an experiment [Mattoso et al., 2010], the cloud and DISC workflow life cycle encompasses a configuration phase that aims at configuring and dimensioning the environment, since both cloud and DISC environments may be not yet *a priori* configured for the workflow execution. Also, there are still issues such as data transfer and movement and the subsequent download of the data for analysis. It is worth noticing that all these phases of the life cycle are associated with the provenance data, that is, either they produce provenance data or consume them in some way.

In the composition phase of the workflow, the scientists elaborate the workflow specification, informing which programs, scripts, or services should be invoked and the data dependencies between them. Also, scientists should inform where input data is stored (e.g., storage in the cloud such as Amazon S3). This specification impacts directly on the configuration and dimensioning of the environment, as we will show in the next chapters. In the configuration phase, the data transfer from the local machine to the cloud or DISC environment is performed, images are created with the programs that are part of the workflow, and the cluster (virtual or not), where the workflow will be executed in parallel, is configured. This phase has a subcycle since the configuration of the cluster is a continuous task, i.e., it does not end while the workflow is not finished. This is because the number of resources allocated to the cluster can increase or decrease depending on the processing capacity demand of the workflow.

In the execution phase, workflow activations are dispatched and executed on the various machines that were instantiated/allocated in the configuration phase. Activation (Task) scheduling is performed at this stage to take advantage of cloud or DISC environments. After the execution, the monitoring phase of the workflow is performed to analyze the occurrence of errors, which activations have already finished, and so on.

In the analysis phase, the data are effectively downloaded to the scientist's machine for analysis. This phase includes a subphase of discovery, where scientists draw conclusions based on the data and verify whether the original research hypothesis has been confirmed or refuted. If it has been refuted, the cycle repeats, changing some input parameters or data. We return to this definition of life cycle throughout the book, pointing out with which stage of the cycle the proposed approaches are associated.

1.3   STRUCTURE OF THE BOOK

This book is composed of four chapters besides Chapter 1. Chapter 2 brings Background Knowledge and workflow formalism necessary to understand the distributed and parallel execution of data-intensive workflows.

Chapter 3 discusses solutions for workflow management in single-site cloud environments. Here we are faced with solutions involving static and dynamic scheduling to handle data and activation scheduling and virtual machines allocation.

However, most clouds are not single-site ones. Typically, a cloud is composed of several sites (or data centers), each with its resources and data. Thus, to use more resources than available at a single site or to access data at different sites, workflows should also be executed in a distributed manner at different sites. Chapter 4 presents the fundamental concepts and solutions to deploy data-intensive SWfMSs in a multi-site cloud. Here we are faced with more complex scheduling challenges that also take into account data transfer among the sites.

More recently, Data-Intensive Scalable Computing (DISC) frameworks (e.g., Apache Spark and Hadoop) and environments have emerged and are being used to execute data-intensive workflows. DISC environments are composed of processors and disks in large-commodity computing clusters connected using high-speed communications switches and networks. The main advantage of DISC frameworks is that they support and grant efficient in-memory data management for data-intensive workflows. Chapter 5 illustrates interesting approaches of data-intensive SWfMSs in DISC environments. Chapter 6 concludes this book by providing interesting research perspectives.

CHAPTER 2

Background Knowledge

Many large-scale scientific experiments take advantage of workflows to model data operations such as loading input data, data processing, data analysis, and aggregating output data. Workflows allow scientists to model and express the entire data processing steps and their dependencies, typically as a Directed Acyclic Graph (DAG). As more and more data is consumed and produced in modern scientific experiments, workflows need to be executed in parallel in distributed environments, e.g., clusters, grids, and clouds, in order to process large-scale data in a timely manner.

An SWfMS is an efficient and sophisticated tool designed to execute workflows and manage datasets in diverse computing environments. We can also develop SWfMS gateways that are systems designed for scientists to execute workflows using different SWfMSs. Several SWfMSs, e.g., Pegasus [Deelman et al., 2005, 2014], Swift/T [Wozniak et al., 2013], Chiron [Ogasawara et al., 2013], SciCumulus [de Oliveira et al., 2010] and gateways such as WS-PGRADE/gUSE [Kacsuk et al., 2012] are now used intensively by various research communities, e.g., astronomy, biology, and computational engineering. Although there are many SWfMSs, the architecture of SWfMSs presents common features, in particular, the capability to produce a Workflow Execution Plan (i.e., WEP) based on a high-level workflow specification.

Besides managing the workflow execution, most of the existing SWfMSs collect metadata to describe the execution, data, and environment related to the workflow. Provenance data [Freire et al., 2008b] is a type of metadata that plays a pivotal role to guarantee traceability and reproducibility of results since it describes the derivation history of a dataset, including the original data sources, intermediate datasets, and the computational workflow steps that were invoked to produce this dataset [Costa et al., 2013, de A. R. Gonçalves et al., 2012, de Oliveira et al., 2012a, Horta et al., 2012].

Since the sequential execution of several data-intensive workflows may take much time, SWfMSs should enable the parallel execution of workflows and exploit vast amounts of distributed resources. Executable activations can be generated based on the activities of the workflow and several types of parallelism and then submitted to the execution environment according to different scheduling approaches and policies.

Some works already survey techniques for SWfMSs. Bux and Leser [2013] provide an overview of parallelization techniques for SWfMSs, including their implementation in real systems, and discuss significant improvements to the landscape of SWfMSs. Some other work [Yu and Buyya, 2005] examines the existing SWfMSs designed for grid computing and proposes taxonomies for different aspects of SWfMSs, including workflow design, information retrieval, workflow scheduling, fault tolerance, and data movement. In this chapter, we focus on providing concepts of workflows, workflow execution in the distributed environment, and provenance data. The main contributions of this chapter are:

1. An introduction of key concepts of SWfs and SWfMSs.

2. A five-layer SWfMS functional architecture, which is useful to discuss the techniques for SWfs.

3. A taxonomy of SWf parallelization techniques and SWf scheduling algorithms, and a comparative analysis of the existing solutions.

4. An introduction of existing SWfMSs and SWf execution environments.

Figure 2.1 illustrates the taxonomy of the main concepts in this chapter. This chapter is organized as follows. Section 2.1 gives key concepts of workflows, including workflow formalism, standards, SWfMSs, workflow algebra, and distributed execution of workflows. Section 2.2 shows the execution of workflows in distributed environments, including clusters, clouds, and DISC environments. Section 2.3 concludes this chapter.

2.1   KEY CONCEPTS

This section introduces the fundamental concepts of workflows. First, we formally define what a workflow is in the context of this book, and then we present some workflow standards, including the definition of SWfs, the difference between workflows and business workflows, and the life cycle of workflows. Then, we detail the architecture of SWfMSs, which contains five layers, i.e., presentation, user services, WEP generation, WEP execution, and infrastructure. Afterward, we present the parallel execution of workflows and workflow scheduling. Finally, we give an overview of existing SWfMSs.

2.1.1   WORKFLOW FORMALISM

A workflow can be formally defined as a directed acyclic graph $W(A, Dep)$, where nodes $A = \{a_1, a_2, ..., a_n\}$ are the activities and the edges Dep represent the data dependencies among activities in A. Although a workflow can be represented as a directed cyclic graph (DCG), it is harder to support since iteration is needed to represent repetition of activities, e.g., with a while-do construct [Yu and Buyya, 2005].

An activity is a description of a piece of work that forms a logical step within a workflow representation. Given $a_i \mid (1 \leq i \leq n)$, let us define $I = \{i_1, i_2, .., i_m\}$ the possible set of input data for an activity a_i, then $input(a_i) \in I$. Moreover, let us consider O as the set of outputs

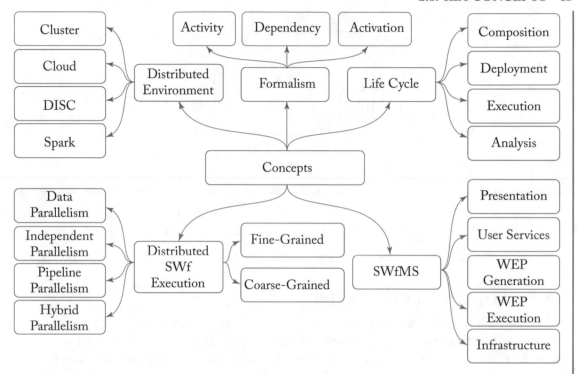

Figure 2.1: Main concepts.

produced by a_i, then $Output(a_i) \in O$. The dependency between two activities a_i and a_j can be represented as $dep(a_i, a_j) \leftrightarrow \exists O_k \in input(a_j)|O_k \in output(a_i)$.

Let us also define *activation* [Ogasawara et al., 2011] as the smallest unit of work that can be processed in parallel and consumes a specific data chunk [Liu et al., 2015]. Let us consider $Ac = \{ac_1, ac_2, \ldots, ac_k\}$ as the set of activations of the workflow W. Each ac_i is associated with a specific activity a_i that is represented as $act(ac_i) = a_j$. Activations also present data dependencies, thus $input(ac_i) \in I$ and $output(ac_i) \in O$ and the dependency between two activations ac_i and ac_j can be represented as $dep(ac_i, ac_j) \leftrightarrow \exists r \in input(ac_j)|r \in output(ac_i) \wedge dep(act(ac_i), act(ac_j))$. Figure 2.2 shows a fragment of SciEvol workflow composed by three activities (1, 2, and 3), each with three activations and their data dependencies. Each activation in Figure 2.2 is associated with an input file of the workflow, i.e., activation 1.a processes one input file, activation 1.b processes another input file, and so forth. In addition, activation 2.a has a data dependency with activation 1.a but not with 2.b and 2.a. The same rationale applies to the remaining activations in this workflow fragment.

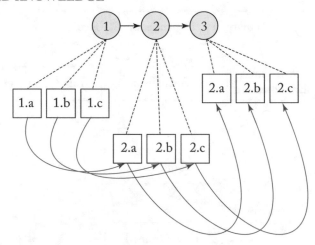

Figure 2.2: An example of workflow activities and activations.

2.1.2   WORKFLOW STANDARDS

Workflows are found in the scientific and business domains. Both types of workflows represent the automation of a process, during which different logical data processing activities process data according to a set of rules. Business workflows are widely used for business data processing in order to make business processes more efficient and more reliable. According to the Workflow Management Coalition (WfMC[1]), a business workflow may be defined as "the automation of a business process, in whole or part, during which documents, information or activations are passed from one participant to another for action, according to a set of procedural rules" [Coalition, 1999].

A business process may be defined as a set of one or more linked procedures or activities that collectively realize a business objective or policy goal, generally within the context of an organizational structure defining functional roles and relationships [Coalition, 1999]. Although business and scientific workflows present some similarities, they are different in three aspects. The first difference is related to the data flows and control flows [Yildiz et al., 2009]. Business workflows focus on procedural rules that generally represent the control flows with different patterns Russell et al. [2016], while scientific workflows highlight data flows that are depicted by data dependencies [Barker and van Hemert, 2008]. This is reasonable since scientific experiments may need to deal with big experimental data. Data-intensive workflows process, manage, and produce vast amounts of data during its execution. Second, compared with traditional business workflows (e.g., purchase order processing), which are rather simple and manipulate small amounts of data, scientific workflows are data-intensive and can be very complex (in terms of number and combinations of activities and activations), thus making execution time a major

[1]www.wfmc.org

issue [Liu et al., 2015]. Third, scientific workflows need to ensure result reproducibility, which requires registering and managing provenance data regarding datasets, intermediate data, and activity executions, which is not strictly necessary for business workflows.

The life cycle of a workflow is a description of the state transitions of a workflow from creation to completion [Deelman et al., 2009, Görlach et al., 2011]. We adopt a combination of workflow life-cycle views [Deelman et al., 2009, Görlach et al., 2011, Mattoso et al., 2010] with a few variations, condensed into four phases.

1. The composition phase [Deelman et al., 2009, Liew et al., 2017, Mattoso et al., 2010] for the creation of an abstract workflow (i.e, only the specification).

2. The deployment phase [Görlach et al., 2011, Liew et al., 2017] for constructing a concrete workflow (i.e., the activations that effectively execute).

3. The execution phase [Deelman et al., 2009, Mattoso et al., 2010] for the execution of workflows.

4. The analysis phase [Görlach et al., 2011, Mattoso et al., 2010] for applying the output data to scientific experiments, analyzing workflow provenance data, and sharing the workflow results.

2.1.3   SCIENTIFIC WORKFLOW MANAGEMENT SYSTEMS

An SWfMS manages a workflow all along its life cycle (Figure 1.3) using some specific techniques. An SWfMS is a complex system that defines, creates, and manages the execution of workflows. In order to execute a workflow in a given environment, an SWfMS typically generates a Workflow Execution Plan (WEP), which is like a program that captures optimization decisions and execution directives, typically produced after compiling and optimizing a workflow specification, before execution. An example of WEP can be found in Figure 2.3. The example presented in Figure 2.3 has one activation per activity of SciEvol and is executed in three different computing nodes. Node a is the one with the best processor and memory, and due to that, most activations are executed on it. Activations from 6.1 to 6.6 can be executed in parallel since they are not dependent. This way, they are distributed across the three nodes. Finally, activation 7 is executed in node a.[2] The produced WEP for this example is also presented in Figure 2.3 where each node (a, b, and c is associated with a series of activations, i.e., the activations that are going to execute on that node.

SWfMSs commonly support different additional functionalities, and the functional architecture of an SWfMS can be layered as follows [Altintas et al., 2004, Deelman et al., 2005, Ogasawara et al., 2013, Zhao et al., 2007a]: presentation, user services, WEP generation, WEP

---

[2]It is worth noticing that the algorithm that decides which activation is going to execute in which node is called the scheduling algorithm. A series of scheduling algorithms is discussed in Chapter 3, 4, and 5.

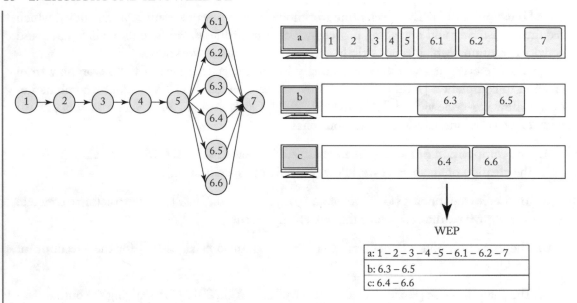

Figure 2.3: A WEP example for SciEvol.

execution, and infrastructure. Figure 2.4 presents this architecture. The higher layers take advantage of the lower layers to perform more concrete functionality. A user interacts with an SWfMS through the presentation layer and chooses the desired functions at the user services layer. A workflow is processed at the WEP generation layer to produce a WEP, which is executed at the WEP execution layer. The SWfMS accesses the physical resources through the infrastructure layer for workflow execution.

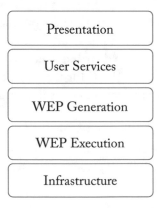

Figure 2.4: Functional architecture of a SWfMS.

The presentation layer serves as a User Interface (UI) for the interaction between users and SWfMSs, i.e., human presentation [Liew et al., 2017], at all stages of the workflow life cycle, including monitoring execution status, expressing workflow steering, and information sharing commands. This interface is responsible for designing a workflow by assembling data processing activities linked by dependencies. The UI can be textual (e.g., Swift/T [Wozniak et al., 2013], Pegasus [Gil et al., 2006], and Chiron [Ogasawara et al., 2013]) or graphical (e.g., Galaxy [Afgan et al., 2018], Taverna [Oinn et al., 2004], VisTrails [Callahan et al., 2006], and Kepler [Altintas et al., 2004]), as shown in Figure 2.5.

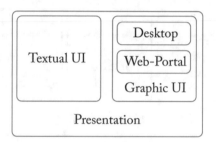

Figure 2.5: UI taxonomy.

Both textual UI and graphical UI (GUI) exploit the textual language, such as XML-based language [Oinn et al., 2004] or JSON format [Abouelhoda et al., 2012], as computer communication Liew et al. [2017] to represent workflows within an SWfMS to support parallel computations on distributed computing and storage resources. The GUI simplifies the designing process of a workflow for the SWfMS users to assemble the components described as icons through drag-and-drop functionality. GUI can be classified as desktop-based GUI (e.g., Taverna [Oinn et al., 2004] and Kepler [Altintas et al., 2004]) and web-portal-based GUI (Galaxy [Goecks et al., 2010]). Desktop-based graphical SWfMSs are typically installed either in a local computer or in a remote server that is accessible through network connection, while web-portal-based SWfMSs are typically installed in a web server, which is accessible through a browser on the client side. Most SWfMS languages support the specification of a workflow in a DAG structure [Wilde et al., 2011], while some SWfMS languages also support iteration for DCG [Dias et al., 2015, Liew et al., 2017].

The user services layer is responsible for supporting user functionality, i.e., workflow monitoring and steering, workflow information sharing, and providing workflow provenance data as shown in Figure 2.6. Workflow monitoring tracks the execution status and displays this information to users during workflow execution [Coalition, 1999]. Through workflow monitoring, an SWfMS user can check if the result is already enough to prove her hypothesis [Costa et al., 2013]. Workflow monitoring can be achieved based on log data (in log files) [Gunter et al., 2011, Vahi et al., 2012] or more general provenance data [Horta et al., 2012], typically in a database [de Oliveira et al., 2010, Mattoso et al., 2014, Ogasawara et al., 2013]. Workflow steering is the interaction between an SWfMS and a user to control the workflow execution progress or configuration parameters [Mattoso et al., 2014]. Through workflow steering, an SWfMS user can control workflow execution dynamically so that the workflow does not need to continue unnecessary execution or execute the workflow again when an error occurs [Costa et al., 2013, de A. R. Gonçalves et al., 2012]. Information-sharing functionality enables workflow information sharing for workflow reusing. An SWfMS can directly integrate a workflow repository to support workflow information sharing among different users in order to reduce repetitive work between different scientist groups.

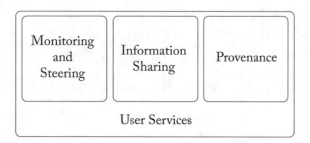

Figure 2.6: Functional modules at the user services layer.

A workflow repository stores workflow information, e.g., workflow data, workflow specifications, and available programs. The repository can contain workflow information for the same SWfMS environments (myExperiment social network [Wolstencroft et al., 2013] for Taverna, the web-based sharing functionality of Galaxy [Goecks et al., 2010], the workflow hosting environment for Askalon [Qin et al., 2008]), or for different SWfMS environments (SHIWA Repository [Terstyánszky et al., 2014]). Provenance data in workflows plays a fundamental role in supporting reproducibility, result interpretation, and problem diagnosis. The provenance data can be generated by semantic-based approach [Kim et al., 2008] or through a practical approach (PROV-Wf [Costa et al., 2013]) from log files [Gadelha Jr. et al., 2013] or event listener interfaces [Altintas et al., 2006] and is generally stored in a database [Costa et al., 2013, Crawl et al., 2011]. The WEP generation can be realized for two data processing models, i.e., batch processing and stream processing [Liew et al., 2017, Liu et al., 2018b]. Batch processing processes the whole datasets and produces their results as bulk data [Liew et al., 2017]. Stream processing processes the continuous incoming data, and the process generally exploits a window to capture the data to process [Özsu and Valduriez, 2011].

The WEP generation layer is responsible for generating a WEP according to a workflow specification. This layer contains three modules, i.e., workflow refactoring, workflow parallelization, and optimization, as shown in Figure 2.7. The workflow refactoring module refines the workflow specification for WEP generation by transformation for execution environments [Ogasawara et al., 2011, 2013]. The transformation can reduce activities [Deelman et al., 2005] or the structure complexity [Boulakia et al., 2014] to simplify workflow. Also, the transformation can also partition a workflow into several fragments [Chen and Deelman, 2012b, Tanaka and Tatebe, 2012] to yield distributed [Liu et al., 2014b] or parallel processing and simplified structure. A workflow fragment (or fragment for short) can be defined as a subset of activities and data dependencies of the original workflow (please refer to Ogasawara et al. [2011] for a formal definition of workflow fragmentation). Note that the term workflow fragment is different from the term sub-workflow: fragments are used for execution while sub-workflows are used to refer to the to an entire workflow that can be viewed as an activity in another workflow [van der Aalst et al., 2003]. Workflow parallelization exploits different types of parallelism to generate concrete executable activations for the WEP. The parallelization can be performed at fragment level, i.e., execution of fragments in parallel, or activity level, i.e., execution of activations of the same or different activities in parallel. Finally, workflow optimization captures the results of workflow refactoring and workflow parallelization and inserts additional instructions, e.g., multiple objectives, for workflow scheduling to generate a WEP.

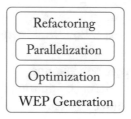

Figure 2.7: Functional modules at the WEP generation layer.

The WEP execution is managed at the WEP execution layer. This layer handles workflow scheduling, activation execution, and fault tolerance, as shown in Figure 2.8. Through workflow scheduling, an SWfMS produces a Scheduling Plan (SP), which aims at making good use of computing resources and preventing execution stalling [Bouganim et al., 2000]. An SP defines the map of activations, activities, or fragments and the execution node or site. An SWfMS can schedule workflow fragments, bags of tasks, or individual activations into computing resources as presented in Section 2.1.4. During activation execution, the input data is transferred to the computing nodes, and the output data is produced. Generally, the provenance data is also generated and captured at this time. The workflow fault-tolerance mechanism deals with failures or errors of activation execution and guarantees the availability and reliability of workflow execution. Fault-tolerance techniques can be classified into proactive and reactive [Ganga and Karthik, 2013]. Proactive fault tolerance avoids faults and errors by predicting the failure and proactively replacing the suspected components from other working components. Reactive fault tolerance reduces the effect of failures after perceiving failures, using checkpointing/restart, replication [Ganga and Karthik, 2013], and activation resubmission techniques [Costa et al., 2012].

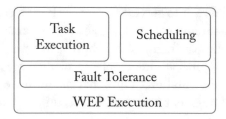

Figure 2.8: Functional modules at the WEP execution layer.

The limitations of computing and storage resources of one computer force SWfMS users to use multiple computers in distributed environments, such as cluster, grid, or cloud infrastructure for workflow execution. This layer provides the interface between the SWfMS and the infrastructure as presented in Section 2.1.4. Also, the infrastructure interface also enables communications among different computing nodes. The operational layer is also in charge of provisioning, which can be static or dynamic. Static provisioning can provide unchangeable resources for SWfMSs during workflow execution, while dynamic provisioning can add or remove resources for SWfMSs at runtime. Based on the types of resources, provisioning can be classified into computing provisioning and storage provisioning.

Computing provisioning means offering computing nodes to SWfMSs, while storage provisioning means providing storage resources for data caching or data persistence. The data storage module generally exploit database management systems and file systems to manage the data during workflow execution. Some SWfMSs such as Taverna put intermediate data and output data in a database. Some SWfMSs use a shared-disk file system (see Section 2.2.2) [Zhao et al., 2008], while some others can exploit distributed file systems (see Section 2.2.2) [Wang et al., 2009] or local file systems in each computing node. Generally, the file systems and the database management systems take advantage of computing nodes and storage resources provided by the provisioning module. SWfMSs can also put some data in the disk cache of one computing node to accelerate data access during workflow execution [Shankar and DeWitt, 2007]. The functional modules are shown in Figure 2.9.

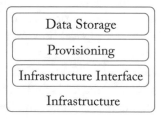

Figure 2.9: Functional modules at the infrastructure layer.

2.1.4   DISTRIBUTED EXECUTION OF WORKFLOWS

Since workflows handle large datasets in large-scale experiments, SWfMSs rely on the effective use of parallel techniques on multiple computers to speed up the workflow execution. Workflow parallelization is the process of transforming and optimizing a (sequential) workflow into a parallel WEP in order to execute it in parallel in multiple computing nodes. This section introduces the basic techniques for the parallel execution of workflows in SWfMSs: workflow parallelism techniques and workflow scheduling algorithms.

Workflow Parallelism

Workflow parallelization identifies the activations that can be executed in parallel in the WEP. There are two parallelism levels: *coarse-grained parallelism* and *fine-grained parallelism*. Coarse-grained parallelism can achieve parallelism by executing workflow fragments (i.e., parts of the workflow) in parallel. On the other hand, fine-grained parallelism performs parallelism by executing different activations in parallel. A workflow can be executed in parallel at a coarse-grained level to parallelize the execution of fragments and then executed in parallel at a fine-grained level to parallelize the execution of activations. According to the dependencies defined in a workflow, different parallelization techniques can result in different WEPs. The degree of parallelism, which is defined as the number of concurrent running computing nodes or threads at any given time [Bux and Leser, 2013], can be used to evaluate the efficiency of workflow parallelization techniques.

Coarse-grained parallelism is performed at the workflow level, which is critical to the execution of meta-workflows or parameter sweep workflows. To execute meta-workflows, the independent sub-workflows are identified as workflow fragments to be submitted to the corresponding workflow execution engine [Terstyánszky et al., 2014]. The execution of a parameter sweep workflow corresponds to the execution of the workflows with different sets of input parameter values. The combination of workflow and each set of input parameter values can be considered independent fragments, which can be executed in parallel [Kacsuk, 2011]. Also, a workflow can achieve coarse-grained parallelism by performing partitioning.

The fine-grained parallelism is performed for a workflow or a workflow fragment. There are three types of parallelism at this level: data parallelism, independent parallelism, and pipeline parallelism. Data parallelism deals with the parallelism within an activity, while independent parallelism and pipeline parallelism handle the parallelism between different activities.

Data Parallelism

Data parallelism is obtained by having multiple activations associated with the same activity, but with each one processing on a different data chunk. As presented in Figure 2.10b, data parallelism happens when the input data of an activity can be partitioned into different chunks so each chunk is processed independently by an activation in a different computing node or processor. Data parallelism can be static, dynamic, or adaptive [Pautasso and Alonso, 2006]. If the num-

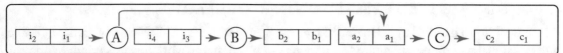

(a) **Sequential execution in one computing node.** Activity B (6.2) starts execution after the execution of activity A (6.1) and activity C (7) starts execution after the execution of activity B. All the execution is realized in one computing node.

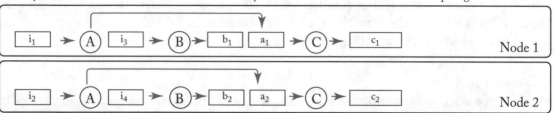

(b) **Data parallelism.** The execution of activities A (6.1), B (6.2), C (7) is performed in two computing nodes simultaneously. Each computing node processes a data chunk.

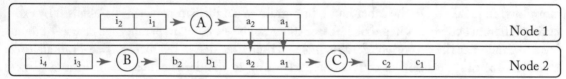

(c) **Independent parallelism.** The execution of activities A (6.1) and B (6.2) is performed in two computing nodes simultaneously. Activity C (7) begins execution after the execution of activities A and B.

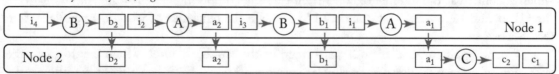

(d) **Pipeline parallelism.** Activity C (7) starts execution once a data chunk is ready. When activities A (6.1) and B (6.2) are processing the second part of data (i_2, i_4), activity C can process the output data of the first part (a_1, b_1) at the same time.

Figure 2.10: **Different types of parallelism.** Circles represent activities. There are three activities: A, B, and C, which can be Activities 6.1, 6.2, and 7 in SciEvol. C processes the output data produced by A and B. Rectangles represent data chunks. "i_1" stands for the first part of input data. "a_1" stands for the output data corresponding to the first part of input data after being processed by activity A.

ber of data chunks is indicated before workflow execution and fixed during execution, the data parallelism is static. If the number of data chunks is determined at runtime, the data parallelism is dynamic. Also, if the number is automatically adapted to the execution environment, the data parallelism is called adaptive. The adaptive data parallelism can determine the best number of data chunks to balance workflow execution to increase parallelism degree while maintaining a reasonable overhead.

Independent Parallelism

Two activities can be either independent, i.e., the execution of one activity does not depend on the outcome of another, or dependent, i.e., there is a data dependency between them. Independent parallelism is achieved by having activations associated with independent activities executed simultaneously. As presented in Figure 2.10c, independent parallelism occurs when a workflow has more than one independent part in the graph, and the activities in each part present no data dependencies with those in another part.

Pipeline Parallelism

With pipeline parallelism (Figure 2.10d), several dependent activities with a producer-consumer relationship are executed in parallel by different activations. One output data chunk of one activity is consumed directly by the next dependent activities in a pipeline fashion. The advantage of pipeline execution is that the result of the producer activity does not need to be entirely materialized. Instead, data chunks can be consumed as soon as they are ready, thus saving memory and disk accesses.

Hybrid Parallelism

As presented in Figure 2.11, the three basic types of parallelism can be combined to achieve higher degrees of parallelism.

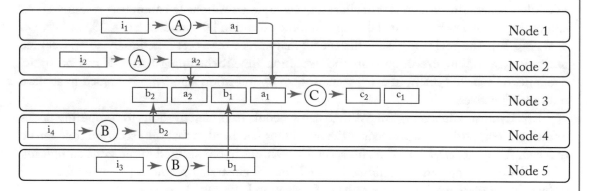

Figure 2.11: **Hybrid parallelism.** Activity A (6.1) is executed through data parallelism at nodes 1 and 2. Activity B (6.2) is executed through data parallelism at nodes 4 and 5. Activities A and B are also executed through independent parallelism. Activities A and C (7), respectively B and C, are executed through pipeline parallelism between nodes (1, 2) and 3, respectively nodes (4, 5) and 3.

We illustrate different types of parallelism, including their combination in hybrid parallelism, with the example shown in Figure 2.10. In this figure, one activation is associated with one activity and the related input data. The Activities A, B, and C can be Activities 6.1, 6.2, and

7 in SciEvol. Figure 2.10a presents the sequential execution of Activity A, B, C and two parts of input data, i.e., i_1 and i_2. Since there is no parallelization, the corresponding activations, i.e., Activity A and Data i_1, Activity A and Data i_2, Activity B and Data i_3, Activity B and Data i_4, and Activity C and Data a_1, b_1, Activity C and Data a_2, b_2 are executed one after another. Figure 2.10b describes the execution with data parallelism. The processing of each part of input data is performed in different computing nodes in parallel, i.e., the processing of input data i_1, i_3 and that of input data i_2, i_4 are done at the same time. Figure 2.10c shows independent parallelism. Activity A and B are executed at different computing nodes concurrently. Figure 2.10d shows pipeline parallelism, i.e., the parallel execution of Activity A (or B) and Activity C. Activity A (or B) can be done at the same time as Activity C while processing the different parts of input data. While Activity C is processing Data a_1 and b_1 at Node 2, which corresponds to the input data i_1 and i_3, Activity A (or B) can process the input data i_2 (or i_4). Figure 2.11 shows hybrid parallelism. Thus, the activations, i.e., Activity A and Data i_1, Activity A and Data i_2, Activity B and Data i_3, and Activity B and Data i_4 can be executed in parallel in different computing nodes. Activity C can begin execution once both Data a_1 and b_1 (or both Data a_2 and b_2) are ready. This parallelism combines data parallelism, independent parallelism, and pipeline parallelism.

Workflow Scheduling

Workflow scheduling is a process of allocating concrete activations to computing resources (i.e., computing nodes) to be executed during workflow execution [Bux and Leser, 2013, de Oliveira et al., 2012b]. The goal is to get an efficient SP that minimizes a cost function based on resource utilization, workflow execution cost, and execution time. Scheduling methods can be static, dynamic, or hybrid. Finally, in many scenarios, an optimization algorithm is needed to achieve multiple objectives.

Activation Clustering An SWfMS can schedule bags of activations to computing nodes or multiple computing nodes to reduce the scheduling overhead so that the execution time can be reduced. A bag of activations contains several activations to be executed in the same computing node. The clustering can be performed using k-means clustering methods [Deng et al., 2011] or by balancing the workload of each bag of activation [Chen et al., 2013].

Static Scheduling Static scheduling generates an SP that allocates all the executable activations to computing nodes before execution, and the SWfMS strictly abides the SP during the whole workflow execution [Bux and Leser, 2013]. Because it is performed before execution, static scheduling yields little overhead at runtime. It is efficient if the SWfMS can predict the execution load of each activation accurately, when the execution environment varies little during the workflow execution, and when the SWfMS has enough information about the computing and storage capabilities of the environment. The static activation scheduling algorithms have two kinds of processor selection methods [Topcuoglu et al., 2002]: heuristic-based and guided random search-based. The heuristic-based method schedules activations according to a predefined rule, while the random search-based method schedules tasks randomly. Static activation scheduling algorithms can also be classified as task-based and workflow-based [Blythe et al., 2005]. The task-based method directly schedules activations into computing nodes, while the workflow-based method schedules a fragment into computing nodes.

Dynamic Scheduling Dynamic scheduling produces SPs that distribute and allocate executable activations to computing nodes during workflow execution [Bux and Leser, 2013]. This kind of scheduling is appropriate for workflows where the workload of activations is challenging to estimate, or for environments where the capabilities of the computers vary a lot during execution (i.e., clouds). Dynamic scheduling can achieve load balancing [Yu and Shi, 2007] in dynamic execution environments, while it takes time to generate SPs during execution dynamically. The scheduling algorithms can be based on the sorted [Maheswaran et al., 1999] queue techniques in a publish/subscribe model with different strategies such as First In First Out (FIFO), adaptive, and so on [Anglano and Canonico, 2008].

Hybrid Scheduling Both static and dynamic scheduling present their advantages, and they can be combined as a hybrid scheduling method to achieve better performance than just using one or the other. For example, an SWfMS might schedule part of the tasks of a workflow, e.g., those activations for which there is enough information, using static scheduling, and schedule the other part during execution with dynamic scheduling Deng et al. [2011].

Scheduling Optimization Algorithms Since there are many criteria to measure workflow execution, SWfMS users may have multiple objectives for optimizing workflow execution, such as reducing execution time, minimizing financial cost [Fard et al., 2014a], and maximizing the throughput [Gu et al., 2013] under different constraints. Therefore, SPs should also be optimized to attain multiple objectives in a given context (cluster, grid, cloud). Unlike query optimizations in a database, this optimization phase is often not explicit and mixed with the scheduling method.

2.1.5 A BRIEF ON EXISTING SWFMSS

In this section, we analyze nine SWfMSs and a workflow gateway to illustrate their techniques: Pegasus [Deelman et al., 2007], Swift/T [Wozniak et al., 2013], Kepler [Altintas et al., 2004], Taverna [Wolstencroft et al., 2013], Chiron [Ogasawara et al., 2013], Galaxy, SciCumulus [de Oliveira et al., 2010], Triana [Taylor et al., 2007a], Askalon [Fahringer et al., 2007], and WS-PGRADE/gUSE [Kacsuk et al., 2012] and detail Chiron, which is used as a case study in this book.

Most SWfMSs implement the five-layer architecture discussed in Section 2.1.3. Pegasus and Swift/T provide excellent support for scalability and high performance of data-intensive workflows, with reported results using more than a hundred thousand cores and terabytes of data during workflow execution [Deelman et al., 2014, Zhao et al., 2007a]. Kepler, Taverna, and Triana provide a GUI for desktop computers. Chiron is widely used because of a powerful algebraic approach for workflow parallelization, similar to the cloud-based SWfMS SciCumulus. Galaxy integrates a GUI that can be accessed through web browsers. Triana is able to use P2P services. Askalon implements both desktop and web GUI and has been adapted to cloud environments. WS-PGRADE/gUSE is a widely used gateway framework, which enables workflow execution in distributed environments using a web interface.

Pegasus, Swift/T, Kepler, Taverna, and WS-PGRADE/gUSE are widely used in astronomy, biology, and so on, while Galaxy can only execute bioinformatics workflows. Pegasus, Swift/T, SciCumulus, and Chiron design and execute a workflow through a textual interface while Kepler, Taverna, Galaxy, Triana, Askalon, and WS-PGRADE/gUSE integrate a GUI for workflow design. All of the nine SWfMSs and the gateway framework support workflow specification in a DAG structure, while Swift/T, Kepler, SciCumulus, Chiron, Galaxy, Triana, and Askalon also support workflow in a DCG structure [Yu and Buyya, 2005]. Users can share workflow information from Taverna, Galaxy, Askalon, and WS-PGRADE/gUSE. All of them support independent parallelism. All of them support dynamic scheduling, and five of them (Pegasus, Kepler, SciCumulus, Chiron, and WS-PGRADE/gUSE) support static scheduling. All nine SWfMSs and the gateway framework support workflow execution in both grid and cloud environments. A brief comparison of these nine SWfMSs and the gateway framework is given in Table 2.1.

Table 2.1: **Comparison of SWfMSs.** A categorization of SWfMSs based on workflow specification (i.e., DAG or DCG), UI types, parallelism types, and scheduling methods. "Activity" means that this SWfMS supports both independent parallelism and pipeline parallelism. WPg represents WS-PGRADE/gUSE.

SWfMS	Spec.	UI	Parallelism	Scheduling
Pegasus	DAG	GUI/Textual	Data and Independent	Static and Dynamic
Swift/T	DCG	Textual	Activity	Dynamic
Kepler	DCG	GUI	Activity	Static and Dynamic
Taverna	DAG	GUI	Data and Activity	Dynamic
Chiron	DCG	Textual	Data, Activity, and Hybrid	Static and Dynamic
SciCumulus	DCG	Textual	Data, Activity, and Hybrid	Static and Dynamic
Galaxy	DCG	GUI	Independent	Dynamic
Triana	DCG	GUI	Data and Activity	Dynamic
Askalon	DCG	GUI	Activity	Dynamic and Hybrid
WPg	DAG	GUI	Data, Activity, and Hybrid	Static and Dynamic

Chiron and Workflow Algebra

Chiron is a database-oriented [Özsu and Valduriez, 2011] SWfMs that aims at managing the parallel execution of workflows. There are six modules in Chiron, i.e., textual UI, activity manager, single-site task scheduler, task executor, provenance data manager, and shared file system. In the presentation layer, it uses the textual UI, which exploits an algebraic data model to express all data as relations and represent workflow activities as algebraic expressions in the presentation layer. Chiron defines that all data consumed and produced by the workflow are stored in relations. A relation contains sets of tuples composed of basic attributes such as integer, float, string, and file references, and so on.

Similar to relational algebra, relations in Chiron can be manipulated by a set of operators: union ($\cup$), intersection ($\cap$), and difference ($-$), as long as their schema are compatible (arity of relations and domain of each attribute are compatible). For example, considering $R(\Re)$ and $S(\Re)$, then $(R \cup S)$, $(R \cap S)$, and $(R - S)$ are all valid expressions. It may be also convenient to write a relation in temporary relation variables. The assignment operator ($\leftarrow$) allows this feature. For example, $T \leftarrow R \cup S$ makes a temporary copy of the union in a relation variable T, which can be reused later in algebraic expressions.

Workflow activities are ruled by algebraic operators that specify the ratio of consumption and production between input and output tuples, which allows for uniform treatment of data-centric activities and to reason about algebraic transformations. The workflow algebra includes six operators: Map, SplitMap, Reduce, Filter, SRQuery, and JoinQuery.

An algebraic expression consists of algebraic activities, additional operands, operators, input relations, and output relations. An algebraic activity contains a program or an SQL expression, and input and output relations. Each relation R has a schema $\Re$, with its typed attributes. An additional operand is the side information for the algebraic expression, which can be relations or a set of grouping attributes. In the user services layer, Chiron supports workflow monitoring, and steering and gathers provenance data based on the algebraic approach.

Figure 2.12 presents an example of MAFFT activity of the SciEvol workflow. MAFFT is ruled by the Map operator, i.e., one tuple in input relation R generates one tuple in the output relation T. MAFFT receives only one parameter as input: the file path that contains all sequences of DNA, RNA, and amino acids (i.e., FASTA file)) in relation R. After processing this FASTA file, MAFFT generates an alignment file (*.mafft). In addition, Chiron is able to extract data from the produced data files and add these data in the relation. In Figure 2.12 *Num_seq* and *length* are parameters found within the .mafft files produced by the execution. Output relation T contains the extracted parameters and the produced alignment file paths. Relation T is then the input relation of the next activity of the workflow. It is worth noticing that each tuple in R can be processed independent of each other, thus opening room for parallelism.

In the WEP generation layer, a workflow is expressed in an XML file called conceptual model. Each activity and its dependencies are analyzed by the activity manager to find executable activities, i.e., unexecuted activities, of which the input data is ready [Ogasawara et al.,

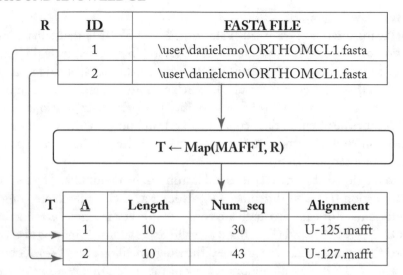

Figure 2.12: An example of the workflow algebra.

2013]. In order to execute an activity, the activity manager generates concrete executable tasks for each activity. Chiron supports all types of parallelism (data parallelism, independent parallelism, pipeline parallelism, hybrid parallelism) and optimizes workflow scheduling by distinguishing between blocking activities, i.e., activities that require all their input data to proceed, and non-blocking, i.e., that can be pipelined. Chiron uses two scheduling policies, called blocking and pipeline, as discussed by Dias et al. [2013]. Let A be a task that produces data consumed by a task B. With the blocking policy, B can start only after all the data produced by A are ready. Hence, there is no parallelism between A and B. In addition, the tasks of each activity are generated independently and the scheduling of the tasks of each activity is done independently. With the pipeline policy, B can start as soon as some of its input data chunks are ready. Hence, there is pipeline parallelism. This pipeline parallelism is inspired by database management system (DBMS) pipeline parallelism in Özsu and Valduriez [2011]. Moreover, Chiron takes advantage of the algebraic approach for workflow execution optimization to generate a WEP.

In the WEP execution layer, Chiron uses an execution module file to specify the scheduling method, database information, and input data information. Chiron exploits the dynamic scheduling method for activation execution. Chiron exploits a master-slave architecture (Figure 2.13) for the execution. During the scheduling process, each time a slave node is available, it requests new activations from the master node, which in turn searches for unexecuted tasks and dispatches them to the slave. This approach is efficient for single-site implementations, where communication latency is negligible, and there is a shared file system. The scheduling process is performed at the beginning of the execution of each activity when the activations are being generated. Then, the activation execution module at each computing node executes the corresponding scheduled activations. When all the activations of the activities are executed, the activity manager analyzes the activities to find new activations to execute. The process of activity analysis, activation scheduling, and activation execution are repeated until all activities have been executed.

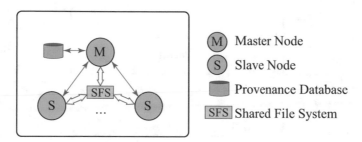

Figure 2.13: Architecture of Chiron.

During workflow execution, the activity manager, the activation scheduler and the activation executor generate provenance data, which is gathered by the provenance data manager. The provenance data manager is located at the master node of the cluster. Chiron gathers execution data, light domain data, and provenance data into a database, i.e., PostgreSQL, structured following the PROV-Wf [Costa et al., 2013] provenance model. The execution of activation in Chiron is based on MPJ [Carpenter et al., 2000], an MPI-like message passing system. In the infrastructure layer, Chiron exploits a shared-disk file system and database for data storage. Since the input data, intermediate data, and output data of workflows are stored in a shared file system, Chiron does not need to manage data transfer between different computing nodes. Chiron can be deployed in a cluster composed of physical computers or virtual machines (VMs) in the cloud. The architecture of the deployment of Chiron is presented in Figure 2.13, where a computing node is a master node and the other nodes are slave nodes.

The provenance model [Ogasawara et al., 2013] is presented in Figure 2.14. In this model, a workflow is composed of several activities. An activity has an operator, i.e., the program for this activity. The status of the activity can be ready, running, or finished. The *activationCommand* of an activity is to execute the activity. The *extractorCommand* is to generate provenance data for the corresponding activations. The time at which the activity execution starts is *executionStart* and the time at which it ends is *executionEnd*. One activity is related to several activations, input relations, and output relations. One relation is the input or output parameters for the activity. Each relation has its attributes and tuples. The activations of an activity are generated based on the input relation of the activity. An activation processes the files associated with the corresponding activity. Each activation has a status, i.e., ready, running, or finished. Also, the start time and end time of its execution is recorded as *ExecutionStart* and *ExecutionEnd*. During execution, the corresponding information of activities, files, and activations are stored as provenance data. Chiron is adapted to the cloud through its extension, Scicumulus [de Oliveira et al., 2010, 2012b]. SciCumulus provides a framework for parallel workflows.

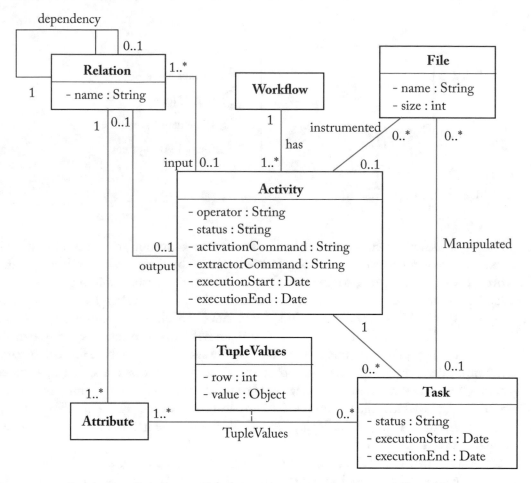

Figure 2.14: Single-Site Provenance Model, based on Ogasawara et al. [2013].

SciCumulus architecture (Figure 2.15) is composed of four main components: SCCore, SCSetup, SCStarter, and SCQP (SciCumulus Query Processor). SCSetup is responsible for storing and retrieving prospective provenance to/from the provenance database. Using this component, scientists insert/update the structure of the workflows in the database. When the structure of the workflow is already inserted in the provenance database, SCStarter can be invoked. SCStarter component is responsible for configuring the environment for executing the workflow. In the case of executions in cloud environments, SCStarter is responsible for deploying virtual machines and configuring storage services before the workflow execution. SCStarter has to be compatible with the cloud API. In the current version, SCStarter works with Amazon AWS API.

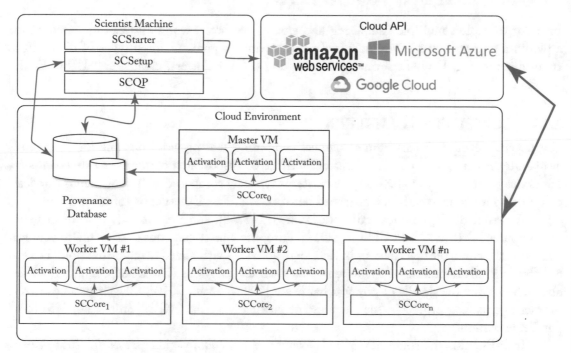

Figure 2.15: SciCumulus Architecture.

When all virtual machines and storage services are running, Starter invokes SCCore in each virtual machine. SCCore is an MPJ (MPI-like)[3] application, so it runs in all virtual machines at the same time using message passing (each virtual machine contains an instance of SCCore according to the rank of the virtual machine, i.e., $SCCore_0$, $SCCore_1$, etc.) SCCore follows a Master/Worker architecture. The SCCore-Master ($SCCore_0$) is responsible for scheduling the workflow activities in the several virtual machines. Also, SCCore-Master is responsible for collecting retrospective provenance data and storing it in the provenance database. All other instances of SCCore-Workers receive activations to execute and request more activations. In the original version of SciCumulus, all data is stored in one single bucket in the S3 service. Thus, it is not fragmented either distributed in different buckets. The same problem occurs with other existing SWfMSs since they do not consider data file distribution and results' confidentiality issues. The SCQP component is responsible for querying the provenance database during or after the workflow execution. It can be used by scientists to steer the workflow or to perform a *post-mortem* analysis of the results. For more information about SciCumulus, please refer to de Oliveira et al. [2010].

[3]http://mpj-express.org/

2.2 DISTRIBUTED ENVIRONMENTS USED FOR EXECUTING WORKFLOWS

In order to exploit multiple computing and storage resources, workflows can be executed in a plethora of distributed environments. In this section, we present three types of distributed environments, i.e., High-Performance Computing (HPC) clusters, clouds, and DISC Environments.

2.2.1 COMPUTING CLUSTERS

Cluster computing is a paradigm of parallel computing that provides high performance and availability. A computing cluster, or cluster for short, consists of a set of interconnected computing nodes [Chowdhury et al., 2011]. A cluster is typically composed of homogeneous physical computers interconnected by a high-speed network, e.g., Fast Ethernet or Infiniband.

A cluster can be composed of nodes in a grid [Foster and Kesselman, 2003] or in a supercomputer [Critchlow and Chin Jr., 2011]. Also, the cluster can consist of virtual machines (VMs) in the cloud (virtual cluster). In the cloud, a VM is a virtualized machine (computer), i.e., a software implementation of a computer that executes programs (like a real computer) while abstracting away the details of physical hardware [Zhang et al., 2010]. Cluster users can rely on message passing protocols, such as message passing interface (MPI) [Snir et al., 1998] for parallel execution.

In HPC clusters, some SWfMSs [Deelman et al., 2005, Ogasawara et al., 2013, Zhao et al., 2007a] can provide workflow parallelization using MPI [Snir et al., 1998] (or an MPI-like language) or a middleware within the system. Since they have full control of the parallel workflow execution, these SWfMSs can leverage parallelism at different levels and yield the maximum level of performance. Some other SWfMSs outsource parallelization and workflow scheduling to external execution tools, e.g., web services or Hadoop MapReduce systems [Wang et al., 2009]. These SWfMSs can achieve activity parallelism but not data parallelism (see Section 2.1.4), which is generally performed in the external execution tools.

2.2.2 CLOUD COMPUTING

Cloud computing encompasses on-demand, reliable services provided over the Internet (typically represented as a cloud) with easy access to virtually infinite computing capacity, storage, and networking resources. This pool of resources is typically exploited by a pay-per-use model, in which guarantees are offered by the cloud provider utilizing customized Service-Level Agreements (SLAs). SLA is a part of a service contract where a service is formally defined [Wieder et al., 2011].

One of the significant differences between grid and cloud is the business model, i.e., the cloud offers a pay-as-you-go method, while the grid is based on resource exchange [Foster et al., 2008]. Also, clouds provide support for pricing, accounting, SLA management, visualization, security control, and so on [Foster et al., 2008]. Cloud services can be divided into three broad categories: Software-as-a-Service (SaaS), Platform-as-a-Service (PaaS), and Infrastructure-as-a-Service (IaaS). SaaS is the delivery of application software as a service such as an email or Microsoft Office 365. PaaS is the delivery of a computing platform with development tools and APIs as a service, e.g., Microsoft Azure. IaaS is the delivery of computing infrastructure (i.e., computing, networking, and storage resources) as a service such as Amazon Elastic Compute Cloud (EC2) and Amazon Web Services (AWS). SaaS, PaaS, and IaaS can be useful to develop, share, and execute workflow components as cloud services. Clouds have already demonstrated their suitability to execute workflows that demand HPC [Sadooghi et al., 2017]. Thus, to execute a workflow in the cloud, all activations have to be scheduled and executed in parallel on a set of VMs $VM = \{vm_1, vm_2, \ldots, vm_d\}$.

However, in the rest of this section, we will focus on IaaS, which will allow for running existing workflows in the cloud. The cloud has some useful features to execute workflows. Infrastructure can scale up and down dynamically based on application resource needs [Foster et al., 2008], e.g., SWfMSs. In particular, the quality of service guaranteed by SLA can yield more stable performance. Juve et al. [2013b] compare the performance of an astronomy application with the Pegasus SWfMS in the grid, the commercial cloud, and the academic cloud. They conclude that the performance is the least stable in a grid and more stable in a commercial cloud than an academic cloud.

In this section, we first present the techniques for data storage in the cloud and the adaptations of SWfMSs for cloud environments, including workflow execution in a single-site cloud and that in multiple cloud sites.

Data Storage in the Cloud

Data storage in the cloud is critical for the performance of workflows. It can be performed using different file systems. A file system is in charge of controlling how information is stored and retrieved in a computer or a cluster [Arkoudas et al., 2004]. In the cloud, IaaS users need a file system that can be concurrently accessible for all the VMs. This can be achieved through a shared-disk file system or a distributed file system. In a shared-disk file system, all the computing nodes of the cluster share some data storage that is generally remotely located. Examples of shared-disk file systems include General Parallel File System (GPFS) [Schmuck and Haskin, 2002], Global File System (GFS) [Preslan et al., 1999] and Network File System (NFS) [Sandberg et al., 1988]. A distributed file system stores data directly in the file system that is constructed by gathering storage space in each computing node in a shared-nothing architecture. Files must be partitioned into chunks, e.g., through a hash function on records' keys, and the chunks are distributed among computing nodes. Different from the shared-disk file system, computing nodes have to load the data chunks from the distributed file system to the local system before local processing. Cloud users can deploy a file system by installing the corresponding frameworks (e.g., GPFS framework or HDFS [hdf]) in the virtual machines with the cloud storage resources such as Microsoft Blob Storage and Amazon Elastic Block Store (EBS). Alternatively, cloud users can mount Amazon Simple Storage Service (S3) into all the Linux-based VMs so all the virtual machines can have access to the same storage resource, as with a shared-disk file system.

Workflow Execution at a Cloud Site

In a single-site cloud environment, SWfMSs can be directly installed in the virtual machines and exploit services deployed in the cloud [de Oliveira et al., 2012a,b, Deelman et al., 2012, Juve and Deelman, 2011a, Wolstencroft et al., 2013]. Existing parallelization techniques, e.g., parallelism techniques (see Section 2.1.4), scheduling techniques (see Section 2.1.4), and existing execution models in HPC clusters [Deelman et al., 2012], can be used to execute a workflow in the cloud.

SWfMSs can exploit some middleware to create or remove VMs and enable the communication between VMs in order to execute workflows in the cloud [Afgan et al., 2010, Hategan et al., 2011, Wang and Altintas, 2012]. Such middleware includes Coasters [Hategan et al., 2011] in Swift/T, Kepler EC2 actors [Wang and Altintas, 2012], CloudMan [Afgan et al., 2010] for Galaxy, and RabbitMQ12 for Triana[4] SWfMS.

These tools can provide computing and storage provisioning for workflow execution or communication between VMs. However, they cannot take advantage of the dynamic provisioning features of the cloud. Some SWfMSs can take advantage of the scalability of the cloud to provision VMs and storage for workflow execution [Afgan et al., 2010] based on a provisioning system [de Oliveira et al., 2012a,b, Fard et al., 2013a, Juve and Deelman, 2011b, Ostermann et al., 2009, 2011]. Since high parallelization degree can lead to less execution time, SWfMSs can dynamically create new VMs in order to reduce execution time under monetary cost constraint. However, if the estimated monetary cost of workflow execution with the current number of VMs exceeds the monetary cost constraint, SWfMSs can remove some VMs from the virtual cluster.

For instance, SciDim [de Oliveira et al., 2013b] is proposed to estimate an initial virtual cluster size through a multi-objective cost function and provenance data under budget and time limits for the execution of workflows in a cloud extension of Chiron, i.e., Scicumulus [de Oliveira et al., 2010, 2012b].

2.2.3   DATA-INTENSIVE SCALABLE COMPUTING CLUSTERS

Several scientists employ SWfMS for the modeling, enacting, and monitoring of the execution of large-scale parallel workflows. SWfMSs provide a series of advantages for scientists, including a variety of scheduling strategies, fault-tolerance techniques, and provenance management mechanisms. However, since one single SWfMS may not be optimized for all classes of scientific workflows [Juve et al., 2013b], some scientists are migrating their IO-intensive workflows

---

[4]Triana in cloud: http://www.trianacode.org/news.php.

to execute in DISC systems, such as Apache Spark.[5] Examples are Kira in astronomy [Zhang et al., 2018], Spark-GA [Mushtaq et al., 2017], GOAT [Kanzki et al., 2016], and ADAM[6] in the bioinformatics domain.

Such data-intensive science [Critchlow and Chin Jr., 2011, Hey et al., 2012] requires the integration of two fairly different paradigms: HPC and DISC. HPC is computer-centric and focuses on high performance of simulation applications, typically using powerful yet expensive supercomputers. DISC [Bryant, 2011], on the other hand, is data-centric and focuses on fault tolerance and scalability of web and cloud applications using cost-effective clusters of commodity hardware. Examples of DISC systems include big data processing frameworks such as Hadoop or Apache Spark, or NoSQL systems (see Bondiombouy and Valduriez [2016], which includes a survey of DISC systems). To harness parallel processing, HPC uses a low-level programming model (such as MPI or OpenMP), while DISC relies on powerful data processing operators (Map, Reduce, Filter, etc.). Data storage is also entirely different: supercomputers typically rely on a shared disk infrastructure and data must be loaded in compute nodes before processing, while DISC systems rely on a shared-nothing cluster (of disk-based nodes) and data partitioning. Spurred by the growing need to analyze big scientific data, the convergence between HPC and DISC has been a recent topic of interest [Asch et al., 2018, Fox et al., 2015]. Following, we explain with more detail the Apache Spark, which is used as a framework in Chapter 5.

2.2.4 APACHE SPARK

Apache Spark is a large-scale data processing framework designed for the optimization of batch and iterative parallel operations on large datasets using different programming languages such as Python, Scala, and Java. Spark not only enables the parallel execution of applications through a sequence of MapReduce-like operations [Zaharia et al., 2010a] (i.e., transformations) but also introduces significant response-time gains by exploiting the memory storage in each machine of the cluster compared with previous MapReduce frameworks [Zaharia et al., 2010a]. Spark is based on a master/worker architecture. There is a driver that interacts with a single coordinator called master (i.e., cluster manager) that manages workers in which executors run according to Figure 2.16. A Spark application usually consists of a driver program that executes the user's primary function and runs several parallel operations in a cluster.

One of the main advantages of using Spark is that it makes use of the Resilient Distributed Dataset (RDD), which can be cached in the memory storage of multiple nodes in a cluster. The RDD is an immutable and distributed collection of objects that are produced and consumed by Spark operators. A dataset in RDD is split into logical partitions, which may be processed on different nodes of the cluster, i.e., data objects are processed in parallel by the workers. RDDs can be created in different ways: (i) by parallelizing an existing collection in the program, or (ii) making a reference to a dataset in external storage, e.g., Hadoop Distributed File System

---

[5]https://spark.apache.org/
[6]https://adam.readthedocs.io/en/latest/

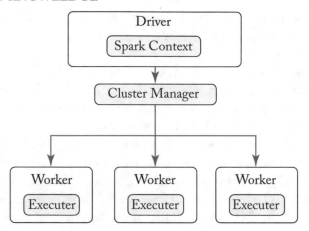

Figure 2.16: Apache spark architecture.

(HDFS). RDDs provide support for two types of operations on data (i) transformations, where a new dataset is created based on a previous one, and (ii) actions, which return results to the driver. One example is presented in Figure 2.17. In Figure 2.17, the input data is loaded to RDD_1 in four partitions. Each partition is consumed by a transformation and generates a new partition for the subsequent RDD until the final result is produced and passed to the driver.

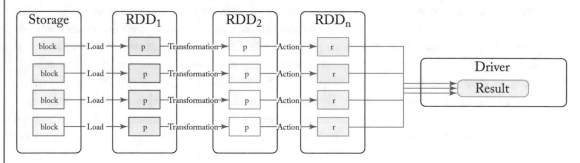

Figure 2.17: Use of RDDs

Since RDDs are immutable collections, every time a transformation is executed, a new RDD is created. This loop continues until an action is performed and a result is generated. Thus, several RDDs may be created during the execution of a Spark application as depicted in the RDD Life Cycle presented in Figure 2.18.

Furthermore, instead of just only using Map and Reduce, Apache Spark also enables the use of other functional programming operators, such as filter, join and collect [Zaharia et al., 2012b]. A typical sequence of an Apache Spark routine is as follows:

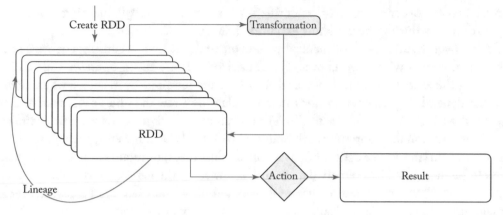

Figure 2.18: The life cycle of RDDs.

1. Building (a set of) RDDs by reading from distributed file systems, caching any (part of) other previously loaded RDD, or parallelizing a collection;

2. Processing each content on the RDD partition by using functions that *(i)* resemble high-level operators, such as filtering, and *(ii)* avoid external parameters; and

3. Reducing the resulting RDDs by using aggregate conditions such as counting, summing, and sorting.

The framework resorts to RDDs abstractions for the management of data collections consumed and produced by either operations or workflow activities. The rationale is that each RDD represents a set of read-only data collections partitioned across the available computational resources [Zaharia et al., 2012b]. Apache Spark caches RDD contents into available memory of distributed and parallel environments, e.g., clusters or clouds, so that it can be recovered whenever an RDD partition is lost.

Accordingly, Spark can employ a mechanism for collecting and querying the fault tolerance lineage of data. Such a fault-tolerant mechanism analyzes the history of activities and the flow of data (i.e., data derivation in a specific application) for the rebuilding of lost partitions [Zaharia et al., 2012b].

Although Spark can be set to *log* some workflow activities [Armbrust et al., 2015, Zaharia et al., 2012b], the framework only targets the lineage of activities as provenance data by recording the name of the activities. Despite the handling of both debugging and activity identifiers, Spark does not register other provenance-related data and provides neither data analytics nor queries regarding domain data [Armbrust et al., 2015]. Such a lack of support for parameterized storage and retrieval of provenance prevents scientific applications from fully benefiting from detailed analyses of results during the workflow execution [Zaharia et al., 2010a].

Moreover, Spark does not manage provenance-related data regarding the execution of black-box programs within workflows. The framework resorts to an operator called *pipe* for transferring the execution control to a black-box program temporarily in such a way that workflows that depend on *pipe* operator for the manipulation of raw data files must read and write from standard I/O. An alternative to the *pipe* operator is redesigning (or rewriting) the entire scientific application for using the Spark Standard I/O to RDDs. However, such an approach is either unfeasible (the source code is not available in most cases) or requires the users to pick between *(i)* the flush of all in-memory data to disk followed by the loading of the obtained results back into main memory, or *(ii)* the use of distributed file system (e.g., HDFS), which removes the major advantages of Spark: data locality and in-memory processing.

2.3 CONCLUSION

In this chapter, we discussed the key concepts of workflows and SWfMSs and the execution environments of workflows. We present the key concepts of workflows in four sections. First, we introduced the definitions of workflows. Then, we presented the definitions and a five-layer functional architecture of SWfMSs and the corresponding functions. The five-layer architecture is composed of presentation, user services, WEP generation, WEP execution, and infrastructure. Afterward, we presented the basic techniques for the parallel execution of workflows in SWfMSs: parallelization and scheduling. We showed how different kinds of parallelism (coarse-grained parallelism, data parallelism, independent parallelism, and pipeline parallelism) can be exploited for parallelizing workflows. The scheduling methods to allocate activations to computing resources can be static or dynamic, with different trade-offs, or hybrid to combine the advantages of static and dynamic scheduling methods. Workflow scheduling may include an optimization phase to minimize a multi-objective function in a given context (cluster, DISC, cloud). However, unlike in database query optimization, this scheduling optimization phase is often not explicit and mixed with the scheduling method. Fourth, to illustrate the use of the techniques, we gave an analysis of nine popular SWfMSs (Pegasus, Swift/T, Kepler, Taverna, Chiron, Galaxy, Triana, SciCumulus, and Askalon) and a science gateway framework (WS-PGRADE/gUSE). Then, we detailed the distributed environments to execute workflows, including HPC clusters, cloud, and DISC environments. In the following chapters, we present existing solutions for managing workflows in single-site and multi-site clouds and DISC environments.

CHAPTER 3

Workflow Execution in a Single-Site Cloud

The cloud provides several different computing resources and appears as appropriate infrastructure for executing data-intensive workflows. However, executing a workflow in the cloud is not a simple task. According to the cloud and DISC workflow life-cycle presented in Figure 1.3, first the SWfMS has to deploy the necessary resources, i.e., virtual machines provisioning is critical for workflow execution. Therefore, since workflow execution takes much time and money, it is fundamental to achieve multi-objectives, i.e., reducing both execution time and financial cost when scheduling the activations to the virtual machines that are part of the virtual cluster.

Although clouds can be single-site and multi-site, in this chapter, we address a problem of how to manage workflows in a single-site cloud. The goal is to present how to provision virtual machines in this environment and to execute a workflow while reducing execution time and financial costs. To the best of the authors' knowledge, a complete solution must present a multi-objective cost model that considers execution time and financial costs, a virtual machine provisioning mechanism, and a scheduling mechanism. This chapter is based mostly on the work of de Oliveira et al. [2012a], de Oliveira et al. [2012b], de C. Coutinho et al. [2014], and Liu et al. [2016a].

3.1   BIBLIOGRAPHIC AND HISTORICAL NOTES

Workflows are used to model large-scale scientific experiments to process significant amounts of data. In order to process big data, the execution of workflows generally takes much time. As a result, it is fundamental to use parallelism techniques to execute such workflows within a reasonable time. As discussed in Chapter 1, some SWfMSs already provide parallel capabilities, which can take advantage of clusters, grids, and clouds to execute data-intensive workflows.

Since the cloud offers several different types of computing resources and virtually infinite computing capacity, it becomes a promising infrastructure for workflow execution. Through Infrastructure-as-a-Service, i.e., IaaS, cloud providers offer virtual machines to the general public, including scientists, through the Internet [Gonzalez et al., 2009, Vaquero et al., 2008]. Several types of virtual machines are available. The virtual machine type determines some parameters such as the number of virtual CPUs, the size of memory, and the default storage size of hard disk. Deployed virtual machines can be used to create a virtual cluster in the cloud.

However, the problem of defining the number and type of virtual machines to deploy and to schedule all activations of these virtual machines remains open for workflow execution in the cloud since this estimation and scheduling involve various parameters, such as virtual machines characteristics, the behavior of each workflow execution, and so on [de C. Coutinho et al., 2014].

3.1.1   EARLY WORK ON SINGLE-SITE VIRTUAL MACHINE PROVISIONING FOR SCIENTIFIC WORKFLOWS

Although there are several virtual machine provisioning approaches already proposed in the literature, most of them are disconnected from the concept of workflows [Alsarhan, 2017, Chandra, 2013, Choi and Lim, 2014, Faragardi et al., 2018, Nhapi et al., 2016, Panagiotou et al., 2015]; others, although focused on provisioning for workflows, support only a single objective [Emeakaroha et al., 2013] or generate provisioning plans without considering the behavior of the workflow execution [Shen et al., 2011, Xu et al., 2012]. On the other hand, some approaches already consider multi-objectives and workflow behavior while deploying virtual machines for workflow execution [de C. Coutinho et al., 2014, de Oliveira et al., 2013b, Liu et al., 2016a].

SciDim [de Oliveira et al., 2013b] is a provisioning mechanism that aims at generating a provisioning plan based on a metaheuristic, i.e., genetic algorithm [Resende and Ribeiro, 2016]. In genetic algorithms, a set of candidate solutions to an optimization problem is evolved in order to find better solutions. Each candidate solution is associated with a set of chromosomes (i.e., a set of properties) that are mutated. In general, the solutions are represented as strings of 0 and 1, but other implementations are also possible, according to Iwamoto et al. [1993]. In the implementation presented by de Oliveira et al. [2013b], each chromosome is composed of four genes, each one associated with a specific type of virtual machine available to use in the workflow executions (in de Oliveira et al. [2013b], the authors follow the Amazon AWS model, and they only consider micro, large, extra-large, and extra-large high capacity virtual machine types). Each allele represents the number of virtual machines of a specific type to be deployed. Users have to specify D_T, the desired execution time, and D_F, the desired financial cost. However, SciDim depends on a dynamic modification of the provisioning plans during workflow execution, which is not supported by most existing SWfMSs.

de C. Coutinho et al. [2014] propose the GraspCC algorithm, based on the GRASP [Martins et al., 1998] metaheuristic, to generate a provisioning plan for workflow execution. However, GraspCC relies on the strong assumption that all activities of a workflows can be executed in parallel, i.e., if there is an activity that cannot be executed in parallel (i.e., there is only one activation associated with that activity), GraspCC determines it can be executed in several virtual machines. Furthermore, it cannot reuse existing deployed virtual machines, and its cost model is simple, e.g., it does not consider the cost of initializing virtual machines, which may be high when many virtual machines have to be deployed. Also, it does not consider the workflow structure for estimating the number of virtual machines to deploy. As a result, real execution time of SciEvol in Amazon AWS [Ama, 2015] may be two times bigger than the estimated time.

Also, some cost models, such as the one proposed by de Oliveira et al. [2012b] for workflow scheduling, cannot be used for estimating an accurate amount of virtual CPUs (CPUs designed to virtual machines) to deploy for workflow execution since they assume, similar to GraspCC, that the entire workload of workflows can be executed in parallel.

In this chapter, we go deeper into the Single-Site Virtual Machine Provisioning (SSVP— Section 3.3.2) approach to estimate the number of virtual machines for workflow execution. The cost model used to estimate the cost of the execution of workflows extends the one proposed by de Oliveira et al. [2012b], which includes two objectives, i.e., execution time and financial cost. SSVP generates virtual machine provisioning plans (i.e., the list of virtual machines and associated types to deploy) for the execution of workflows with minimum cost in a single-site cloud.

3.1.2 EARLY WORK ON SINGLE-SITE WORKFLOW SCHEDULING

Workflow scheduling in clouds is the process of allocating concrete activations to virtual machines to be executed concurrently during the workflow execution. Activation (i.e., task) scheduling is a well-known NP-complete problem even in simple scenarios, according to Liu and Layland [1973].

The main objective of the scheduling process is to generate an optimized scheduling plan (*SP*), i.e., *SP* defines which activation runs in which virtual machine to minimize some cost such as execution time and financial costs. Scheduling algorithms can be static, dynamic, or hybrid [Liu et al., 2015].

In the last few years, several approaches have been proposed for scheduling workflows in clouds [Arabnejad et al., 2016, Boeres et al., 2011, de Oliveira et al., 2012a,b, Durillo et al., 2013, 2015, Fard et al., 2013b, 2014b, Janetschek et al., 2017, Orhean et al., 2018, Qin and Jiang, 2005, Teylo et al., 2017, 2018, Wang et al., 2014]. Each one of these approaches aims at generating an optimal (or sub-optimal) *SP* for a specific workflow.

However, scheduling and executing the workflows in clouds is still an open, yet important, problem due to several reasons. First, the cloud's pricing model has to be determined to fit in the budget informed by scientists. On the other hand, cloud providers allow for acquiring resources on demand, based on the pay-per-use pricing model, e.g., users pay according to the used-time quantum (e.g., minutes, hours, days, etc.).

Second, clouds are changing environments, and they may be susceptible to performance variations during the execution course of the workflow, thus requiring adaptive/dynamic scheduling solutions. Elastic scaling of resources is a key characteristic of clouds. To provide this feature, resources are allocated and reallocated as needed by the provider, and users are not aware of those changes unless they are an administrator. For example, if scientists execute their workflows using Amazon AWS spot instances [Ama, 2015], virtual machines can be unallocated or moved as the provider needs more CPU capacity in a specific data-center. In the case of Amazon, the demand varies during the year, which means that they may need more resources to handle their Thanksgiving and Christmas rush than they do the rest of the year, for example. These moves and instabilities can produce negative impacts on the scheduling of workflow activations.

Third, in clouds, virtual machine failures are no longer an exception but rather a characteristic of such environments [Jackson, 2012]. Although the cloud provider tries to guarantee the reliability of the environment, workflow scheduling has to consider possible failures when scheduling activations to execute on several distributed virtual machines. Thus, we present some existing approaches for scheduling workflows in clouds.

Durillo et al. [2015] propose a new version of the Heterogeneous Earliest Finish Time (i.e., HEFT) workflow scheduling heuristic for handling multiple conflicting objectives and approximating the Pareto frontier optimal schedules. This new version of HEFT was evaluated using two criteria: performance and financial cost. Authors used synthetic and real-world applications DISC and federated clouds environments.

Similar to the work of Durillo et al. [2015], Arabnejad et al. [2016] proposes the Deadline–Budget Constrained Scheduling (DBCS) heuristic scheduling algorithm that considers two significant constraints for workflow scheduling; time and cost. When using DBCS, users have to inform deadline and budget constraints, and DBCS looks for a feasible solution that accomplishes both constraints.

Janetschek et al. [2017] introduce a Manycore Workflow Runtime Environment (MWRE) that manages workflows on many-core computing architectures. MWRE translates workflows represented in XML to C++ program for execution. This program efficiently schedules the workflow activities using a callback mechanism that resolves dependencies, transfers data, and handles composite activities.

Durillo et al. [2013] propose a bi-objective optimization approach by considering both makespan and energy as objectives. The authors used a Pareto-based workflow scheduling algorithm called MOHEFT using energy consumption and performance models for activity executions.

Boeres et al. [2011] introduce a cost function developed for the Makespan and Reliability Cost Driven (MRCD) algorithm that integrates reliability and performance (execution time) objectives simultaneously in the same formula. This article was the inspiration for the cost model proposed in our approach. However, authors do not consider the financial costs involved in the execution.

Qin and Jiang [2005] present a dynamic scheduling heuristic for parallel real-time jobs on heterogeneous clusters. It is assumed that DAGs model jobs and that they arrive at the system following a Poisson process. The algorithm considers the reliability measure, and there is an admission control so that a parallel real-time job whose deadline cannot be guaranteed is rejected. Although this approach focuses on meeting deadlines (restriction), it does not take into account the financial cost or limit the budget proposed by scientists as well.

Fard et al. [2013b] propose a pricing model and a truthful mechanism for scheduling single activities considering two objectives: financial cost and execution time. Authors analyzed the truthfulness and the efficiency of the mechanism and presented extensive experimental results showing a significant impact of the selfish behavior of the cloud providers on the efficiency of the whole system.

Teylo et al. [2018] propose a static scheduling approach for HPC applications which are composed of independent tasks (bag-of-task) with deadline constraints and considering temporal failures. The scheduling algorithm proposed in this work aims at minimizing financial costs of bag-of-task applications in AWS cloud, respecting its deadline and avoiding temporal failures.

Orhean et al. [2018] propose a reinforcement learning [Busoniu et al., 2010] algorithm to solve the scheduling problem in distributed systems. Reinforcement learning takes into consideration the heterogeneity of the machines and the arrangement of activities in a DAG of dependencies, thus determining a scheduling policy for better execution time.

Teylo et al. [2017] propose a new scheduling approach named Task Scheduling and Data Assignment Problem (TaSDAP) for scientific workflows that considers both task scheduling and the data file assignment problems together. The authors propose a new workflow representation, where nodes of the DAG represent either tasks or data files. The authors implemented a hybrid evolutionary algorithm for solving it named HEA-TaSDAP.

Fard et al. [2014b] propose a generic multi-objective optimization framework supported by a list scheduling heuristic for scientific workflows in heterogeneous DCIs, which includes clouds. The authors performed experiments with a four-objective case. The study comprising makespan, economic cost, energy consumption, and reliability as optimization objectives.

Although all approaches as mentioned earlier consider multi-objectives for scheduling workflow activities in clouds, all of them are static, i.e., they do not take into account the variation of the virtual resources.

In this chapter, we go deeper into the Site Greedy (SGreedy) scheduling algorithm originally proposed by de Oliveira et al. [2012b]. The SGreedy approach is based on a greedy scheduling algorithm and a load balancing algorithm that adapts *SP* according to cloud performance variations. Also, SGreedy aims at meeting deadline and the limit budget informed by users.

3.1.3   CHAPTER GOALS AND CONTRIBUTIONS

In this chapter we consider a single-site cloud, e.g., a single cloud provider in the same data center. The scenario of a multi-site cloud (with single or multiple cloud providers) is beyond the scope of this chapter (it will be presented in Chapter 4).

The main contributions of this chapter are:

1. the design of a multi-objective cost model that includes execution time and financial costs to estimate the cost of executing workflows at a single-site cloud;

2. a single-site virtual machine provisioning approach (SSVP) to generate provisioning plans to execute workflows at a single site;

3. the Site Greedy (SGreedy) scheduling algorithm to generate an *SP* that can be adapted to cloud performance variations; and

4. an experimental evaluation, based on the implementation of SSVP and SGreedy approaches in Microsoft Azure, and using SciEvol [Ocaña et al., 2012b], a bioinformatics workflow for molecular evolution reconstruction, that shows the advantages of the approaches compared with baseline algorithms.

Next, we present the multi-objective cost model, SSVP and SGreedy in details.

3.2   MULTI-OBJECTIVE COST MODEL

In this section, we discuss a multi-objective cost model, which is used to estimate the cost of executing workflows at a single-site cloud. Although there are several available cost models [Arabnejad et al., 2016, Boeres et al., 2011, de Oliveira et al., 2012a,b, Durillo et al., 2013, 2015, Fard et al., 2013b, 2014b, Janetschek et al., 2017, Orhean et al., 2018, Qin and Jiang, 2005, Teylo et al., 2017, 2018, Wang et al., 2014], the cost model presented in this chapter is composed of time cost, i.e., execution time, and financial cost for the execution of workflows in clouds, which are the most common objectives. This cost model is going to be used in the virtual machine provisioning and in activation scheduling. A cost model is composed of a set of formulas to estimate the cost of the execution of workflows according to a scheduling plan. The formalism presented here is an extension of the model proposed by de Oliveira et al. [2012a,b] and Boeres et al. [2011].

The total cost of executing a workflow W can be defined by Equation (3.1):

$$Cost(W, P_L) = \omega_t * T_n(W, P_L) + \omega_m * F_n(W, P_L), \tag{3.1}$$

where ω_t and ω_m represent the weights informed by users to prioritize minimizing the execution time or financial costs, which are positive values such as $\omega_t + \omega_m = 1$. $T_n(W, P_L)$, and $M_n(W, P_L)$ are normalized values that are defined in Sections 3.2 and 3.2. Since the values for execution time and financial costs are normalized, the cost has no unit. In the rest of this chapter, cost represents the normalized cost, which has no real unit. P_L is the provisioning plan, which defines the number and the types of virtual machines to deploy.

Similarly, we can define the cost of executing an activation ac_i in virtual machine vm_j as presented in Equation (3.2):

$$Cost(ac_i, vm_j) = \omega_t * T_n(ac_i, vm_j) + \omega_m * F_n(ac_i, vm_j). \tag{3.2}$$

In the following sections we detail how $T_n(W, P_L)$ and $F_n(W, P_L)$ are modeled.

Execution Time

In this section, we present how to estimate the execution time of a workflow W. Following the formalism presented in Chapter 2, we have a set of activations $AC = \{ac_1, ac_2, ..., ac_n\}$. The execution time of an activation ac_i in a specific virtual machine vm_j is given by $P(ac_i, vm_j)$. Consider also that the virtual machine provisioning plan P_L defines the set of virtual machines to deploy to create a virtual cluster V_C, i.e., $P_L = \{vm_1, vm_2, ..., vm_{pl}\}$ and $P_L \subseteq VM$. Then we may define the execution time of all activations AC in a workflow W as $T(W, P_L)$. Thus, the normalized execution time T_n used in Equation (3.1) can be defined as Equation (3.3):

$$T_n(W, P_L) = \frac{T(W, P_L)}{D_T}, \tag{3.3}$$

where D_T is the user-defined desired time to execute W. Both D_T and D_F (desired financial cost—see Section 3.2) are set by users. Note that some combinations of D_T and D_F may lead to unfeasible scheduling for the execution of the W. We take D_T and D_F into consideration in the cost model, while the real execution time and financial costs may be bigger or smaller depending on the real execution environment.

In order to execute W, the SWfMS needs to initialize the corresponding execution environment and to run the programs in the virtual machines. The initialization time is the total time needed to deploy and initialize virtual machines for the execution of W. The deployment of a virtual machine is the action of creating it under a user account in the cloud. The deployment of the virtual machine defines the type and location, i.e., the cloud site, of the virtual machine. The initialization is the process of starting the virtual machine, installing programs, and configuring parameters of the virtual machine so that it can be used for executing the activations of W. This way, the total time needed for the execution of W can be estimated by the following Equation (3.4):

$$T(W, P_L) = I_T(P_L) + E_T(W, P_L), \tag{3.4}$$

$I_T(P_L)$ represents the time to initialize the environment for a deployment plan P_L and E_T is the effective time to run the programs invoked in W using the deployment plan P_L. The time to provision the virtual machines is estimated by Equation (3.5).

$$I_T(P_L) = m * A_{I_T}. \tag{3.5}$$

A_{I_T} represents the average time to provision a virtual machine. The value of A_{I_T} can be configured by users according to the used cloud environment, which can be obtained by measuring the average time to start, install the required programs, and configure several virtual machines. In the rest of this chapter, we assume that the provisioning plan P_L deploys $|P_L| = m$ virtual machines and that there is only one virtual machine being started at a Web domain at the same time, which is true in Microsoft Azure cloud and many other providers.

Assuming that the provisioning plan P_L corresponds to the deployment of n_{cpu} virtual CPU cores to execute W, according to Amdahl's law [Sun and Chen, 2010], the execution time can be estimated by Equation (3.6):

$$E_T(W, P_L) = \frac{(\frac{\alpha}{n_{cpu}} + (1 - \alpha)) * W_l(W, I_D)}{C_{spc}},\qquad(3.6)$$

where α represents the percentage of the workload W_l that can be executed in parallel. α can be obtained by measuring the total execution time of SWf consuming a small amount of input data I_D a few times with different numbers of virtual CPUs. For instance, let us assume that we have t_1 for n_{cpu} virtual CPUs and t_2 for m_{cpu} virtual CPUs. We can obtain α using Equation (3.7):

$$\alpha = \frac{m_{cpu} * n_{cpu} * (t_2 - t_1)}{m_{cpu} * n_{cpu} * (t_2 - t_1) + n_{cpu} * t_1 - m_{cpu} * t_2}.\qquad(3.7)$$

C_{spc} represents the average computing performance of each virtual CPU core, which is measured by FLOPS (FLoating-point Operations Per Second), following the same approach proposed by de C. Coutinho et al. [2014]. According to Com, we can use the following formula to calculate the computing speed of a virtual CPU core. The unit of CPU frequency F_{eq} is GHz and the unit of computing speed C_{spc} is GFLOPS:

$$C_{spc} = 4 * F_{eq}.\qquad(3.8)$$

Finally, W_l represents the workload of W with specific amounts of input data I, which can be measured by the number of FLOP (FLoat-point Operations) [de C. Coutinho et al., 2014]. All parameters α, W_l and C_{spc} should be configured by the user according to the features of the cloud and the W to be executed. In this chapter, we calculate the workload of a W using the following function where ac_j is one activation of W and w_l represents the workload of activation ac_j consuming input data defined by $input(ac_j)$. We can also define $I = \{i_1, i_2, ..., i_m\} = \bigcup_{j=1}^{m} input(ac_j)$.

$$W_l(W, I) = \sum_{ac_j \in W} w_l(ac_j, input(ac_j)).\qquad(3.9)$$

The workload of an activation with a specific amount of input data is estimated according to the workflow being executed.

Financial Cost

In this section, we present the formalization used to estimate the financial cost to execute W with a provisioning plan P_L. The normalized financial cost F_n used in Equation (3.1) can be defined by Equation (3.10):

$$F_n(W, P_L) = \frac{F(W, P_L)}{D_F},$$

(3.10)

where F is the financial cost associated with the execution of W using the virtual machines defined by P_L. In addition, D_F is the desired financial cost informed by the user.

Let us assume that each activation has a user-defined workload $W_l(act_j, input(ac_j))$ similar to the one previously defined. Similar to Formula (3.4) for estimating the execution time, the financial cost also contains two parts, i.e., initialization and W execution, as defined in Equation (3.11).

$$F_n(W, P_L) = I_{fc}(P_L) + E_{fc}(W, P_L),$$

(3.11)

where I_{fc} represents the financial cost associated with the provision of virtual machines for executing W and E_{fc} is the financial cost to effectively execute W.

The financial cost to initialize the execution environment is estimated by Equation (3.12), i.e., the sum of the financial cost of provisioning each virtual machine.

$$I_{fc}(P_L) = \sum_{i=1}^{m} \left(F(vm_i, s) * \frac{(m - i) * I_T}{T_Q} \right),$$

(3.12)

$F(vm_i)$ is the financial cost to use a virtual machine vm_i per time quantum at site s. I_T represents the average time to provision a virtual machine as previously defined. T_Q is the time quantum in the cloud, which is the smallest possible discrete unit of time to calculate the cost of using a virtual machine. For instance, if the time quantum is 1 min and the price of a virtual machine is 0.5 dollars per hour, the cost to use the virtual machine for the time period of T ($T \geq (N - 1)$ min and $T < N$ min) is $\frac{N*0.5}{60}$ dollars.

The parameter m (determined by SSVP) represents that m virtual machines must be deployed to execute W. Similar to the execution time estimation, we assume that there is only one virtual machine being started at a Web domain at the same time. Also, during the provisioning process, the virtual machine that has fewer virtual CPU cores is provisioned first in order to reduce the financial cost for waiting for the provisioning of other virtual machines. Thus, the order of vm_i is also in this order in Equation (3.12), i.e., vm_i begins with the virtual machine that has less virtual CPU cores.

The financial cost for W execution can be estimated by Equation (3.13), i.e., the financial cost of using n virtual CPU cores during the workflow execution.

$$E_{fc}(W, P_L) = n * F_{cpc} * \lfloor \frac{E_T(W, P_L)}{T_Q} \rfloor. \tag{3.13}$$

$E_T(SWf, P_L)$ is defined in Formula (3.6). The parameter F_{cpc} represents the average financial cost to use one virtual CPU core in one-time quantum in the cloud, which can be the price of virtual machines divided by the number of virtual CPU cores. We assume that the financial cost of each virtual CPU in the virtual machines of different types is the same in the cloud. T_Q represents the time quantum in the cloud.

3.3   SINGLE-SITE VIRTUAL MACHINE PROVISIONING (SSVP)

A cloud provides diverse computing resources and appears as appropriate infrastructures for executing SWfs. However, the problem of choosing the number and the type of VMs remains a critical problem for SWf execution in the cloud since the estimation involves various parameters, such as VM types, and different SWfs [de C. Coutinho et al., 2014]. Although some existing VM provisioning solutions exist [de C. Coutinho et al., 2014, de Oliveira et al., 2013a, Emeakaroha et al., 2013, Shen et al., 2011, Xu et al., 2012], they either focus on a single objective or rely on the strong assumption that the entire workload of SWfs can be executed in parallel. In this section, we present a Single-Site VM Provisioning (SSVP) approach based on the multi-objective cost model presented in Section 3.2. SSVP generates VM provisioning plans for the execution of SWfs with minimum cost for SWf execution at a single cloud site. A VM provisioning plan defines how to provision VMs. The SSVP approach is based on the assumption that part of the workload can be executed only sequentially. Next, we first define the problem to address and then present the SSVP approach.

3.3.1   PROBLEM DEFINITION

The aforementioned virtual machine deployment scenario can be described as a mathematical formulation named CC-IP [de C. Coutinho et al., 2014]. Let P be the set of virtual machine types provided by cloud providers during a set of time quanta. A set of scientists' requirements such as the maximum financial cost C_M , maximum allowed workflow execution time T_M , disk storage D_S, memory capacity MC, and a processing demand of G_f Gflops is defined. Each virtual machine type $p \in P$ has an associated financial cost c_p (i.e., the cost of deploying a virtual machine for one-time quantum, the time quantum varies according to the cloud provider. It can be 1 h, alternatively, 1 min) and computing resources as disk storage dp, memory capacity m_p and processing power of g_p Gflop per time quantum (Gflopt). Moreover, it is a common practice that cloud providers limit the total amount of virtual machines that a single user can deploy. Let us set NM as the maximum number of virtual machines that a user can deploy in a cloud provider. It is worth noticing that the availability of virtual machines is not considered here.

Thus, a binary variable x_{pit} for each $p \in P$, $i \in \{1, \ldots, NM\}$ and $t \in T = \{1, \ldots, TM\}$, such that $x_{pit} = 1$ if and only if virtual machine i of type p is deployed at time t, otherwise $x_{pit} = 0$ is set. Also, consider variable tm as the last-time quantum that a virtual machine was used by the user. In scheduling, this variable is also called the makespan. Since we are aiming at minimizing the amount of virtual machines to deploy, the aforementioned scenario can be formalized as follows:

$$\min \left(\alpha_1 \sum_{p \in P} \sum_{i=}^{N_M} \sum_{t \in T} c_p x_{pit} + \alpha_2 t_m \right), \tag{3.14}$$

where $\alpha_1 + \alpha_2 = 1$.

The objective function presented in Equation (3.14) seeks both the minimization of financial costs and total execution time. The weights α_1 and α_2 define the relevance of each objective in the opinion of users/scientists. This allows for fine tuning of the model, i.e., one can choose if he/she wants a "fast" workflow execution or a "low budget" workflow execution. Generally, since these objectives are conflicting, both objectives cannot arrive at optimal levels simultaneously. For example, if the value of α_1, is close to 1, the model prioritizes "low budget" solutions with high execution time.

Although this model was initially designed for general tasks (standalone applications), it can be easily adapted to be applied in workflows since we can we estimate the number of virtual machines to deploy before each activity execution. However, this approach is not suitable when users run workflows using a pipeline model, since activations from different activities may be executing at the same time. Figure 3.1 presents how we can invoke this model during execution of SciEvol, where the virtual cluster was redimensioned after the execution of activity 4 (from 2 virtual machines to 4 virtual machines).

However, it is well known that exact procedures such as CC-IP and brute-force search have often proved incapable of finding solutions, as they are incredibly time-consuming, particularly for real-world problems as SciEvol workflow. This way, the effective use of heuristics and metaheuristics provides sub-optimal solutions in a reasonable time. Actually, in the scientific workflow domain, these sub-optimal solutions are acceptable since many existing SWfMSs can adapt the number of virtual machines on the execution course of the workflow. Next we go deeper in the Single-Site Virtual Machine Provisioning (SSVP) approach.

3.3.2   SSVP ALGORITHM

Based on the equations presented in Section 3.2, we can now estimate the total execution cost (which considers the execution time and financial cost) to execute a workflow W without considering the cost of site initialization according to Equation (3.15). Equation (3.15) is used to estimate an optimal number of virtual machines, which is used to generate the provisioning plan in SSVP, of virtual CPU cores to deploy for the execution of W.

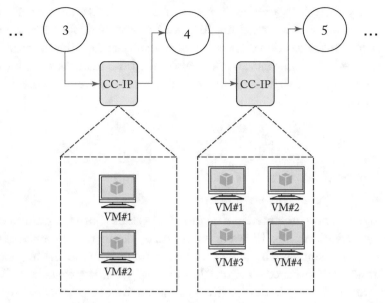

Figure 3.1: Invoking CCIP during SciEvol execution.

$$E_C(W, P_L) = \omega_t * \frac{E_T(W, P_L)}{D_T} + \omega_m * \frac{E_{fc}(W, P_L)}{D_M}. \tag{3.15}$$

In Equation (3.15), $E_T(W, P_L)$ is defined in Equation (3.6), $E_{fc}(W, P_L)$ is defined in Equation (3.13), and D_T and D_M are defined by users. In order to get a general formula to estimate the optimal number of virtual CPUs, we use Formula (3.16), which presents no floor function, for $E_{fc}(W, P_L)$.

$$E_{fc}(W, P_L) = n * F_{cpc} * \frac{E_T(W, P_L)}{T_Q}. \tag{3.16}$$

Finally, the execution cost E_C can be expressed as Equation (3.17) with the parameters defined in Equations (3.18), (3.19) and (3.20).

$$E_C(W, P_L) = a * n + \frac{b}{n} + c, \tag{3.17}$$

given:

$$a = \frac{\omega_m * F_{cpc} * W_l(W, I_D) * (1 - \alpha)}{C_{spc} * T_Q * D_M} \tag{3.18}$$

$$b = \frac{\omega_t * \alpha * W_l(W, I_D)}{C_{spc}(s) * D_T} \tag{3.19}$$

$$c = \left(\frac{\omega_m * \alpha * F_{cpc}}{D_M * T_Q} + \frac{\omega_t * (1 - \alpha)}{D_T} \right) * \frac{W_l(W, I_D)}{C_{spc}(s)}. \tag{3.20}$$

Based on Equation (3.17), we can estimate the minimal execution cost $EC_{\min}$ and an optimal number of virtual CPUs, i.e., n_{opt}, according to Equation (3.21) and Equation (3.22):

$$EC_{\min}(SWf, s) = 2 * \sqrt{a * b} + c \tag{3.21}$$

$$n_{opt} = \sqrt{\frac{b}{a}}. \tag{3.22}$$

When SSVP provisions virtual machines of n_{opt} virtual CPUs, the cost is the minimal based on Equation (3.15), namely $EC_{\min}$, for the execution of W.

It is worth noticing that we consider that a, b, and n are positive numbers; we can calculate the derivative of function (3.17) as:

$$E_C'(N, W, s) = \frac{d}{dn} E_C(n, W, s) = a - \frac{b}{n^2}. \tag{3.23}$$

When n is smaller than $\sqrt{\frac{b}{a}}$, $E_C'(n, W, s)$ is negative and $E_C(n, W, s)$ declines when n grows. When n is bigger than $\sqrt{\frac{b}{a}}$, $E_C'(n, W, s)$ is positive and $E_C(n, W, s)$ increases when n grows. So $E_C(n, W, s)$ has a minimum value when $E_C'(n, W, s)$ equals zero, i.e., $n = \sqrt{\frac{b}{a}}$. And we can calculate the corresponding value of $E_C'(n, W, s)$ as presented in Equation (3.21).

In order to provision virtual machines in a cloud, SSVP uses Algorithm 3.1 to generate a P_L, which minimizes the cost based on the cost model and n_{opt}. In Algorithm 3.1, Line 2 calculates the optimal number of virtual CPUs to deploy according to Formulas (3.18), (3.19), (3.20), and (3.22). Since the number of virtual CPUs should be a positive integer, we take $\lceil \sqrt{\frac{b}{a}} \rceil$ as the optimal number of virtual CPUs to deploy. Lines 4–9 optimize the provisioning plan to reduce the cost to execute W. Lines 4 and 6 calculate the cost to execute SWf based on Formulas (3.3), (3.4), and (3.11). Line 5 improves the provisioning plan by inserting, modifying, or removing an existing virtual machine. If the optimal number of virtual CPUs *CPUNumber* is bigger than the number *ExistingCPUNumberEC* of virtual CPU cores with the consideration of current provisioning plan, and existing virtual CPU cores, a virtual machine is planned to be inserted in the provisioning plan. The virtual machine is of the type that can reduce the difference between *CPUNumber* and *ExistingCPUNumberEC*. If *CPUNumber* is smaller than

---

Algorithm 3.1 Single-Site VM Provisioning (SSVP)

Input : W: the workflow to execute;

m: the number of existing virtual CPUs;

E_{VM}: existing VMs;

limit: the maximum number of virtual CPU cores to deploy at Site s;

Output : P_L: virtual machine provisioning plan

1: $P_L \leftarrow \emptyset$
2: $CPUNumber \leftarrow$ CalculateOptimalNumber(W)
3: **while** $Cost < CurrentCost$ **do**
4:      $CurrentCost \leftarrow$ CalculateCost(W, m, E_{VM}, PL)
5:      $PL' \leftarrow$ improve$(P_L, m, E_{VM}, limit, CPUNumber)$
6:      $Cost \leftarrow$ CalculateCost(W, m, E_{VM}, P'_L)
7:      **if** $Cost < CurrentCost$ **then**
8:          $P_L \leftarrow P'_L$
9:      **end if**
10: **end while**

ExistingCPUNumberEC, the difference between *CPUNumber* and *ExistingCPUNumberEC* is not considerable and the difference can be reduced by modifying the type of an existing virtual machine; the type is planned to be modified in the provisioning plan. Otherwise, an existing virtual machine is planned to be removed in the provisioning plan. The virtual machine to be removed is selected from all the existing ones in order to most reduce the difference between *CPUNumber* and *ExistingCPUNumberEC*. If the cost to execute W can be reduced by improving P_L, the provisioning will be updated (Line 8), and the improvement of P_L continues (Line 9). Note that the direction in the *improve* function of SSVP is determined by comparing *CPUNumber* and *ExistingCPUNumberEC*, while the function in GraspCC [de C. Coutinho et al., 2014] compares the current provisioning plan with all possible solutions by changing one virtual machine in the P_L.

While choosing the type of virtual machine to be added, modified, or removed, storage constraints,[1] specifying that the scheduled site should have enough storage resources for executing *SWf*, should be considered. If the storage constraint is not met, more storage resources are planned to be added to the file system of the virtual cluster[2] at the site. Note that the number of virtual CPU cores to be deployed in P_L, generated by Algorithm 3.1, may be smaller than n_{opt} because the cost (time and financial costs) to initialize the site is also considered.

---

[1] All virtual machine types (A1, A2, A3, and A4) previously mentioned can execute the activities of SciEvol in terms of memory.

[2] We assume that a virtual cluster exploits a shared file system for W execution. In a shared file system, all the computing nodes in the virtual cluster share some data storage that is generally remotely located [Liu et al., 2014a].

3.4   SGREEDY SCHEDULING ALGORITHM

In this section we present SGreedy scheduling algorithm, proposed by de Oliveira et al. [2012a]. Let us consider $\varphi(W, VM)$ as a scheduling of all activations of AC of W on VM. Formally, given a workflow W that includes a set of activities $A = \{a_1, a_2 ..., a_n\}$ and a set $AC = \{ac_1, ..., ac_k\}$ of activations created for parallel workflow execution, let $\varphi(W, VM) = \{sched_1, sched_2, ..., sched_g\}$ for AC. Let us also consider as $sched(ac_i, vm_j, start, end)$ where $start$ and end are the start and end time of an activation cai executing on vm_j. Since the cloud environment is a changing environment (virtual machines are deployed and destroyed during the execution course of the workflow) we cannot create an *a priori* scheduling plan. Thus, the several $sched$ have to be generated during the course of the experiment. We define $ord(sched_i)$ to be the position of $sched_i$ in the sequence of all schedules. We say that $sched_i \leq sched_j \leftrightarrow ord(sched_i) \leq ord(sched_j)$.

In clouds, the search space for scheduling is bi-dimensional (execution time and financial cost). In fact, in this context, the scheduling solutions represent the trade-offs between these two criteria. SGreedy scheduling algorithm is then based on minimizing execution time and financial cost criteria. To schedule based on these two objectives, we use the weighted cost function presented in Equation (3.2).

SGreedy works as follows: for each vm_j in VM that is idle and requests for an activation to execute, it then performs a search for the best ac_i in the list of available activations AC' (the ones ready to be executed) to execute in vm_j following the bi-objective cost model (Equation (3.2)). Thus, given $vm_j \in VM$ as the next virtual machine to execute an activation, SGreedy has to find $ac_i \in AC'$, which minimizes the cost function. Note that the chosen ac_i is the one that satisfies Equation (3.24), as follows:

$$C(ac_i, vm_j) = \min_{\forall vm_j \in VM} Cost(ac_i, vm_j). \tag{3.24}$$

The weights associated with each criterion, i.e., ω_t and ω_m, are variables in the form $0 \leq \omega_t \leq 1$ and $0 \leq \omega_m \leq 1$, which represents the level of relevance for each criterion for the scientist (where $\omega_t + \omega_m = 1$). By allowing scientists to inform ω_t and ω_m, we provide a way to perform a fine tuning in the workflow execution parameters.

Using SGreedy we are able to solve three different scenarios: (S1) to find the fastest scheduling plan, i.e., $\omega_m \leq \omega_t$; (S2) to find the plan with the smallest financial cost, i.e., $\omega_t \leq \omega_m$; and (S3) to find a balanced scheduling plan (each one of the criterion — total execution time and financial cost — have equal weight), i.e., $\omega_m = \omega_t$. To implement each one of these scenarios we have to set different values of ω_m and ω_t in order to focus on each specific criterion.

However, independently of the particular scenario that is being solved we execute the same scheduling algorithm, i.e., SGreedy, just varying weights in the cost function presented in Equation (3.24). SGreedy is based on a greedy scheduling algorithm [de Oliveira et al., 2012a,b] and a load balancing algorithm that scales up and down virtual machines involved in the execution to meet the deadline and the limit budget informed by users as follows.

Algorithm 3.2 SGreedy Workflow Scheduling

Input : W: the workflow to execute;

E_{VM}: a set of existing VMs;

Deadline: The deadline informed by scientists;

Budget: the budget informed by scientists

ω_t: execution time criterion weight

ω_m: financial cost criterion weight

Output : $\varphi(W, E_{VM})$: The schedule of W on E_{VM}

1: $loadBalance(E_{VM}, Deadline, Budget)$
2: $\varphi(W, E_{VM}) \leftarrow \emptyset$
3: $available \leftarrow \{ac_i \in AC | \forall ac_j \in AC \wedge \neg dep(ac_i, ac_j)\}$
4: $ready \leftarrow \{vm_i \in VM | \forall vm_j \in VM \wedge idle(vm_j)\}$
5: **while** $available \neq \emptyset$ **do**
6:   **for** $vm_j \in ready$ **do**
7:    **for** $ac_i \in available$ **do**
8:     $cost \leftarrow \omega_t * T_n(ac_i, vm_j) + \omega_m * F_n(ac_i, vm_j)$
9:     $possible \leftarrow possible + \{sched(ac_i, vm_j, cost)\}$
10:    **end for**
11:    $chosen \leftarrow \min possible$
12:    $\varphi(W, E_{VM}) \leftarrow \varphi(W, E_{VM}) + chosen$
13:    $perform(chosen)$
14:    $ready \leftarrow ready - \{vm\} + \{vmj \in VM | idle(vm_j)\}$
15:    $available \leftarrow \{ac_i \in AC | ac_j \in AC \wedge \neq dep(ac_i, ac_j)\}$
16:   **end for**
17: **end while**
18: **return** $\varphi(W, E_{VM})$

Algorithm 3.2 is responsible for choosing the most suitable activation ac_i to execute for a given idle virtual machine vm_j based on the proposed cost model. Algorithm 3.2 starts by calling a load balancing procedure (Algorithm 3.3) that allows for SGreedy to adapt the number of resources to fit the deadline and the limit budget informed by scientists. After that, SGreedy loads the list of available activations without data dependencies, i.e., ready to be executed, (line 3) and the list of idle virtual machines (line 4). Then the algorithm starts analyzing if there are idle virtual machines (line 6) and available activations to be executed (line 7). If there is at least one activation to execute, the algorithm searches for the best activation for a specific virtual machine. It is worth noticing that Algorithm 3.2 orders the available virtual machines according to their capacity and the scenario (S1, S2, or S3). If the scenario is S1, then the algorithm orders the virtual machines from the least powerful one to the most powerful one. On the other hand, if the considered scenario is S2, then the algorithm orders the list of available virtual machines from the most powerful one to the least powerful one.

For each activation ready to be executed, SGreedy calculates the cost of executing activation ac_i in virtual machine vm_j (line 8). All possible schedules are stored (line 9), and once all activations are analyzed, the schedule with minimum cost is chosen (line 11). After that, the scheduling plan is updated (line 12) and the activation is performed (line 13). Finally, the lists of available activations and idle virtual machines are updated (lines 14 and 15). At the end of the algorithm, the final schedule plan is provided (line 18).

Algorithm 3.3 focuses on allowing the SWfMS to adapt the number of resources to fit the deadline and the limit budget informed by scientists. Thus, Algorithm 3.3 allows for SWfMS to quickly scale virtual cluster capacity, both up and down, as your computing requirements (deadline and budget) cannot be met. Algorithm 3.3 starts by verifying if the throughput (activations finished per unit of time) has varied (line 6). If not, nothing changes in the set of available virtual machines. If the throughput has reduced, the algorithm simulates the new normalized time (T_n') and the new normalized financial cost (F_n') (lines 7–8). If (T_n') is larger than the deadline and (F_n') is smaller than the informed budget, the number of virtual machines is scaled up in order to meet the deadline (lines 9–15). On the other hand, if the deadline is met, but the financial cost is over budget, then the algorithm scales down the number of virtual machines involved in the execution (lines 17–21). This reduction in the number of virtual machines may cause some interruption in the execution of activations. Therefore, some activations should be rescheduled.

3.5   EVALUATING SSVP AND SGREEDY

In order to evaluate the SSVP and SGreedy, we used a fragment of SciEvol with only two analysis phases as presented in Figure 3.2. This simplified version of SciEvol is composed of only nine activities.

The experiments show the advantages of SGreedy executing in a virtual cluster deployed using SSVP over one deployed using GraspCC in two aspects. The first aspect is that SSVP can estimate cost more accurately than GraspCC based on the cost as mentioned in earlier model. The second aspect is that the provisioning plans generated by SSVP and used by SGreedy incur less financial cost than that generated by GraspCC. All experiments presented in this chapter are based on the execution of the SciEvol in the Japan East region of the Microsoft Azure cloud. During the experiments, the life circle of virtual machines is composed of creation, start, configuration, stop, and deletion. The creation, start, stop, and deletion of a virtual machine was managed by using Azure CLI.

Algorithm 3.3 Load Balancing

Input : E_{VM}: a set of existing virtual machines;
Deadline: The deadline informed by scientists;
Budget: the budget informed by scientists
AC: the list of available activations

Output : -

1: *throughput* $\leftarrow \infty$
2: *prevThroughput* $\leftarrow \infty$
3: **while** $AC \neq \emptyset$ **do**
4:      $E'_{VM} \leftarrow E_{VM}$
5:      *throughput* $\leftarrow \frac{|E_{VM}||AC|}{T(W, E_{VM})}$
6:      **if** *throughput* $\leq$ *prevThroughput* **then**
7:          $T_n \leftarrow simulateT_n(E_{VM}, AC)$
8:          $F_n \leftarrow simulateF_n(E_{VM}, AC)$
9:          **if** $(T_n \geq Deadline) \wedge (F_n \leq Budget)$ **then**
10:             **while** $(T_n' \leq Deadline) \wedge (F_n' \leq Budget)$ **do**
11:                 $E'_{VM} \leftarrow E'_{VM} + 1$
12:                 $T_n' \leftarrow simulateT_n(E'_{VM}, AC)$
13:                 $F_n' \leftarrow simulateF_n(E'_{VM}, AC)$
14:             **end while**
15:             $E_{VM} \leftarrow E'_{VM}$
16:         **end if**
17:         **if** $(MS \leq Deadline) \wedge (F_n \geq Budget)$ **then**
18:             **while** $(T_n' \leq Deadline) \wedge (MC' \leq Budget)$ **do**
19:                 $E'_{VM} \leftarrow E'_{VM} - 1$
20:                 $T_n' \leftarrow simulateT_n(E'_{VM}, AC)$
21:                 $F_n' \leftarrow simulateF_n(E'_{VM}, AC)$
22:             **end while**
23:             $E_{VM} \leftarrow E'_{VM}$
24:         **end if**
25:         **if** $(T_n \geq Deadline) \wedge (F_n \geq Budget)$ **then**
26:             $E_{VM} \leftarrow \emptyset$
27:             $AC \leftarrow \emptyset$
28:         **end if**
29:     **end if**
30: **end while**

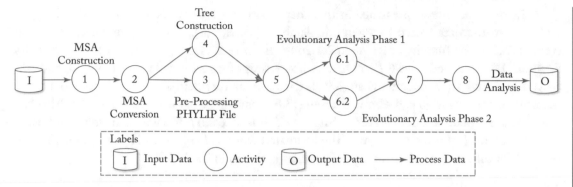

Figure 3.2: A fragment of SciEvol workflow.

In the experiments, the execution of the workflow is performed by a modified version of Chiron SWfMS [Liu et al., 2016a, Ogasawara et al., 2013]. The goal is to show that SGreedy + SSVP is suitable to dynamic provisioning of virtual machines and activation scheduling by making a good trade-off among different objectives for the workflow execution. Microsoft Azure provides five tiers of virtual machines, which are basic tier, standard tier, optimized compute, performance optimized compute, and compute intensive. Each tier contains several types of virtual machines. In one Web domain, users can deploy different types at the same tier. In our experiments, we consider four types, namely $A1$, $A2$, $A3$, and $A4$, in the standard tier. The features of the types are summarized in Table 3.1. In Azure, the time quantum is 1 min. In addition, the average time to provision a virtual machine is estimated at 2.9 min. Each virtual machine uses Linux Ubuntu 12.04 (64-bit) and is configured with the necessary software for SciEvol. All virtual machines are configured to be accessed using Secure Shell (SSH).

Table 3.1: Parameters of different types of virtual machines. Type represents the type of virtual machines. vCPUs represents the number of virtual CPUs in a virtual machine. RAM represents the size of memory in a virtual machine. Disk represents the size of the hard disk in a virtual machine. C_{spc} represents the computing capacity of the virtual machine. F_{cpc} represents the associated financial cost.

Type	vCPUs	RAM	Disk	C_{spc}	F_{cpc}
A1	1	1.75	70	9.6	0.0604
A2	2	3.5	135	19.2	0.1208
A3	4	7	285	38.4	0.2416
A4	8	14	605	76.8	0.4832

In the experiments presented in this chapter, we use 100, 500, and 1,000 fasta files generated from the data stored in a genome database [Oma, a,b]. The programs used are mafft (version 7.221) for Activity 1, ReadSeq 2.1.26 for Activity 2, raxmhpc (7.2.8 alpha) for Activity 4, pamlX1.3.1 for Activities 6.1 and 6.2, in-house script for Activity 3 and Activity 8, and Activity 5 and Activity 7 exploit a PostgreSQL database management system to process data. The percentage of the workload, i.e., α in Formula (3.6), that can be parallelized is 96.43%. Also, the input data is stored at a data server of Site 3, which is accessible to all sites in the cloud using *SCP* command (a Linux command). The estimated workload (in GFLOP) of each activity of SciEvol for different numbers of input fasta files is shown in Table 3.2.

Table 3.2: SciEvol workload estimation.

Activity	Number of Fasta Files		
	100	500	1,000
	Estimated Workload (in GFLOP)		
1	1,440	10,416	20,833
2	384	2,778	5,556
3	576	4,167	8,333
4	1,440	10,416	20,833
6.1	5,760	41,667	83,334
6.2	10,560	76,389	152,778
6.3	49,920	361,111	722,222
6.4	59,520	430,556	861,111
6.5	75,840	548,611	1,097,222
6.6	202,560	1,465,278	2,930,556
8	6,720	48,611	97,222

In Table 3.3, the unit of time is minute, the unit of financial cost is Euro, the unit of RAM and Disk is gigabytes (GB), the unit of data is megabyte (MB), the computing capacity of virtual machines is GigaFLOPS (GFLOPS) and the unit of workload is GigaFLOP (GFLOP). ω_t represents the weight of time cost. $A1$, $A2$, $A3$ and $A4$ represent the types of virtual machines in Azure platform. [Type of VM] * [number] represents provisioning [number] of virtual machines of [Type] type, e.g., $A1 * 1$ represents provisioning one virtual machine of $A1$ type. WE represents West Europe; JW Japan West, and JE Japan East. The financial cost corresponds to the price in Euro of Azure on July 27, 2015.

SciEvol was executed consuming 100 fasta files for different weights of execution time and financial costs. We assume that the limitation of the number of virtual CPU cores is 32. The estimated workload of this workflow fragment is 192,000 GFLOP. The desired execution time

Table 3.3: VM provisioning results

Algorithm		SSVP			GraspCC		
ω_t		0.1	0.5	0.9	0.1	0.5	0.9
P_L		$A3 * 1$	$A4 * 1$	$A4 * 3$	$A1 * 6$	$A2 * 3$	
Estimated	E_T	95	55	34	60		
	E_{fc}	0.38	0.44	0.75	0.36		
	E_C	1.3094	1.1981	0.7631	1.1882	1.104	1.0208
Real	E_T	98	54	35	113	100	
	E_{fc}	0.40	0.43	0.81	0.64	0.60	
	E_C	1.3472	1.1748	0.7879	2.1181	1.8199	1.6973

is set to 60 min and the maximum execution time is defined as 120 min. The desired financial cost is configured as 0.3 Euros, and the maximum acceptable financial cost is 0.6 Euros. The deployment plans presented in Table 3.3 are respectively generated by SSVP, and GraspCC [de C. Coutinho et al., 2014]. Table 3.3 shows the result of the experiments to execute SciEvol with different weights of execution time and financial costs. The execution time, financial cost, and execution cost is composed of the time and the cost of provisioning and workflow execution. For SSVP, the difference between estimated and real execution time ranges from 1.9–3.1%, the difference for financial cost ranges from 2.0–6.5%, and the difference for the execution cost is between 2.0–3.2%. The difference between the estimated and real values also depends on the parameters configured by the users. Table 3.3 shows that SSVP can make an acceptable estimation based on different weights of objectives, i.e., time and financial costs.

As aforementioned, GraspCC is based on two strong assumptions. The first assumption is that the entire workload of each activity can be executed in parallel, which may not be realistic since some activities cannot be parallelized. The second one is that more virtual machines can reduce execution time without any harmful impact on the cost, e.g., financial cost, for the whole execution of a workflow. These two assumptions lead to inaccuracies greater of the estimation of execution time and financial costs. Also, as it is only designed for the time quantum of 1 h, GraspCC always generates a provisioning plan that contains the most possible significant number of virtual CPUs to reduce the execution time to one-time quantum, i.e., 1 h. In Azure, since the time quantum is 1 min, it is hard to reduce the execution time to one-time quantum, i.e., 1 min. In order to use GraspCC in Azure, we take the time quantum of 1 h for GraspCC. GraspCC does not take into consideration the execution cost (time and financial costs) for provisioning virtual machines, which also brings inaccuracy to the estimated time. Moreover, GraspCC is not sensitive to different values of weight, which are ω_t and ω_m. However, SSVP is sensitive to different values of weight because of using the optimal number of virtual CPUs calculated based using the cost model. The final provisioning plan of GraspCC is listed in Table 3.3.

GraspCC generates the same provisioning plan for different values of ω_t (0.5 and 0.9). In addition, the difference between the estimated time and the real execution time is 88.3% ($\omega_t = 0.1$) and 66.7% ($\omega_t = 0.5$ and $\omega_t = 0.9$). However, the difference corresponding to the cost model of SSVP is under 3.1%. Finally, compared with SSVP, the corresponding real cost of the GrapsCC algorithm is 57.2% ($\omega_t = 0.1$), 54.9% ($\omega_t = 0.5$), and 115.4% ($\omega_t = 0.9$) bigger.

Figure 3.3 shows the cost for different provisioning plans and different weights of execution time and financial costs. According to the provisioning plan generated by SSVP, 4, 8, and 24 virtual CPU cores are deployed when ω_t is 0.1, 0.5, and 0.9. The corresponding cost is the minimum value in each polyline. The three polylines show that SSVP can generate a good provisioning plan, which reduces the cost based on the cost model. The differences between the highest cost and the cost of corresponding good provisioning plans are: 56.1% ($\omega_t = 0.1$), 26.4% ($\omega_t = 0.5$), and 122.1% ($\omega_t = 0.9$).

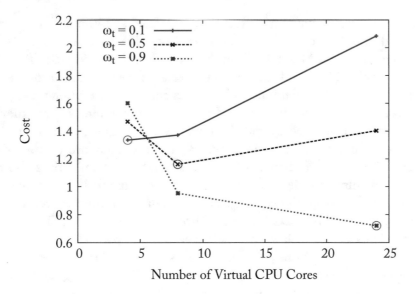

Figure 3.3: Cost for different values of ω_t with three provisioning plans. The circled points represent the number of virtual CPU cores corresponding to the provisioning plan generated by SSVP and the corresponding cost of the execution of SciEvol.

SciEvol was also executed consuming 500 and 1,000 fasta files. The setup parameters are listed in Table 3.4 and the results are presented in Tables 3.5 and 3.6. Since it needs bigger computing capacity to process more input fasta files, we increase the limitation of the number of virtual CPUs, i.e., 64 virtual CPUs for 500 fasta files and 128 virtual CPUs for 1,000 fasta files. From the tables, we can see that as the estimated workload and desired financial cost of the

Table 3.4: Setup Parameters. "Number" represents the number of input fasta files. "Limit" represents the maximum number of virtual CPUs that can be deployed in the cloud. Maximum values are twice the desired values.

Number			500	1,000
Desired	Execution Time		60	60
	Monetary Cost		2	6
Maximum	Execution Time		120	120
	Monetary Cost		4	12
Limit			64	128
Estimated Workload			1,401,600	2,803,200

workflow increase, more virtual CPUs are planned to be deployed in the cloud. SSVP generates different provisioning plans for each weight of execution time. However, for the same number of input fasta files, GraspCC generates the same provisioning plan for different weights of execution time, namely $A1 * 1$, $A3 * 10$ for 500 fasta files, and $A2 * 1$, $A4 * 10$ for 1000 fasta files. The execution time corresponding to both SSVP and GraspCC exceeds the maximum execution time. However, SSVP has some important advantages, e.g., precise estimation of execution time and smaller corresponding cost.

Table 3.5: SSVP Provisioning Results. "Number" represents the number of input fasta files. The provisioning plan represents the plan generated by the corresponding algorithms. "E_T" represents execution time and "E_{fc}" represents financial cost.

Number		500			1,000		
ω_t		0.1	0.5	0.9	0.1	0.5	0.9
Provisioning Plan		$A3 * 1, A4 * 1$	$A4 * 3$	$A4 * 7$	$A4 * 2$	$A4 * 6$	$A4 * 11$
Estimated	E_T	328	194	150	473	290	260
	E_{fc}	3.29	4.60	7.93	7.59	13.62	21.70
	E_C	2.0263	2.7640	2.6419	1.9271	3.5462	4.2602
Real	E_T	299	177	136	424	294	244
	E_{fc}	2.99	4.42	8.34	6.90	14.71	23.21
	E_C	1.8438	2.5800	2.4572	1.7417	3.6758	4.0468

The difference between estimated time and real-time is calculated based on Equation (3.25). As presented in Figure 3.4, the difference between estimated execution time and real execution time corresponding to GraspCC with SGreedy is much greater than that corre-

Table 3.6: GraspCC Provisioning Results. "Number" represents the number of input fasta files. The provisioning plan represents the plan generated by the corresponding algorithms.

Number	500			1,000		
P_L	$A1 * 1, A3 * 10$			$A2 * 1, A4 * 10$		
Estimated	E_T	60			60		
	E_{fc}	2.48			4.95		
	E_C	1.2144	1.1191	1.0238	0.8429	0.9127	0.9825
Real	E_T	166			257		
	E_{fc}	6.19			22.43		
	E_C	3.06	2.93	2.80	3.79	4.01	4.23

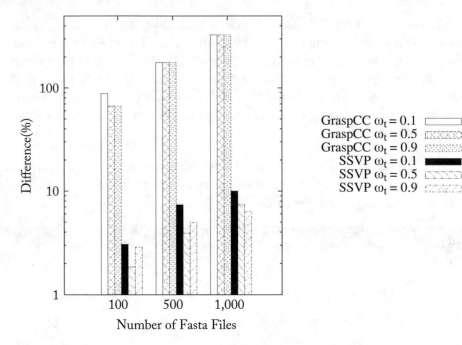

Figure 3.4: Difference between estimated time and real time.

sponding to the cost model of SSVP with SGreedy, which ranges between 66.7% and 328.3%. This result reveals that our cost model can be up to 76.7% more precise than that of GraspCC. As the number of fasta files increases, the difference also increases, i.e., it is more difficult to estimate the time. However, the difference corresponding to the cost model of SSVP is always under 11%.

$$Difference = \frac{EstimatedTime - RealTime}{RealTime} * 100\%. \qquad (3.25)$$

The cost corresponding to different numbers of fasta files is shown in Figure 3.5. It can be seen from the figure that the cost corresponding to GraspCC is always greater than that corresponding to SSVP with different amounts of input data because SSVP is based on a more accurate cost model and is designed for the quantum of 1 min. Based on Equation (3.26), compared with GraspCC, the cost corresponding to SSVP is up to 53.6% smaller. The cost for GraspCC is a line in Figures 3.5b and 3.5c, since GraspCC is not sensitive to the weights of time cost and it generates the same virtual machines provisioning plans, the cost of which is a line. However, since SSVP is sensitive to different values of the weights of execution time, it can reduce the cost at large.

$$Difference = \frac{Cost(GraspCC) - Cost(SSVP)}{Cost(SSVP)} * 100\%. \qquad (3.26)$$

From the experimental results presented in this chapter, we can conclude that SSVP allied to SGreedy can generate better provisioning and scheduling plans than GraspCC because of accurate cost estimation of the cost model.

3.6   CONCLUSION

In this chapter, we discussed in detail a virtual machine provisioning approach, namely SSVP, to generate provisioning plans for workflow execution with multiple objectives in a single-site cloud using SGreedy scheduling algorithm. The cost model aims at minimizing two costs: execution time and financial costs. We used a real workflow, i.e., SciEvol, with real data from the bioinformatics domain as a use case. We evaluated our approaches by executing SciEvol in Microsoft Azure cloud. The results show the provisioning approach (SSVP) allied to SGreedy generates better provisioning plans for different weights of time cost to execute a workflow at a site compared with other existing approaches, namely GraspCC with SGreedy. The advantage of using SSVP can be up to 53.6%. Also, our cost model can estimate the cost within an acceptable error limit, and it is 76.7% more precise than that of GraspCC.

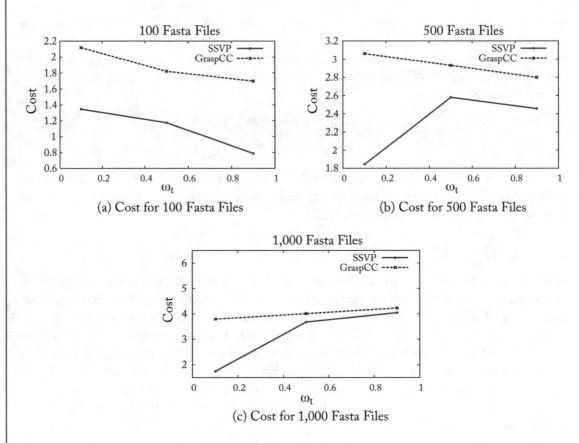

Figure 3.5: Cost for different numbers of fasta files.

CHAPTER 4

Workflow Execution in a Multi-Site Cloud

By offering virtually infinite resources, several different scalable services, stable service quality, and pay-as-you-go payment policies, clouds are an appealing solution for workflow execution. In Chapter 3, we discussed workflow executions in a single-site cloud. However, most clouds are multi-site by nature, i.e., they are composed of several sites (or data centers), each with its resources and data.

Due to the low latency and proprietary issues, several scientific data sources are already stored in clouds. For instance, the climate data in the Earth System Grid [Williams et al., 2009], large amounts of raw data from Quantum Chromodynamics (QCD) [Perry et al., 2005], the 1,000 genome project[1] [Clarke et al., 2017], the data of the ALICE project [ali], and the data of business workflows are stored in geographically distributed cloud-based storages. As a consequence, the input data of a workflow can be geographically distributed in several cloud sites and, thus, the workflow execution should be adapted to a multi-site cloud while exploiting distributed computing or storage resources beyond a single site. Nowadays, communities have been using workflow technologies to automate their computational experiments while exploiting more and more geographically dispersed and independently managed computing infrastructures [Liew et al., 2017].

Figure 4.1 presents one example of SWf execution in different cloud sites spread across the globe. Notice that multi-site workflows are also common in the domain of business, such as the one presented in Figure 4.2 based on Beheshti et al. [2016]. Here the workflow product order is executed many times with very high throughput, and it consumes and generates a large volume of data. There are several activities in the workflow. For instance, the order is first received by the company through an ordering system with the input data distributed at three sites, e.g., Asia, America, and Europe. After order verification, the order is executed at the site of Europe. During or after processing the order, emails and invoices are sent to the clients, and the products are shipped through the shipping system from the site of Asia. Two main scenarios require scheduling taking into account data. The first case is when the script of the ordering activity together with the corresponding input data are both stored at the cloud site located in Europe, while that of the shipping system activity together with the shipping data is located in Asia. This means that the execution of the two activities is correspondingly carried out at the site of

---

[1]https://cloud.google.com/genomics/docs/public-datasets/1000-genomes

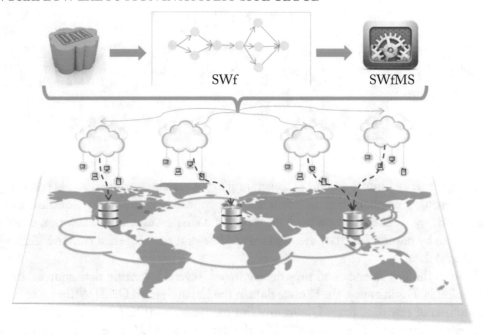

Figure 4.1: Workflow execution in a multi-site cloud.

Europe and Asia. For efficiency, it would better to execute the two activities at a single site. Here, the problem is how to schedule the execution of different activities, e.g., ordering system, email system, and invoice system, among the three sites in order to reduce the overall execution time and monetary cost. The second scheduling scenario occurs if the input data is placed in all sites, and the tasks of each activity can be executed at different sites depending on the site load. The problem of how to schedule the tasks and how to place the data of each activity is essential to reduce the overall workflow execution time.

The goal of this chapter is to discuss how to parallelize and schedule the execution of workflows in a multi-site cloud, where each site has its virtual cluster, data, and programs, in order to achieve some objectives. First, we present the main concepts and basic approaches to executing workflows in a multi-site cloud. Then, we focus on the direct workflow execution in a multi-site cloud in two ways, i.e., fine-grained and coarse-grained approaches. The fine-grained approach directly schedules activations of each activity into a site in order to reduce execution time, while the coarse-grained approach schedules workflow fragments, each of which corresponds to the whole execution of one or several activities, into different sites. The main contributions of this chapter are:

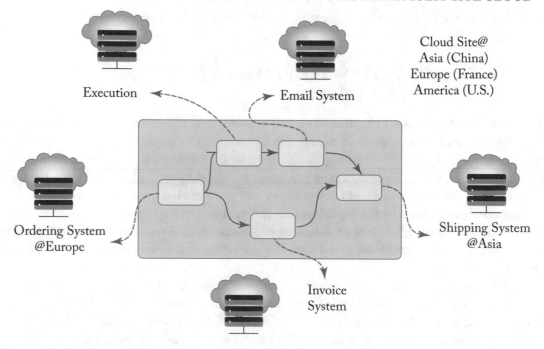

Figure 4.2: **Product order workflow at multiple cloud sites.**

1. a fine-grained and a coarse-grained approach to execute SWfs in a multi-site cloud;

2. scheduling algorithms, i.e., DIM and ActGreedy, for the fine-grained approach and the coarse-grained approach;

3. a local distributed storage based strategy to optimize the access to hot metadata and the combination of the local distributed strategy and scheduling algorithms for the fine-grained approach;

4. the design of a multi-objective cost model that includes execution time and financial costs to estimate the cost of executing SWfs at a multi-site cloud for the coarse-grained approach; and

5. an experimental evaluation of different scheduling algorithms.

The rest of the chapter is organized as follows. Section 4.1 presents an overview of workflow execution and shows two approaches, i.e., execution with a multi-site cloud platform and direct workflow execution in a multi-site cloud. Then, Sections 4.2 and 4.3 detail two approaches to directly execute a workflow in a multi-site cloud, i.e., fine-grained workflow execution and coarse-grained workflow execution. Finally, Section 4.4 presents a taxonomy and summarizes this chapter.

4.1   OVERVIEW OF WORKFLOW EXECUTION IN A MULTI-SITE CLOUD

As discussed in the previous chapters, the cloud provides virtually infinite computing and storage resources, and thus, appears as a cost-effective solution to deploy and to run workflows. In order to provide scalability and high availability, cloud providers such as Amazon and Microsoft typically have multiple data centers located at different geographically distributed sites. Also, there are important cases where workflows will need to be deployed at several sites, e.g., because the data accessed by the workflow is in different research groups' databases at different sites or because the workflow execution needs more resources than those that can be deployed in a single site. Therefore, multi-site cloud workflow management becomes an open, yet important problem.

A multi-site cloud is a cloud composed of several sites (or data centers), each from the same or different providers and explicitly accessible to cloud users [Nguyen and Thoai, 2012]. In the context of this chapter, the term "explicitly accessible" has two meanings: (i) each site is separately visible and directly accessible to cloud users, and (ii) cloud users can decide to deploy their data and applications at specific sites while the cloud providers do not change the location of their data. In this chapter, we consider a multi-site cloud environment from a single provider since the case of federated clouds (with multiple cloud providers) is relatively new to cloud users [Abdi et al., 2017, Sun et al., 2018, Toosi et al., 2014].

The execution of workflows in a multi-site cloud differs from the execution in a single-site cloud and other execution environments. The multi-site cloud environment is different from the geographically distributed environment, which only needs to deal with multiple servers without considering the execution within each server. A multi-site cloud environment is composed of multiple cloud sites, each of which contains distributed nodes (servers) connected by a fast local network, e.g., Infiniband, while the inter-site connection commonly presents limited bandwidth. Thus, both intra-site and inter-site execution must be considered, as well as the interplay between them. Furthermore, compared with data processing frameworks for DISC environments, e.g., Apache Spark [Zaharia et al., 2010a] or Apache Hadoop [Had, Shvachko et al., 2010] (both discussed in Chapter 5), multi-site workflow execution must handle data in multiple virtual clusters and use existing programs at specific cloud sites, with limited network connections among these sites. In addition, compared with Peer-to-Peer (P2P) [Martins et al., 2008, Pacitti and Valduriez, 2012] environments, a significant difference is that multi-site cloud does not have as many sites and that the security issue in multi-site cloud is more important than in P2P environments, e.g., some data cannot be moved to another site.

In multi-site cloud environments, most SWfMSs start executing the workflow only after gathering all the needed data in a shared-disk file system at a single site, which is time-consuming and jeopardize performance. There are two basic approaches to execute workflows by exploiting resources distributed at multiple sites in a multi-site cloud. The first approach is to execute workflows on top of a multi-site cloud platform, which manages the resources at different cloud sites, and the second approach is to directly execute workflows in a multi-site cloud with an SWfMS that offers multi-site features instead of using multi-site cloud platform. Next we discuss in details each of these approaches.

4.1.1 WORKFLOW EXECUTION WITH A MULTI-SITE CLOUD PLATFORM

A multi-site cloud platform is a solution that manages several sites (or data centers) of single or multiple-cloud providers, using a uniform and transparent interface for cloud users. An SWfMS can be deployed on top of a multi-site cloud platform to execute workflows in a multi-site cloud, as presented in Figure 4.3. We classify the multi-site cloud platform into three types, i.e., full platform, network platform, and execution platform.

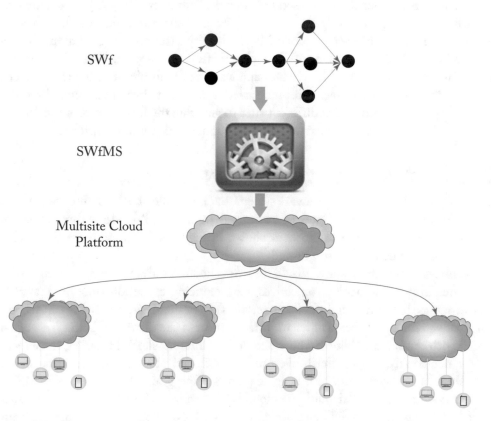

Figure 4.3: Workflow execution with a multi-site cloud platform.

A full platform manages computing, storage, and network resources through a uniformed API [Hume et al., 2012]. For instance, BonFIRE [Hume et al., 2012] provides large-scale, virtualized computing, storage, and networking resources with full control of the user on resource deployment. It also provides in-depth monitoring and logging of physical and virtual resources. BonFIRE currently comprises several (seven at the time this book was written) geographically distributed cloud sites across Europe while offering a uniform API.

A network platform only provides an illusion that all the resources are within a single site. For instance, U-chupala et al. [2013] is a network platform based on a Virtual Private Network (VPN) and a smart virtual machine scheduling mechanism. It is composed of a virtual infrastructure layer, an overlay network layer, and a physical resource layer. The virtual machine containers lie in the physical resource layer. The overlay network connects all the physical resources and enables the virtual infrastructure layer to use a cloud framework that gives the illusion of a single pool of resources. This pool can provide scalable resources to users while hiding the complexity of the physical infrastructure underneath.

General frameworks for distributed computing can also be used. For instance, workflows can be executed using MapReduce-based frameworks [Wang et al., 2009], which are extended to deal with a multi-site cloud [Luo and Plale, 2012, Tudoran et al., 2012]. A MapReduce framework can manage the execution of a MapReduce application, which contains Map activities and Reduce activities. The Map and Reduce activities correspond to multiple activations in a workflow. In order to execute a MapReduce application at multiple sites, the execution of Map and Reduce activities is partitioned and scheduled at different sites. Then, global reducer processes the output data produced at different sites to generate the final results of the MapReduce application. MapReduce frameworks are discussed in more detail in Chapter 5.

4.1.2   DIRECT WORKFLOW EXECUTION

A multi-site SWfMS is a multi-site aware system that is capable of using computing and storage resources distributed at different sites to execute. A multi-site SWfMS is directly deployed in a multi-site cloud to execute workflows as shown in Figure 4.4. A multi-site SWfMS can be classified as fine-grained or coarse-grained.

The fine-grained multi-site SWfMS directly schedules the activations of each activity into different sites in order to achieve objectives, e.g., reducing execution time or financial costs. When the data is distributed at different sites, this type of multi-site SWfMSs can schedule the execution of activities to different sites in order to process the distributed data (i.e., activations associated with the same activity can be scheduled to different sites). However, the effective use of fine-grained SWfMS incurs much overhead for each activation during workflow execution.

Askalon [Fahringer et al., 2007] can be used as a fine-grained multi-site SWfMS that executes workflows in a federated multi-site cloud [Ostermann et al., 2009], i.e., a multi-site cloud composed of resources from different cloud providers. Nevertheless, it schedules activations in computing nodes at different sites without considering the organization of computing nodes,

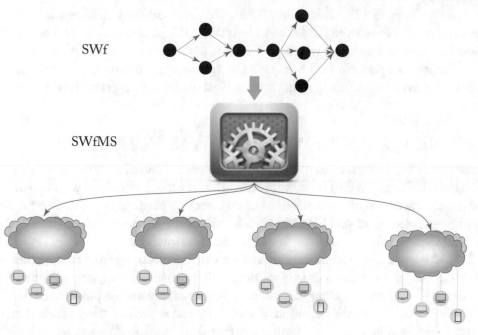

Figure 4.4: Direct workflow execution in a multi-site cloud.

i.e., which virtual machines are at the same site, for optimization. This method takes the computing nodes as the nodes at a single-site cloud without considering the features of multi-site resources, e.g., the difference of data transfer rate, resource sharing for intra-site and inter-site, and so on. The Decentralized-Metadata Multi-Site Chiron (DMM-Chiron) [Liu et al., 2016a] is also a fine-grained multi-site SWfMS that exploits different scheduling algorithms (see details in Section 4.2.2) and metadata management strategies (see details in Section 4.2.1) to execute workflows in a multi-site cloud.

The coarse-grained SWfMS first partitions a workflow into fragments and then schedules each fragment at a specific site for execution. This type of SWfMS can reduce the overhead of activation scheduling, which is performed in parallel at multiple sites, and performs load balancing at two levels: inter-site and intra-site.

Inter-site load balancing is performed by scheduling fragments, with a global scheduler, and intra-site load balancing is performed by local activation scheduling. This two-level approach makes the scheduling process more straightforward. However, the coarse-grained SWfMSs cannot schedule the execution of activities at different sites. Swift/T [Wozniak et al., 2013] and Pegasus [Deelman et al., 2007] can be used as coarse-grained SWfMSs that achieve multi-site execution through workflow partitioning.

Swift/T performs workflow partitioning by generating corresponding abstract WEPs for each site [Zhao et al., 2007a,b], while Pegasus performs partitioning through several methods

[Chen and Deelman, 2012b, Chen et al., 2013]. The first method partitions a workflow under storage constraints at each site [Chen and Deelman, 2012b]. The second method partitions a workflow into several fragments which present almost the same workload [Chen et al., 2013]. This last method can perform load balancing for the homogeneous multi-site environment, in which each site has the same computing capacity. Next we detail fine-grained and coarse-grained approaches.

4.2   FINE-GRAINED WORKFLOW EXECUTION

In several scenarios, the input data of a workflow may be distributed at different sites and cannot be moved to other sites. To enable workflow execution in a multi-site cloud with this distributed input data, the execution of the activations of each activity needs to be carried out at different sites. A fine-grained multi-site SWfMS, which enables the execution of activities at different sites to deal with the distributed data, is suitable for this situation.

SWfMSs generally generate, capture and store metadata during workflow execution. Such metadata describe the workflow execution, the execution environment, and all data consumed and produced during the workflow execution. This metadata is named provenance data [Freire et al., 2008b], which traces the execution of workflows and the relationship between input data and output data, and is sometimes more important than the workflow execution itself due to reproducibility issues [Freire et al., 2008a].

Due to the difference between the inter-site network latency and the intra-site network latency, there are two design principles for the architecture of a fine-grained multi-site SWfMS as discussed by Liu et al. [2018a]. The first principle is the two-layer multi-site workflow management, i.e., *intra-site* and *inter-site* layer. The intra-site layer operates as a single-site SWfMS, while the inter-site layer coordinates the interactions at the site level, typically through a master/slave architecture (one site being the master site). A node, e.g., a master node in a master/slave architecture, at each site is responsible for synchronization and data transfers.

The second principle is the eventual consistency for high-latency communication. While high-speed networks normally interconnect sites, the latency is ultimately bounded by the physical distance between sites, and communication time might reach the order of seconds [azu]. Under these circumstances, it is unreasonable to aim for a system with an entirely consistent state in all of its components at a given moment without strongly compromising the performance of the workflow. With a reasonable delay due to the greater latency propagation, the system is guaranteed to be eventually consistent (please refer to Özsu and Valduriez [2011] for details on eventual consistency).

For instance, Figure 4.5 shows the architecture of a multi-site workflow execution:

1. At the inter-site level, all communication and synchronization are handled through a set of master nodes (M), one per site. One site acts as a global coordinator (master site) and is responsible for scheduling activities/activations to each site using a two level (2L) scheduling approach (see details in Section 4.2.2), or to each computing nodes at each site using a

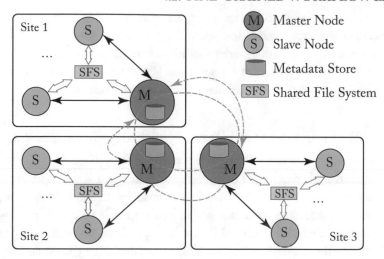

Figure 4.5: Multi-site workflow execution architecture with decentralized metadata. Dotted lines represent inter-site interactions.

one level (1L) scheduling approach (see details in Section 4.2.2). Every master node holds a *metadata store*, which is part of the global metadata storage and is directly accessible to all other master nodes. At this level, the messages can be transferred using a queue system, while the files can be transferred using a peer-to-peer approach.

2. At the intra-site level, the typical master/slave scheme is widely used: the master node schedules activations within the site when using a 2L scheduling approach and coordinates a group of slave nodes, which execute the activations. All nodes within sites are connected to a shared file system to access consumed and produced data. *Metadata updates* are propagated to other sites through the master node.

The fine-grained workflows execution in a multi-site cloud is carried out as follows. First, the data dependencies of each activity are analyzed to identify the available activities to execute, i.e., the input data of which is ready [Ogasawara et al., 2013]. Then, the activations are generated for the available activities. Afterward, the activations are scheduled to each site, and the data, i.e., input files of activations, are transferred to the scheduled sites. The activations are scheduled to computing nodes within a single site and are executed in such computing nodes. When the activations of all the activities are executed, the execution of a workflow is finished.

During the fine-grained workflow execution, there are two critical problems to be considered. During the execution, metadata is produced and plays a vital role in the performance of workflow execution. Thus, the first problem is how to efficiently manage metadata with high inter-site network latency in order to reduce workflow execution time. Also, smart scheduling algorithms, which are to decide at which sites and in which computing node to execute the activations, may benefit from such metadata and are also essential to reduce workflow execution time. The second problem is the activation scheduling, which is how to schedule activations to which computing node of which site in order to achieve some objectives, e.g., reducing execution time or financial costs. Next, we present the solutions for two critical problems of a fine-grained multi-site SWfMS, i.e., metadata management and activation schedule.

4.2.1 USING DISTRIBUTED DATA MANAGEMENT TECHNIQUES

Metadata management significantly impacts the performance (execution time) of computing systems that must deal with thousands or millions of individual files, as with workflows. Figure 4.6 shows a general metadata model for workflow execution in a multi-site cloud. A workflow contains one or multiple activities, and each activity corresponds to one or multiple activations. Each activation is scheduled and executed in a virtual machine at a site and processes one or multiple files. **Activation metadata** is the metadata associated with the execution of activations, which is composed of the command, parameters, start time, end time, status, and execution site. During execution, the status and the activations are queried many times by each site to search for new activations to execute and determine if an activity is finished. Also, the status of an activation may be updated several times. As a result, it is essential to acquire these metadata quickly.

File metadata is relative to the size, location, and possible replicas of a given piece of data. Knowledge about file metadata allows for the SWfMS to schedule the corresponding activation to where the data is, or vice versa. This is especially relevant in multi-site settings: timely availability of the file metadata enables moving data before they are needed, hence reducing the impact of low-speed inter-site networks. In general, other metadata such as file ownership are not critical, yet interesting for different reasons, for the execution.

In the context of multi-site workflow execution, metadata can be classified to two types, i.e., *hot metadata* and *cold metadata*. Hot metadata refers to the metadata, e.g., activation metadata and file metadata, that needs to be frequently accessed [Levandoski et al., 2013] and placed in fast and easy-to-query storage [Hsieh et al., 2006] for workflow execution. Less frequently accessed metadata is denoted cold metadata.

The hot metadata can be statically identified by users and marked using tags in the workflow definition file, e.g., XML or JSON files. However, the "temperature" of metadata may vary during execution, and trying to predict hot metadata before execution can be tedious and error-prone. Some frameworks assess the data "temperature" *offline*, i.e., they perform a later analysis on a frequency-of-access log to avoid overhead during the operation [Levandoski et al., 2013]. More interestingly, *online* approaches maintain a rank on the frequency of access to the metadata alongside the execution in adaptive replacement cache [Megiddo and Modha, 2003], and the hot metadata is dynamically identified. Furthermore, according to Liu et al. [2018a], the advantage of dynamic hot metadata identification can consume up to 26% in terms of the total workflow execution time in a multi-site cloud. This is because of the wrong notification

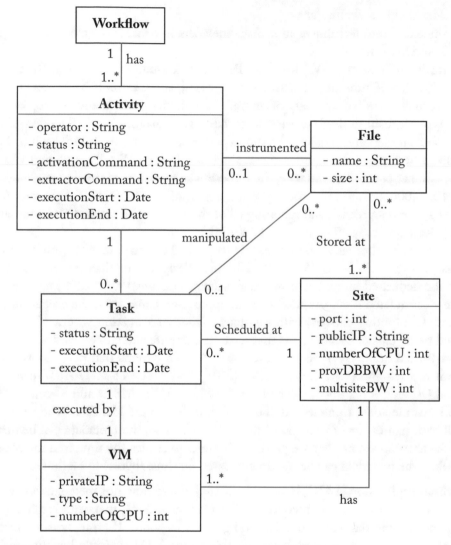

Figure 4.6: Multi-site metadata model, based on Liu et al. [2016c].

of hot metadata by the users, while the dynamic hot metadata can dynamically mark the right metadata as hot.

Managing the metadata in a multi-site cloud environment is essential. In this section, we present how to use distributed data management techniques to manage the metadata efficiently.

Metadata Management Techniques

There are three different techniques to manage metadata in a multi-site cloud, i.e., centralized, distributed, and hybrid.

Centralized In some SWfMSs, e.g., Pegasus [Deelman et al., 2005], Swift/T [Wozniak et al., 2013], SciCumulus [de Oliveira et al., 2010], and Chiron [Ogasawara et al., 2011], metadata is usually handled by means of centralized registries implemented on top of relational databases, typically using a single server at a centralized site that processes all requests. However, the single metadata server can quickly become a performance bottleneck with high I/O pressure and penalized by the overheads from transactions and locking [Stonebraker and Çetintemel, 2005, Stonebraker et al.]. For instance, the CyberShake workflow [Deelman et al., 2006] runs more than 800,000 activations, processing and aggregating over 80,000 input files (approximately 200 TB of data reads), and requiring all of these files to be tracked and annotated with metadata [Deelman et al., 2006, Juve et al., 2013a].

A lightweight alternative to databases is to index the metadata, although most indexing techniques [Wang et al., 2010, Wu et al., 2010] are designed for data rather than metadata. However, the dedicated index-based metadata schemes [Leung et al., 2009] use a centralized index. Most centralized metadata management approaches come from the execution in High-Performance Computing clusters, with solutions relying on low-latency networks for message passing and tiered cluster deployments that separate compute and storage nodes.

Distributed Some SWfMSs rely on distributed file systems that partition the metadata and store it at each site (e.g., Gehani et al. [2010] and Malik et al. [2010]), using a hashing method [Brandt et al., 2003, Corbett and Feitelson, 1996, Miller and Katz]. The hashing method assigns metadata to nodes based on a hash code of a file identifier. The hash code can be the full path names [gir] or the ID of the path [lus]. Also, the metadata can be distributed based on the location where they are produced in order to reduce the time to transfer data [Liu et al., 2018a]. The metadata can be distributed based on three following methods.

Local without replication (LOC) [Liu et al., 2018a] Every new hot metadata entry is stored at the site where it has been collected. For read operations, metadata is queried at each site, and the site that stores the data will give the response. If no reply is received within a time threshold, the request is resent. This method will typically benefit pipeline-like workflow structures, where consecutive activations are usually co-located at the same site. Compared with the centralized strategy, LOC can manage the hot metadata in parallel by three instances instead of one.

Hashed without replication (DHT) [Pineda-Morales et al., 2015] Hot metadata is queried and updated following the principle of a distributed hash table (DHT). A simple hash function determines the site location of a metadata entry applied to its key attribute, *filename* in case of file metadata, and *activation-id* for activation metadata. The linear complexity of reading operations compensates the impact of inter-site. The use of DHT may outperform the centralized version. However, performance degradation may happen for large-scale workflows since there is a larger number of long-distance hot metadata operations when using DHT compared to the centralized strategy. With the hashed technique, more operations are carried out on average among different sites than the site that needs to read the metadata. In the centralized strategy, the hot metadata is always stored in a centralized site. Thus, some long latency operations are reduced. Thus, while the DHT strategy might seem efficient due to linear read and write operations, it is not well suited for geo-distributed executions, which favor locality and penalize remote operations.

Hashed with local replication (REP) [Pineda-Morales et al., 2015] This method combines the two previous techniques by keeping both a local record of the hot metadata and a hashed copy. Intuitively, this would reduce the number of inter-site reading requests. This hybrid method is expected to highlight the trade-offs between metadata locality and DHT linear operations. Since REP takes time to replicate the data, the performance of REP is better than the centralized strategy for the workflows of small scales, while it may be worse than the centralized strategy for big scale workflow execution in a multi-site cloud.

Hybrid In order to execute activations in multiple sites, the workflow metadata storage scheme should be adapted. However, maintaining an updated version of all metadata across a multi-site environment may consume a significant amount of communication time, also incurring high financial costs. To reduce this impact, metadata can be managed by a hybrid approach, i.e., the combination of the centralized and distributed approaches [Liu et al., 2018a, Zhao et al., 2013]. In the hybrid approach, one part of the metadata, e.g., the cold metadata, is handled with a centralized approach, while the other part of the metadata, e.g., the hot metadata, is managed based on a distributed method, e.g., LOC, DHT, or REP. Different distributed storage techniques can be exploited for hot metadata during the workflow execution while keeping cold metadata stored locally and synchronizing such cold metadata only during the execution of the activity. Since the execution of workflows in a multi-site cloud favors data location, the hybrid strategy with LOC can reduce the whole execution time of a workflow in a multi-site cloud by 28% compared with the centralized strategy when using OLB (see details in Section 4.2.2) according to Pineda-Morales et al. [2016].

Metadata Operations

The slave nodes trigger the metadata operations at each site, which are the actual executors of the workflow activations. There are two types of metadata operations, i.e., metadata write and metadata read. The different metadata management techniques are used in the metadata write process. We present the following protocols, as an example, to illustrate the two types of metadata operations.

Metadata Write As presented in Figure 4.7a, a new metadata record is passed on from the slave to the master node at each site. If the metadata is not classified to hot or cold, each metadata record is addressed with one metadata strategy as presented later in this section.

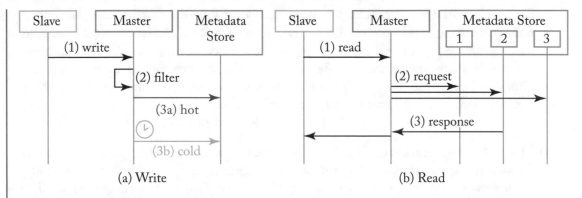

Figure 4.7: Metadata protocols.

Otherwise, upon reception, the master may filter the record as either hot or cold. The master node assigns the hot metadata to the metadata storage pool at the corresponding site(s) according to one metadata technique presented in Section 4.2.1. Created cold metadata is kept locally and propagated asynchronously to the master site during the execution of the activity.

Metadata Read Each master node has access to the entire pool of metadata stores so that it can get hot metadata from any site. Figure 4.7b shows the process. When a slave requests a read operation (1), a master node sends a request to each metadata store (2), and it processes the response that comes first (3), provided such response is not an empty set. This mechanism ensures that the master node gets the required metadata in the shortest time. The metadata read can also be used for activation scheduling process, which is presented in Section 4.2.2.

When the metadata is classified as hot and cold metadata, cold metadata operations are filtered out in order to ensure that hot metadata operations are managed with high priority over the network, and that cold metadata updates are propagated only during periods of low network congestion. The filter is generally located in the master node of each site (see Figure 4.8). It separates hot and cold metadata, prioritizing the propagation of hot metadata, and thus alleviates congestion during metadata-intensive periods.

4.2.2   ACTIVATION SCHEDULING IN A MULTI-SITE CLOUD

Activation scheduling is the key to the performance of workflow execution in a multi-site cloud. The objective of activation scheduling is generally to reduce the execution time of a workflow. However, as previously discussed in Chapter 3, the activation scheduling process may have multiple objectives, e.g., reducing the execution time and the financial costs at the same time. In the rest of this section, we consider a single objective, i.e., reducing total execution time. Thus, we do not consider multiple objectives.

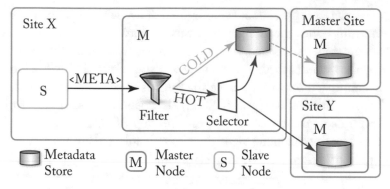

Figure 4.8: The hot metadata filtering component.

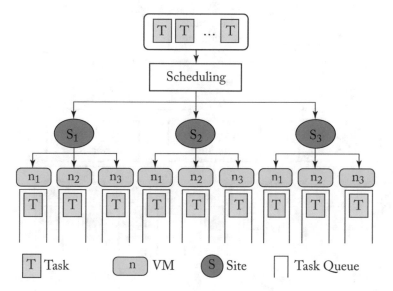

Figure 4.9: 1L scheduling. A scheduler directly schedules activations to the computing nodes at different sites.

The activations can be scheduled by two approaches, i.e., **one Level (1L)** and **two Level (2L)**. The 1L approach [Duan et al., 2014] directly schedules activations to computing nodes at different cloud sites as shown in Figure 4.9. A scheduler is a component within the SWfMs that implements a specific scheduling algorithm to schedule activations to computing resources, e.g., a site or a computing node. Since the 1L approach corresponds to a centralized scheduler, it is easy to implement. However, it is difficult to achieve load balance at the site level because of significant scheduling complexity [Schenk and Gärtner, 2002], and the 1L approach cannot reuse the scheduling algorithms within a single-site SWfMS.

The 2L approach [Liu et al., 2016c] is composed of two levels as shown in Figure 4.10. The first level performs multi-site scheduling, where each activation is scheduled to a site. Then, the second level performs single-site scheduling, where each activation is scheduled to a computing node of the site by the default scheduling strategy of a single-site SWfMS. Compared with 1L approach, this 2L approach may well reduce the multi-site scheduling complexity [Liu et al., 2016c]. According to Schenk and Gärtner [2002], 2L scheduling also significantly outperforms 1L scheduling in terms of performance, i.e., the speedup of execution. Both the 1L and 2L approaches need to exploit scheduling algorithms to schedule activations to a site or computing nodes. Next, we present different scheduling algorithms.

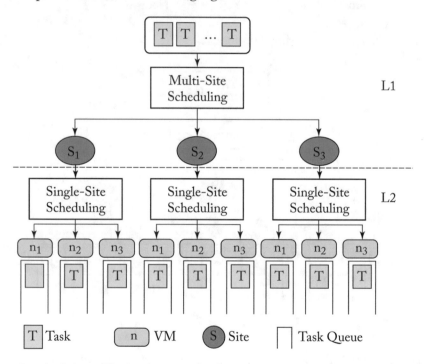

Figure 4.10: 2L scheduling. The multi-site scheduler schedules activations to different sites and the activations are scheduled to each computing nodes by the single-site scheduler.

Activation Scheduling Algorithms

There are three types of activation scheduling algorithms, i.e., classic, data-intensive, and multi-objective. All three types of algorithms can be directly used or adapted to be used in the 1L approach or at the two levels of the 2L approach.

There are many classic scheduling algorithms that can be applied to this scenario, e.g., Opportunistic Load Balancing (OLB) [Maheswaran et al., 1999], Minimum Completion Time (MCT) [Maheswaran et al., 1999], min-min [Etminani and Naghibzadeh, 2007], max-min [Etminani and Naghibzadeh, 2007], and Heterogeneous Earliest Finish Time (HEFT) [Topcuoglu et al., 2002], each with pros and cons.

These algorithms schedule activations to different computing resources, i.e., a computing node in the 1L scheduling and a site in the 2L scheduling. The OLB algorithm randomly assigns each activation to an available computing resource without considering the characteristics of the activation or the computing node. The MCT algorithm schedules each activation to a computing resource that can finish the execution first. HEFT gives priority to each activation according to the dependencies of activations and the workload of the activation. Then, it schedules the activations with the highest priority to the site that can finish the execution earlier. The min-min algorithm schedules the activation, which takes the least time to execute, to the site that can finish the execution first. The max-min algorithm schedules the activation, which takes the most significant time to execute, to the site that can finish the execution first. The activations of the same activity are generally independent of each other since each activation processes a different data chunk. Thus, the HEFT, min-min, and max-min algorithms degrade to the MCT algorithm for this kind of activations. Some other scheduling solutions extend the well-known scheduling algorithms. For instance, min-min is adapted for executing multiple workflows [Smanchat et al., 2009], and HEFT [Yu and Shi, 2007] is adapted to a dynamic scheduling algorithm and is implemented in Askalon [Wieczorek et al., 2005].

Data-intensive activations have a characteristic of taking much time to transfer data. Thus, it may take less time to schedule the activations to where the data are. Based on this characteristic, a basic data-intensive activation scheduling algorithm is to schedule activations as close as possible to where the data are [Dean and Ghemawat, 2004]. However, this basic algorithm may suffer from hot data spots [Liu et al., 2018b], i.e., some computing resources may receive several activations to execute because of the stored data in the nodes while others nodes remain idle. If most data is stored at some computing resources, the activations are eventually scheduled to these nodes.

Thus, the data generated by the activations are always stored in the few computing resources. As a result, more and more activations are scheduled at these nodes, and more data is stored in the same nodes, which become hot, while the other computing resources remain idle. In this situation, the execution time of a workflow may be prolonged. Data-Intensive Multi-Site activation scheduling (DIM—Algorithm 4.4), proposed by Liu et al. [2016c], is based on the basic data-intensive activation scheduling algorithm, while it can achieve good load balance to avoid the hot data spots. DIM algorithm presents two steps. First, DIM schedules a bag of activations to where their input data are stored. Then, DIM adjusts the scheduling of activations at different computing resources until load balance is achieved to reduce the execution time. The load balancing is calculated based on the estimation of the execution time of all the activations at each computing resource. The execution time of the activations at a computing resource can be estimated based on Amdahl's law with consideration of generating provenance data and inter-site data transfer.

Algorithm 4.4 Data-Intensive Multisite Activation Scheduling (DIM)

Input : T: a bag of activations to be scheduled; S: a set of cloud sites *Output* : $SP(T, S)$: the scheduling plan for T in S

1: $SP(T, S) \leftarrow \emptyset$
2: **for** $t \in T$ **do**
3:     $s \leftarrow GetDataSite(\text{Dist}(t, S))$
4:     $SP(T, S) \leftarrow SP(T, S) \cup \{(t, s)\}$
5:     TotalTime($SP(T, S)$)
6: **end for**
7: **while** MaxunbalanceTime($SP(T, S)$) is reduced in the last loop **do**
8:     $sMin \leftarrow MinTime(S)$
9:     $sMax \leftarrow MaxTime(S)$
10:     $SP(T, S) \leftarrow \text{ActivationReschedule}(sMin, sMax, SP(T, S))$
11: **end while**

The details of the DIM algorithm are explained in Algorithm 4.4. First, the activations are scheduled according to the location of input data, i.e., the site that stores the most significant amount of input data (Lines 2–5), which is similar to the scheduling algorithm of MapReduce [Dean and Ghemawat, 2004]. Line 3 searches the site that stores the biggest part of input data corresponding to Activation t. Line 4 schedules Activation t at Site s. The scheduling order (the same for Algorithm 4.5) is based on the *id* of each activation. Line 5 estimates the total time of all the activations scheduled at Site s with consideration of generating provenance data and inter-site data transfer. Then, the total time at each site is balanced by adjusting the whole bag of activations scheduled at that site (lines 6–9). Line 6 checks if the maximum difference of the estimated total time of activations at each site can be reduced by verifying if the difference is reduced in the previous loop or if this is the first loop. While the maximum difference of total time can be reduced, the activations of the two sites are rescheduled as described in Lines 7–9. Lines 7 and 8 choose the site that has the minimum total time and the site that has the maximum total time, respectively. Then, the scheduler calls the function *ActivationReschedule* to reschedule the activations scheduled at the two selected sites to reduce the maximum difference of total time.

In order to balance the load of each computing resource, DIM reschedules some activations from the computing resource that takes the longest time to finish its execution to the computing resource that takes the shortest time to finish its execution until the difference of the execution time of all the computing resources is acceptable. Let us assume that we have n activations to be scheduled at m sites and $n \gg m$. Then, the complexity of the DIM algorithm is $\mathcal{O}(m \cdot n \cdot \log n)$. Since m is much smaller than n, it is only a little bit larger than those of OLB and MCT, which is $\mathcal{O}(m \cdot n)$, but yields high reduction in workflow execution. According

Algorithm 4.5 Activations Rescheduling

Input : s_i: a site that has bigger total time for its scheduled activations;
s_j: a site that has smaller total time for its scheduled activations;
$SP(T, S)$: original scheduling plan for a bag of activations
T in multisite S *Output :* $SP(T, S)$: modified scheduling plan

1:   $Diff \leftarrow CalculateExecTimeDiff(s_i, s_j, SP(T, S))$ {Absolute value}
2:   $T_i \leftarrow GetScheduledActivations(s_i, SP(T, S))$
3: **for** $t \in T_i$ **do**
4:     $SP'(T, S) \leftarrow ModifySchedule(SP(T, S), \{(t, s_j)\}$
5:     $Diff' \leftarrow CalculateExecTimeDiff(s_i, s_j, SP'(T, S))$ {Absolute value}
6:     **if** $Diff' < Diff$ **then**
7:       $SP(T, S) \leftarrow SP'(T, S)$
8:       $Diff \leftarrow Diff'$
9:     **end if**
10: **end for**

to Liu et al. [2016c], DIM can reduce the execution time of a workflow in a multi-site cloud by 24.3% compared with MCT and 49.6% compared with OLB, when it is used as at the multi-site scheduling level in the 2L approach with a centralized metadata management strategy.

There are two methods for activation scheduling with multiple objectives, i.e., *a priori* and *a posteriori*. In the *a priori* method, preference information is given by users, and then the best solution is generated. This method is focused on minimizing a weighted sum of objectives similar to the one proposed by de Oliveira et al. [2012b] and discussed in Chapter 3.

The advantage of such an approach is that predetermined weights automatically guide it, while the disadvantage is that it is hard to determine the right values for the weights [Blagodurov et al., 2015]. Let us take an example of the greedy activation scheduling algorithm based on provenance data for workflow execution [de Oliveira et al., 2012b]. This algorithm schedules a bag of activations that take the least cost to be executed for each computing node. The cost to execute a bag of activations is estimated based on the provenance data stored in provenance database and a weighted function in a cost model (see details in Section 4.3.2) composed of the execution time, financial cost, and reliability.

In contrast, *a posteriori* methods produce a Pareto front of solutions [Duan et al., 2014] without predetermined values [Arabnejad et al., 2016, Blagodurov et al., 2015, Fard et al., 2014a]. Each solution is better than the others concerning at least one objective, and users can choose one from the produced solutions. However, this method requires users to choose the most suitable solution. Also, when the users have a clear idea of the importance of objectives, the results of the *a priori* method are also equivalent to a Pareto optimal solution [Marler and Arora, 2004, Zadeh, 1963].

One example of an *a posteriori* method is the Game-Multi-Objective (GMO) algorithm. It is based on game theory [Duan et al., 2014] to schedule activations to multiple sites. GMO has three steps. The first step initiates the distribution of bags of activations among computing resources. The relation between a bag of activations and a computing resource is the probability that the bag is scheduled to the computing resource. Then, the second step repeats, modifying the distribution to reduce the cost based on a cost model, composed of execution time and financial cost. When the distribution of some bags of activations is stable, i.e., equals 1, the third step removes these bags of activations from the iteration and schedules them to the computing resources. The second and third steps repeat until the entire distribution of all the bags of activations is stable. This algorithm chooses the earliest generated solution in order to reduce execution time.

Combining Activation Scheduling and Metadata Management

In order to efficiently schedule the activations at different sites, the scheduling process of MCT and DIM needs to get the information about where the input data of each activation is located. This information is available in the metadata, i.e., file metadata. Thus, the metadata have to be provisioned to the multi-site activation scheduler [Liu et al., 2018a]. Also, the metadata should be loaded in the memory once, and then be used for the whole scheduling process in order to reduce frequent interaction between the scheduler and the hot metadata manager. The combination of good scheduling algorithms and metadata management techniques can significantly reduce the complete execution of a workflow in a multi-site cloud (up to 55% according to Liu et al. [2018a]). Figure 4.11 shows the advantage (up to 38%) of the combination of scheduling and distributed metadata management for the execution of the Buzz workflow at three cloud sites.

4.3 COARSE-GRAINED WORKFLOW EXECUTION WITH MULTIPLE OBJECTIVES

When the input data of an activity is not distributed at different sites, the execution of an activity can be carried out at a single site, which resembles what was described in Chapter 3. However, the execution of different activities may need the stored data distributed at different specific sites. The stored data can be the configuration parameters or some intermediate data, which are necessary for the execution of some activities. Because of the large volume of the data or the configurations, e.g., security configuration of a database, the stored data can be accessed only within the corresponding site. In this situation, the execution of different activities should be scheduled at different sites, while each activity can be executed within a single site.

In this section, we present coarse-grained workflow execution with multiple objectives in a multi-site cloud with the assumption that the execution of each activity can be carried out at a single-site cloud. The coarse-grained execution partitions a workflow into fragments and then

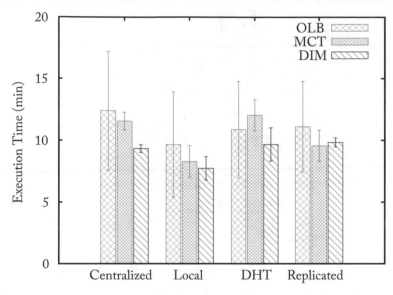

Figure 4.11: Execution time of the Montage SWf (0.5 degree) with different scheduling algorithms and metadata management techniques. Avg. intermediate data shown in parenthesis.

exploits ActGreedy algorithm (detailed in Chapter 3) to schedule each fragment to a single-site cloud in order to achieve multiple objectives based on the previously defined cost model.

When a fragment is scheduled to a site, the execution of its associated activities is scheduled to the same site. Since workflow execution may take a long time and cost much money, the multiple objectives are generally composed of reducing execution time and financial costs. Also, a data constraint, which specifies that some data should not be moved, because it is either too big or for proprietary reasons, exists.

Figure 4.12 shows a general architecture of a coarse-grained multi-site SWfMS [Liu et al., 2014b, 2016b]. The architecture has four modules: workflow partitioner, multi-site scheduler, single-site initialization, and single-site execution—the workflow partitioner partitions a workflow into fragments. Then, the fragments are scheduled to sites by the multi-site scheduler. Then, the single-site initialization module prepares the execution environment for the fragment, using two components, i.e., virtual machine provisioner (detailed in Chapter 3) and multi-site data transfer. At each site, the virtual machine provisioner component deploys and initializes virtual machines for the execution of workflows. The deployment process defines the type and location, namely the cloud site, of the virtual machine.

The multi-site data transfer module transfers the input data of fragments to the site where they will be executed. Finally, the single-site execution module starts the execution of the fragments at each site. This can be performed by an existing single-site SWfMS, e.g., Chiron [Ogasawara et al., 2013] or SciCumulus [de Oliveira et al., 2010]. Within a single site, when the

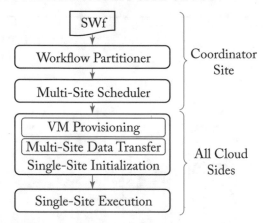

Figure 4.12: System architecture.

execution of its fragment is finished, and the output data is moved to other sites, the virtual machines are shut down. When the execution of the fragment is waiting for the output data produced by other sites and the output data at this site are transferred to other corresponding sites, the virtual machines can be shut down to avoids unnecessary financial cost. When the necessary data is ready, the virtual machines are restarted to continue the execution of the workflow fragment.

In a multi-site cloud, there are two types of sites, i.e., coordinator and participant. The coordinator is responsible for coordinating the execution of fragments at different participants. Two modules, namely workflow partitioner and multi-site scheduler, are deployed at the coordinator site. Both the coordinator and participants execute the scheduled fragments. The initialization module and single-site execution module are implemented at both the coordinator and participants.

Since a single-site SWfMS executes the fragments at each site, some metadata is placed where it is produced. Also, since there is a coordinator that controls the overall workflow execution, the rest of the metadata is centralized at the coordinator site. Thus, the metadata is managed in a hybrid strategy with the LOC method (see details in Section 4.2.1) in the coarse-grained execution.

During the coarse-grained workflow execution in a multi-site cloud, there are two critical problems to be considered. The first is the workflow partitioning problem, which is how to partition a workflow into fragments in order to achieve objectives. The second is the multi-site fragment scheduling problem, which is how to schedule the fragments into different cloud sites in order to achieve multiple objectives while taking into account the impact of resources distributed at different sites, e.g., different bandwidths and data distribution at different sites, and different prices for virtual machines. In this section, we used the SciEvol workflow as a case study (see details in Chapter 1), as shown in Figure 4.13, to present the solutions to address the two critical problems.

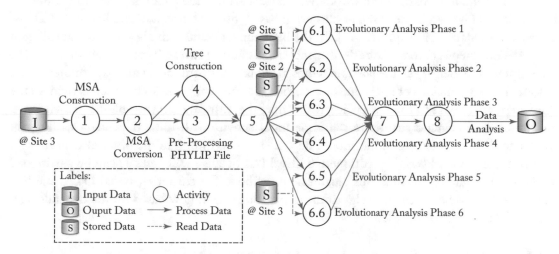

Figure 4.13: SciEvol workflow.

In Figure 4.13, *read data* represents that one activity just reads the stored data without modifying it and that the activity should be executed at the corresponding site to read data since the stored data is too big to be moved and can be accessed only within the corresponding site because of configurations, e.g., security configuration of a database. Thus, Activities 6.1 and 6.2 are fixed at Site 1, 6.3 and 6.4 at Site 2, and 6.5 and 6.6 at Site 3 because of the stored data constraints.

4.3.1   WORKFLOW PARTITIONING

Workflow partitioning is the process of dividing a workflow structure and input data into several fragments so that each fragment can be executed in parallel or not at a different site. It can be performed by DAG partitioning and data partitioning. DAG partitioning transforms a DAG composed of activities into a DAG composed of fragments, while each fragment is a DAG composed of activities and dependencies. Data partitioning divides the input data of a fragment generated by DAG partitioning into several datasets, each of which is encapsulated in a newly generated fragment.

This section focuses on DAG partitioning. There are three DAG partitioning methods, i.e., basic, load balanced, and Data Transfer Minimization (DTM). The primary method encapsulates each activity in one fragment, which is also called activity encapsulation partitioning method. Load balanced methods balance the workload in each fragment [Karypis and Kumar, 1998] or balance the workload according to the capacity of cloud sites [Liu et al., 2014b]. The load balanced methods may have different constraints, e.g., storage constraints of each site [Chen and Deelman, 2012a].

DTM methods partitions a workflow in order to minimize data transfer among different fragments. DTM can be heuristic or clustering based. For instance, a heuristic method DTM contains four steps [Liu et al., 2014b]. In the beginning, several activities are fixed at different sites. The first step is to remove the dependencies that connect two activities at the same site. The second step is to identify all the possible routes to connect the activities at any two different sites. A route is a combination of a pipeline of activities and the dependencies between activities. The third step is to choose the dependencies, which have the least data transfer volume in each route, and other dependencies that share the same input activity with these dependencies. Fourth, we delete the dependencies in the chosen dependencies according to the order of data transfer volume until the workflow is partitioned. SciEvol (see details in Chapter 1) can be partitioned as shown in Figure 4.14 using this partitioning method. The clustering-based DTM method exploits the K-Means clustering algorithm to partition a workflow based on the dependencies among data and activities [Deng et al., 2011].

4.3.2   FRAGMENT SCHEDULING ALGORITHMS

In general, to map the execution of activities to distributed computing resources is an NP-hard problem [Yu and Buyya, 2005]. Different scheduling algorithms can generate different scheduling plans. In order to evaluate the performance of different scheduling plans, cost models are used. In this section, we build upon the cost model defined in Chapter 3 and then present different types of fragment scheduling algorithms.

Cost Model

Since the workflow execution in a multi-site cloud may consume much time and financial cost, we consider a cost model composed of execution time cost and financial cost for the execution of workflows as an example. The cost model is generally implemented in the scheduling module and under a specific execution environment, i.e., multi-site cloud. The presented cost model [Liu et al., 2016b] is an extension of the model proposed in de Oliveira et al. [2012b] and discussed in Chapter 3. Thus, the cost of executing a workflow in a multi-site cloud can be defined by:

$$Cost(W, S) = \omega_t * T_n(W, S) + \omega_m * F_n(W, S), \tag{4.1}$$

where ω_t and ω_m represent the weights informed by users to prioritize minimizing the execution time or financial costs, which are positive values such as $\omega_t + \omega_m = 1$. $T_n(W, S)$ and $M_n(W, S)$ are normalized values that are defined in Equations (4.2) and (4.3) and represent the time cost and financial cost of executing workflow W on sites S. Since the values for execution time and financial costs are normalized, the cost has no unit. In the rest of this chapter, cost represents the normalized cost, which has no real unit. D_T represents the desired execution time to execute

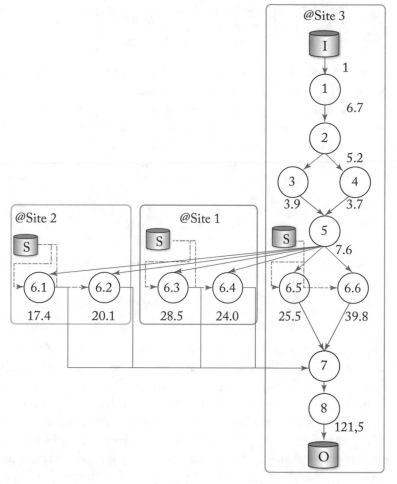

Figure 4.14: Workflow partitioning and data location based scheduling. The number represents the relative (compared with the input data) amount of output data for corresponding activities.

the workflow and D_F is the desired financial cost for the execution. Both D_T and D_F are configured by the users. Note that these may be unfeasible to obtain for the execution of the workflow similar to the single-site execution. We take the desired execution time and financial costs into consideration in the cost model, while the real execution time and financial costs may be bigger or smaller depending on the real execution environment. $T(W, S)$ and $F(W, S)$ are the real execution time and real financial cost for the execution of the W on sites S.

$$T_n(W, S) = \frac{T(W, S)}{D_T},$$

(4.2)

$$F_n(W, S) = \frac{F(W, S)}{D_F}. \tag{4.3}$$

However, it is still difficult to estimate the execution time and financial costs for the whole workflow even with a scheduling plan according to Equation (4.1) since it is hard to generate a virtual machine provisioning plan for each site with global desired execution time and financial costs. A virtual machine provisioning plan defines the types and the number of virtual machines at a site to execute fragments at the site. As shown in Equation (4.4), we decompose the cost model as the sum of the cost of scheduling each fragment wf_i on the sites.

$$Cost(W, S) = \sum_{\substack{wf_i \in W}}^{sched(wf_i, s_j) = 1} Cost(wf_i, s_j). \tag{4.4}$$

The cost of executing a fragment at a site can be defined as presented in Equation (4.5), which is an adaptation of Equation (3.1):

$$Cost(wf, s) = \omega_t * T_n(wf, s) + \omega_m * F_n(wf, s), \tag{4.5}$$

ω_t and ω_m are the same as that in Formula (4.1), and represent the weights for the execution time and the financial cost to execute Fragment wf at Site s. $T_n(wf, s)$ can be calculated based on Amdahl's law [Sun and Chen, 2010] with the consideration of the time to start virtual machines and the time to transfer data. Moreover, $F_n(wf, s)$ can be calculated based on $T_n(wf, s)$, the virtual machine provisioning plan, the price to use virtual machines at the scheduled site and a scheduling plan. The virtual machine provisioning plan can be generated based on a single-site virtual machine provisioning plan, e.g., SSVP (see Section 3.3.2), and the fragment scheduled at the site according to the scheduling plan. $sched(wf_i, s_j) = 1$ is a binary variable that represents that fragment wf_i is scheduled at site s_j.

Fragment Scheduling Algorithm

There are basically four types of fragment scheduling algorithms, i.e., classic, Site Greedy (SGreedy), data location-based (LocBased), and Activity Greedy (ActGreedy). As explained in Section 4.2.2, many classic scheduling algorithms, e.g., HEFT [Wieczorek et al., 2005], min-min [Etminani and Naghibzadeh, 2007], max-min [Etminani and Naghibzadeh, 2007] and Opportunistic Load Balancing (OLB) [Maheswaran et al., 1999] can be used for fragment scheduling while focusing on a single objective, i.e., reducing execution time.

Also, a brute-force method can generate an optimal scheduling plan. The brute-force method generates all the possible solutions and chooses the best solution. However, its complexity is very high. Furthermore, genetic algorithms [Wieczorek et al., 2005] can generate near-optimal scheduling plans. The principle of a genetic algorithm is to encode possible scheduling plans into a population of chromosomes, and subsequently to transform the population using standard operations of selection, crossover, and mutation, producing successive generations, until the convergence condition is met. For example, a simple genetic algorithm has two steps. The first step initiates the several scheduling plans as chromosomes of a population defined by users. The population is the number of scheduling plans (chromosomes). The second step is to repeat a process to optimize the scheduling plan until the cost of the scheduling is smaller than a predefined threshold. The repeated process contains two operations. The first operation is to generate a new set of scheduling plans based on the existing ones. Then, if the cost of a scheduling plan in the newly generated scheduling plan is smaller than a predefined threshold, the algorithm stops. Alternatively, the scheduling plans that correspond to small cost are selected as chromosomes in order to continue the algorithm. The number of selected scheduling plans equals the predefined population. The disadvantage of the genetic algorithm is that it is difficult to configure parameters, e.g., populations, threshold [Wieczorek et al., 2005] and that the scheduling time is very long.

The greedy activation scheduling algorithm [de Oliveira et al., 2012b] presented in Section 4.2.2 can be adapted to a multi-site, multi-objective fragment scheduling algorithm as discussed by Liu et al. [2016b]. The adapted algorithm is denoted by Site Greedy (SGreedy). SGreedy schedules the fragment, which takes the smallest cost based on a multi-objective cost model, to each site. However, it incurs a high cost to transfer the data among different sites. In order to use SGreedy, the activity encapsulation partitioning method is used to partition a workflow. The scheduling plan generated by SGreedy is shown in Figure 4.15.

Algorithm 4.6 describes SGreedy. When there is a fragment that is not scheduled (Line 3), for each site (Line 4), the fragment that takes the least cost is scheduled to each site (Lines 5–10). The fragments are selected from the available fragments (Lines 5 and 12). Lines 7–8 estimate the total cost to execute Fragment wf at the site. Line 9 chooses the optimal fragment, i.e., wf_{opt}, that needs the smallest total cost to be executed for the site. Line 10 schedules the optimal fragment to the site. Line 11 updates the fragments that need to be scheduled. Line 13 prepares available fragments to be scheduled for the next site.

The goal of LocBased (data location-based) [Liu et al., 2014b] is to reduce the time to transfer data, which also reduces the financial cost to use virtual machines. LocBased schedules the fragment where its input data or fixed stored data is; the corresponding scheduling plans are shown in Figures 4.14. The stored data is necessary for the execution of specific activities, while it can only be accessed at the site where it is stored. LocBased is used with the DTM workflow partitioning method in order to reduce data transfer among different sites.

LocBased (data location-based) is given in Algorithm 4.7. Line 2 partitions a Fragment wf using DTM (see details in Section 4.3.1) as shown in Figure 4.14. Then, each fragment wf (Line 3) is scheduled to a data site (Lines 4–5). If the fragment contains a fixed activity, the scheduled data site is the one that stores the required data (i.e., stored data) of the fixed activity.

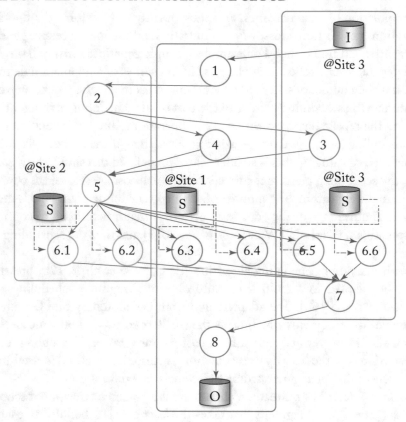

Figure 4.15: Site greedy scheduling.

If the fragment does not contain a fixed activity, the scheduled data site is the one that stores the biggest part of the input data of the fragment.

ActGreedy is based on LocBased and SGreedy. During the scheduling process of Act-Greedy, all the fragments are scheduled at a corresponding site, which takes the minimum cost calculated based on a cost model composed of multiple objectives, e.g., reducing execution time and financial cost. Similarly to LocBased, ActGreedy schedules fragments of multiple activities. ActGreedy can schedule a pipeline of activities to a site in order to reduce data transfer between different fragments, i.e., the possible data transfer between different sites. A pipeline is a group of activities with a one-to-one, sequential relationship between them [Rodriguez and Buyya, 2015]. However, ActGreedy is different from LocBased since it makes a trade-off between time and financial costs. Different from SGreedy, which chooses the best fragment for an available site, ActGreedy chooses the best site for an available fragment. An available fragment indicated that its previous activities are already scheduled, which means that the location of the input data of the fragment is known.

Algorithm 4.6 Site Greedy Scheduling

Input : *swf*: a scientific workflow; S: a set of sites *Output* : *SP*: scheduling plan for *swf* in S

1: $SP \leftarrow \emptyset$
2: $WF \leftarrow partition(WF)$ {According to basic partitioning method (see details in Section 4.3.1}

3: **while** $WF \neq \emptyset$ **do**
4:   **for** $s \in S$ **do**
5:     $WFA \leftarrow GetAvailableFragments(WF)$
6:     **if** $WFA \neq \emptyset$ **then**
7:       **for** $wf \in WFA$ **do**
8:         $Cost[i] \leftarrow EstimateCost(wf, s)$ {According to the cost estimation method}
9:       **end for**
10:       $wf_{opt} \leftarrow GetFragment(s, Cost)$ {Get the fragment that takes the minimal cost for the execution at Site s}
11:       $SP \leftarrow SP \bigcup \{Schedule(wf_{opt}, s)\}$
12:       $WF \leftarrow WF - wf_{opt}$
13:       $WFA \leftarrow GetAvailableFragments(WF)$
14:     **end if**
15:   **end for**
16: **end while**

Algorithm 4.7 Data Location Based Scheduling

Input : *swf*: a scientific workflow; S: a set of sites *Output* : *SP*: scheduling plan for *swf* in S

1: $SP \leftarrow \emptyset$
2: $WF \leftarrow partition(WF)$
3: **for** $wf_i \in WF$ **do**
4:   $s_j \leftarrow GetDataSite(wf_i, S)$ {get Site s_j that stores its required data or the biggest amount of input data}
5:   $SP \leftarrow SP \bigcup \{Schedule(wf_i, s_j)\}$
6: **end for**

As shown in Algorithm 4.8, ActGreedy chooses the best site for each fragment. First, it partitions the SWf according to the activity encapsulation partitioning method (Line 3). Then, it groups the fragments of three types into bigger fragments to be scheduled (Line 6). The first type is the pipeline of activities. We use a recursive algorithm presented in Rodriguez and Buyya [2015] to find pipelines. Then, the fragments of the corresponding activities of each pipeline

---

Algorithm 4.8 Activity Greedy Scheduling

Input : *swf*: a scientific workflow; *S*: a set of sites *Output* : *SP*: scheduling plan for *swf* in *S*

1: $SP \leftarrow \emptyset$
2: $SWfCost \leftarrow \infty$
3: $WF \leftarrow partition(swf)$
4: **while** not all the fragments $\in WF$ are scheduled **do**
5:   $SP' \leftarrow \emptyset$
6:   $WF \leftarrow Group(WF)$
7:   **while** $CurrentSWfCost < SWfCost$ **do**
8:     $WFA \leftarrow GetAvailableFragments(WF, SP')$
9:     **if** $WFA \neq \emptyset$ **then**
10:       **for** $wf \in WFA$ **do**
11:         $s_{opt} \leftarrow BestSite(wf, S)$
12:         $SP' \leftarrow SP' \bigcup \{Schedule(wf, s_{opt})\}$
13:         update $CurrentSWfCost$
14:       **end for**
15:     **end if**
16:   **end while**
17:   **if** $CurrentSWfCost < SWfCost$ **then**
18:     $SP \leftarrow SP'$
19:     $SWfCost \leftarrow CurrentSWfCost$
20:   **end if**
21: **end while**

---

are grouped into a fragment. If there are stored activities of different sites in a fragment of a pipeline, the fragment is partitioned into several fragments by DTM (see details in 4.3.1) in the *Group* function. The second type is the control activities. If it has only one preceding activity, a control activity is grouped into the fragment of its previous activity. If it has multiple preceding activities and only one following activity, a control activity (Activity 7) is grouped into the fragment of its following activity (Activity 8). If it has multiple preceding activities and multiple following activities, a control activity (Activity 5) is grouped into the fragment of one of its preceding activities (Activity 3), which has the most data dependencies among all its preceding activities, i.e., the amount of data to be transferred in the data dependency is the largest. It reduces data transfer among different fragments, namely the data transfer among different sites, to group the fragments for pipelines and control activities. The third type is the activities that are scheduled at the same site and that have dependencies to connect each activity. Afterwards, Line 8 gets the available fragments to be scheduled to the best site (Lines 11–12), which incurs the least cost among all the sites to execute the fragment. The cost is estimated based on the cost model presented in Section 4.3.2. When estimating the cost, if the scheduled fragment has data dependencies with fixed activities, the cost to transfer the data in these data dependencies will be taken into consideration. The loop (Lines 7–16) schedules each fragment to the best site, while the big loop (Lines 4–20) improves the scheduling plans by rescheduling the fragments after grouping the fragments at the same site, which ensures that the final scheduling plan corresponds to smaller cost to execute an SWf.

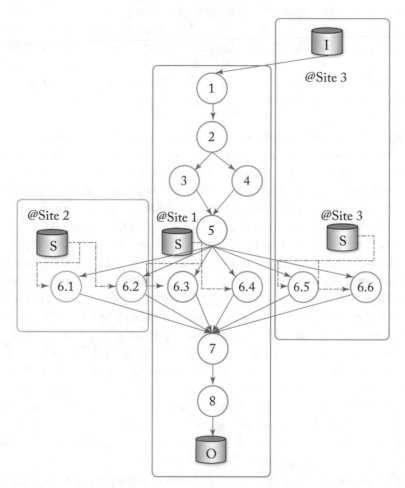

Figure 4.16: Activity greedy scheduling.

The ActGreedy scheduling algorithm is also combined with the activity encapsulation method. The scheduling plan generated by ActGreedy is shown in Figure 4.16. ActGreedy has relatively small granularity compared with LocBased. ActGreedy exploits data location information to select the best site in order to make a trade-off between the cost for transferring data among different sites and another cost, i.e., the cost to provision the virtual machines and the cost to execute fragments. If the amount of data increases and the desired execution time is small, Activity 7 and Activity 8 may be scheduled at Site 3, which takes less cost to transfer data.

4.3.3   PERFORMANCE ANALYSIS

In order to compare the performance of different scheduling algorithms, we present an experimental evaluation of the fragment scheduling algorithms. All experiments are based on the execution of the SciEvol SWf in Microsoft Azure multisite cloud. In the experiments, we consider three Azure [Azu] sites to execute SciEvol SWf, namely West Europe as Site 1, Japan West as Site 2, and Japan East as Site 3. We use 100, 500, and 1,000 fasta files generated from the data stored in a genome database [Oma, a,b]. We use SSVP, presented in Chapter 3, to deploy VMs at a single site to execute an SWf fragment.

LocBased is optimized for reducing data transfer among different sites. The scheduling plan generated by this algorithm is shown in Figure 4.14. However, the different financial costs of the three sites are not taken into account. Also, this algorithm directly schedules a fragment, which contains multiple activities. Some activities are scheduled at a site, which is more expensive to use virtual machines. As a consequence, the scheduling plan may correspond to a higher cost. SGreedy schedules a site to the available activity, which takes the least cost. SGreedy does not take data location into account and may schedule two continuous activities, i.e., one preceding activity and one following activity, to two different sites, which takes time to transfer data and to provision virtual machines. As a result, this algorithm may lead to a higher cost.

ActGreedy can schedule each fragment to a site that takes the least cost to execute it, which leads to smaller cost compared with LocBased and SGreedy. Also, ActGreedy can make the adaptive modification for different numbers of input fasta files. Note that workflow partitioning algorithms may also have an impact on the performance of the scheduling algorithm. For instance, LocBased is based on a workflow partitioning algorithm to reduce data transfer among different workflow fragments. According to Liu et al. [2016b], the cost of ActGreedy is up to 21.75% (compared with LocBased) and 74.51% (compared with SGreedy) smaller based on Equations (4.4) and (4.5), as shown in Figure 4.17. In addition, the cost of ActGreedy is up to 10.7% (compared with LocBased) and 17.2% (compared with SGreedy) smaller, calculated according to Equation (4.1) as shown in Figure 4.18.

Although Genetic and Brute-Force can generate a near-optimal or optimal solution, their scheduling time is much longer than ActGreedy (up to 577 times and 128 times, as shown in Figure 4.19 [Liu et al., 2016b]). Genetic may perform worse than Brute-Force for a small number of activities or sites with the specific configuration. The scheduling time of Genetic is smaller than that of Brute-Force when the number of activities or sites increases. Even though when the number of activities and the number of sites is small, the scheduling time is negligible compared with the execution time, it becomes significant when the numbers of activities or

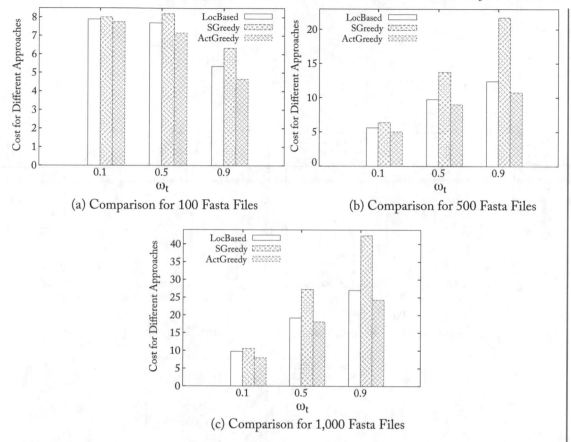

(a) Comparison for 100 Fasta Files

(b) Comparison for 500 Fasta Files

(c) Comparison for 1,000 Fasta Files

Figure 4.17: Cost for different scheduling algorithms. The cost is calculated according to Formula (4.4).

sites increase. For instance, with a significant number of activities or sites, the scheduling time of Brute-Force and Genetic exceeds the execution, while the scheduling time of ActGreedy remains small, as shown in Figure 4.19. This is because of the high complexity of Brute-Force and Genetic algorithms. Because of long scheduling time, Genetic and Brute-Force algorithms are not suitable for most workflows [Liu et al., 2016b]. Although the scheduling time of ActGreedy is much longer than that of SGreedy and LocBased, it remains reasonable compared with the overall workflow execution time.

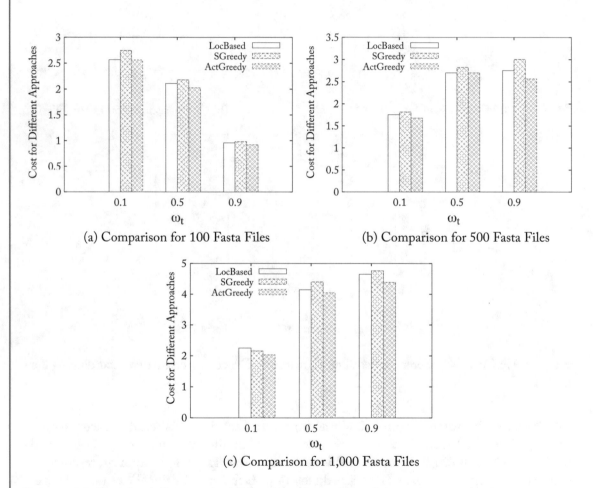

(a) Comparison for 100 Fasta Files

(b) Comparison for 500 Fasta Files

(c) Comparison for 1,000 Fasta Files

Figure 4.18: Cost for different scheduling algorithms. According to Formula (4.1).

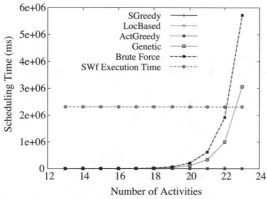

(a) Scheduling time corresponding to different numbers of activities.

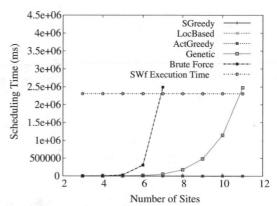

(b) Scheduling time corresponding to different numbers of sites.

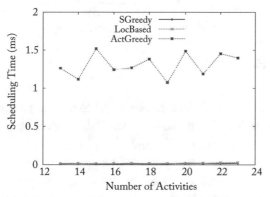

(c) Scheduling time corresponding to different numbers of activities (zoom on LocBased, SGreedy, and ActGreedy).

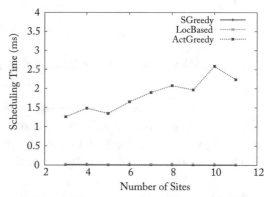

(d) Scheduling time corresponding to different numbers of sites (zoom on LocBased, SGreedy, and ActGreedy).

Figure 4.19: Scheduling time.

4.4   CONCLUSION

In this chapter, we presented the solutions to execute workflows in a multi-site cloud, where the data and computing resources may be distributed at different cloud data centers. Figure 4.20 summarizes the techniques for workflow execution in a multi-site cloud.

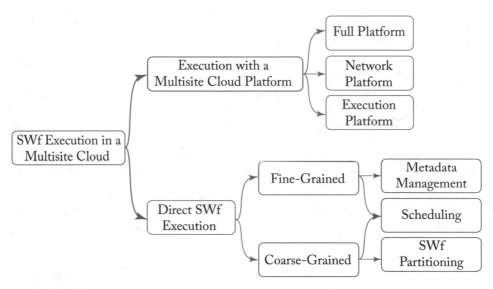

Figure 4.20: Workflow execution in a multi-site cloud.

The workflow execution in a multi-site cloud can be divided between the execution with a multi-site cloud platform and direct workflow execution. The multi-site cloud platform contains three types, i.e., full platform, network platform, and execution platform. The full platform integrates all the resources of each site, while the network platform provides a single-site network environment. The execution platform offers a specific execution environment, e.g., multi-site MapReduce system, for workflow execution in a multi-site cloud.

Workflows can be directly executed in a multi-site cloud using two approaches, i.e., fine-grained and coarse-grained. Each approach has its own corresponding SWfMSs and architectures. The metadata management is important for fine-grained workflow execution. There are three strategies to manage the metadata, i.e., centralized, distributed, and hybrid. The centralized strategy stored the metadata at a centralized site. The distributed strategy typically exploits LOC, DHT, or REP metadata placement method to store the metadata at the corresponding site. In addition, the hybrid combines the centralized and distributed strategy by storing a part of the metadata, e.g., hot metadata, at a site according to a metadata placement method and the other metadata, e.g., cold metadata, at a centralized site. The metadata management strategies can be combined with scheduling strategies to achieve good performance.

During the coarse-grained workflow execution, a workflow is partitioned to fragments. A workflow can be partitioned by activity encapsulation method or by balancing the workload for computing resources. DTM partitioning method can partition a workflow by minimizing the data transfer among different fragments. The partitioning methods should be used with corresponding scheduling algorithms in order to have good performance. Also, the coarse-grained workflow execution can achieve multiple objectives, e.g., reducing execution time and financial cost, based on a cost model, which is used to calculate the cost based on a scheduling plan.

Scheduling is critical to both the fine-grained and coarse-grained workflow execution. Figure 4.21 shows a taxonomy of scheduling techniques. According to the workflow execution approaches, scheduling techniques can be classified as activation scheduling in the fine-grained workflow execution and fragment scheduling in the coarse-grained workflow execution. The activation scheduling can be performed with a 1L scheduling approach and 2L scheduling approach. The 1L scheduling approach directly schedules activations to the computing nodes at different sites, which is very complex and challenging to achieve load balance. The 2L scheduling approach has two levels. The first level is the multi-site level, which schedules activations or bags of activations into different sites. Then, the activations at each site are scheduled with a default scheduling algorithm of a single-site SWfMS. The fragment scheduling schedules the fragments at different sites.

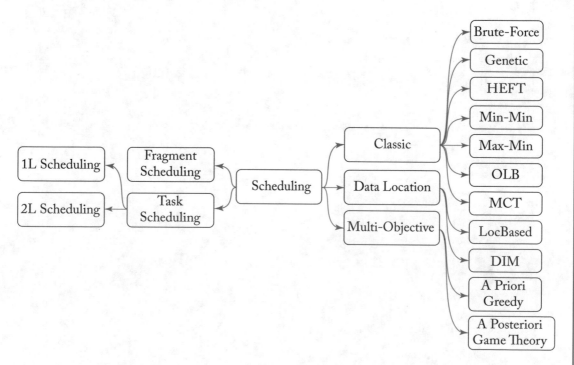

Figure 4.21: Scheduling techniques in SWf execution in a multisite cloud.

Different scheduling algorithms are directly used or adapted to fragment scheduling and activation scheduling. The scheduling algorithms can be classified into three types, i.e., classic, data location-based, and multi-objective. Most scheduling algorithms are based on the classic scheduling algorithms, e.g., Brute-Force, genetic, HEFT, MCT, and so on. The data location-based scheduling algorithms schedules the activations or fragments to where the data is. DIM further balances the load among different sites after scheduling activations at the site where the input data is. The classic and data location scheduling algorithms generally have a single objective, i.e., reducing execution time.

There are two types of scheduling algorithms to achieve multiple objectives, i.e., *a priori* and a posteriori. The *a priori* scheduling approaches generally exploit a greedy method, which schedules a fragment to a best site or schedules a site to the best fragment. "Best" represents that the scheduling plan corresponds to the least cost estimated based on a cost model. The *a posteriori* scheduling approaches typically exploit game theory to generate a Pareto front of solutions and pick the first generated solution in order to reduce scheduling time.

CHAPTER 5

Workflow Execution in DISC Environments

As previously discussed, workflows rely on large-scale processing to corroborate scientific hypotheses, which requires the execution of data-intensive operations such as data loading, transformations, and aggregations [Liu et al., 2016a].

Although both shell and Python scripts may be employed for the implementation of workflows [Pimentel et al., 2017], they may be not suitable for executing activations that require the controlling of parallel processing on High-Performance Computing environments. Such activations require native distributed computing protocols, e.g., MPI, as well as efficient serialization protocols for the distribution of objects among computational nodes [Dalcin et al., 2011].

Thus, Scientific Workflow Management Systems (SWfMS), such as Pegasus [Deelman et al., 2005], SciCumulus [de Oliveira et al., 2012b], and Swift/T [Wozniak et al., 2013] are used for the modeling, enacting, and monitoring of the execution of large-scale parallel workflows. SWfMSs provide a series of advantages for scientists, including a variety of scheduling strategies, fault-tolerance techniques, and provenance management mechanisms. These systems support the execution of workflows in clusters and clouds using a shared-disk model, inherited from High-Performance Computing systems. However, for processing big datasets, moving data through the network may jeopardize workflow execution. Thus, data locality also becomes an issue.

Some scientists are already migrating their IO-intensive workflows to execute in Data-Intensive Scalable Computing (DISC) frameworks due to their popularity, high scalability, and vast support community of users. Examples are Kira in astronomy [Zhang et al., 2018], Spark-GA [Mushtaq et al., 2017], GOAT [Kanzki et al., 2016], and ADAM[1] in the bioinformatics domain.

Although there are several DISC frameworks [Had, Hey et al., 2012, Spark, 2012], in this chapter we go deep in Apache Spark.[2] Differently from Hadoop and other DISC frameworks, Spark benefits from in-memory storage of intermediate data, data movement, and processing, thus providing better performance when compared to Hadoop if the available memory is enough for the execution demand of the workflow in question [Gu et al., 2013]. Frameworks such as Apache Spark control the execution of each activity regarding distinct data partitions to provide

---

[1]https://adam.readthedocs.io/en/latest/
[2]https://spark.apache.org/

automatic dataflow parallelism between activities. Key Apache Spark data abstractions are the *Resilient Distributed Datasets* (RDDs), which are essentially in-memory collections of immutable and partitioned data instances to be processed in parallel [Zaharia et al., 2010b, 2012a].

Although Spark represents a step forward, it is not designed to support scientific applications and workflows. Hence, there are critical issues that have yet to be addressed on the usage of Spark for the execution of scientific workflows.

1. Although Spark-based workflows are executed faster even when using default configuration parameters, a **fine tuning of Spark configuration parameters** can considerably improve the performance. The problem is that Spark (and other frameworks) has more than 100 configuration parameters that can be adjusted to provide an optimized execution of the workflow. This fine tuning is not a trivial task to be accomplished.

2. Another limitation when using Spark with workflows is the case of the **usage of black-box applications** that communicate with each other through *data files*. In this scenario, Spark is unable to benefit from RDDs for the management of swapped data without flushing them to disk.

3. Spark does not **capture provenance data** since the design of a solution for capturing and storing provenance data to Spark has several challenges [Wang et al., 2015] as the gathering of provenance data cannot jeopardize the workflow performance.

4. Spark does not partition the activity inputs in the Spark RDDs to avoid unnecessary data transfers during the workflow execution. To achieve this, a **data placement and a scheduling algorithm** are needed.

In this chapter, we address a problem of how to manage workflows in DISC environments using the well-known DISC framework Apache Spark. The goal is to present how to fine tune Spark, collect provenance data and execute the workflow efficiently. This chapter is based mostly on the work of Gaspar et al. [2017], Guedes et al. [2018], and Oliveira et al. [2019].

5.1 BIBLIOGRAPHIC AND HISTORICAL NOTES

Spark-based workflows are used to model large-scale *in silico* scientific experiments to process significant amounts of data on commodity clusters. Spark has gained much attention from the scientific community in recent years because it is fundamental to use parallelism techniques to execute these workflows within a reasonable time. As discussed in Chapters 1, 2, and 3, several SWfMSs already provide parallel capabilities, which can take advantage of clusters, grids, and clouds to execute data-intensive workflows.

However, such capabilities are not found in Apache Spark and other DISC frameworks since Spark is not designed to support scientists' daily duties. The problems of setting Spark parameters, collecting, and storing provenance data and scheduling activations in Spark remain open for workflow execution in Spark [Guedes et al., 2018]. This section discusses existing work on these topics.

5.1.1 EARLY WORK ON FINE TUNING PARAMETERS OF DISC FRAMEWORKS

Several approaches aim at tuning parameters in DISC frameworks. Most of these approaches are based on Apache Hadoop. These approaches have been idealized for specific application classes or specific environments, such as configuration and allocation of cloud resources to minimize financial cost [Lama and Zhou, 2012] and I/O [Popescu et al., 2013].

AROMA [Lama and Zhou, 2012] aims at automating resource and task allocation in Hadoop for heterogeneous clouds by meeting SLA (Service Level Agreement) requirements while minimizing financial costs involved in the execution. AROMA is based on machine learning algorithms using a clustering algorithm. This clustering algorithm consumes information related to CPU, network, and disk utilization in order to create clusters of applications with similar profiles and resource consumption. After that, AROMA collects resource usage data while the Hadoop application is executing. Using the collected information, AROMA finds a resource allocation and a parameter setting based on the corresponding identified pattern.

PREDIcT [Popescu et al., 2013] is another system that performs runtime prediction for I/O intensive iterative algorithms implemented in Hadoop framework. PREDIcT aims at estimating the number of iterations and the expected execution time for each iteration of the application based on data collected from previous executions. Similar to AROMA, PREDIcT also relies on machine learning algorithms to achieve a satisfactory predictive result. It requires extensive training datasets for generating prediction models, which can lead to poor prediction when no data history is available.

Starfish [Herodotou and Babu, 2011, Herodotou et al., 2011] is a system that implements a cost-based optimization approach to help users identify the best parameter values for MapReduce applications. Starfish has a profiler that gathers workflow execution statistics at runtime. After the profiler collects statistics, a *what-if* model determines the impact of a parameter setting on performance based on the data obtained by the profiler. Finally, an optimizer provides the settings that perform a better execution by querying the *what-if* module. The effectiveness of this approach depends on the accuracy of the em what-if module that is based on estimations and in simulations. Also, the cost-based method, implemented by Starfish [Herodotou, 2012], is an approach where an in-depth knowledge is required about the system's internal features, and also about the workflow behavior. This challenge has motivated the exploration of optimization methods that are agnostic of the workflow/application [Wang et al., 2016, Yigitbasi et al., 2013].

Yigitbasi et al. [2013] adopt a machine-learning approach to generate the predictive model of parameter configuration for Apache Hadoop. The approach proposed by Yigitbasi et al. [2013] is based on Support Vector Regression (SVR) mode, and results show a precise and efficient prediction. The results pointed out that this approach can provide equal or better performance than Starfish [Herodotou et al., 2011] when a small number of parameters is considered for workflow execution. Although SVR classification method presents less risk of over-fitting with a lower training cost of the model, this method is not interpretable by human beings.

Wang and Khan [2015] present an accurate prediction model obtained through simulations on the performance of workflows in Spark systems. However, the model is used to predict the execution time and memory usage of Spark workflows with the default parameter setting. Wang et al. [2016] propose a method to optimize Spark workflows through the configuration of Spark parameters based on machine learning techniques. The method proposed by Wang et al. [2016] is based on binary classification and multi-classification [Han et al., 2011]. A set of classification algorithms is explored in order to obtain a better predictive model, in which it is possible to identify a parameter configuration that leads to efficient execution of the Spark workflow. Similar to the method mentioned above, the method proposed by Wang et al. [2016] is based on the training data obtained from previous executions to extract execution statistics, which makes it more robust and flexible.

Although there are solutions to obtain an efficient set of configuration parameter values through the machine learning methods as in Wang et al. [2016], they do not consider essential features such as the data partitioning strategy [Herodotou et al., 2011, Wang et al., 2016]. The parameters related to data partitioning (partitioning strategy and partitions size) influence workflow execution time.

Thus, in this chapter, we go deeper into the SpaCE approach (Section 5.2) approach to fine tuning spark parameters. SpaCE focuses on generating predictive machine learning models (i.e., decision trees), and then extracts useful rules (i.e., patterns) from this model that can be applied to configure parameters of future executions of the Spark-based workflow.

5.1.2 EARLY WORK ON PROVENANCE CAPTURE IN DISC FRAMEWORKS

Spark enhances the execution of several types of parallel applications, including workflows, but the framework has some limitations to support provenance management. Some work provides provenance support for DISC frameworks, such as Newt [Logothetis et al., 2013] and Reduce and Map Provenance (RAMP) [Ikeda et al., 2011] systems. Other approaches propose complete isolated applications for capturing and storing provenance, such as Titian [Interlandi et al., 2015] and BigDebug [Gulzar et al., 2016].

Spark includes a simplified provenance component named Spark Log [Armbrust et al., 2015], which was designed for monitoring Spark workflow executions. Spark log can be accessed by either a web interface or a text file. In the web front-end, scientists may visualize the DAG of transformations (i.e., activities) and check the status of their execution. Although it presents fixed statistics, such as memory consumption and elapsed time, if scientists need to analyze the domain-specific data, i.e., what was produced by the workflow, they will need to parse and process the data files.

Newt [Logothetis et al., 2013] aims at using provenance for finding errors in the outcome of workflows. The tool captures provenance data by using code instrumentation, in which users are responsible for setting an identifier for each data instance of the experiment and provide their relationship beforehand. Provenance data are stored in the relational and clustered MySQL DBMS in such a way high-level SQL queries can be issued for determining the tracking of all identifiers involved in experimental parts that culminate in the output error.

RAMP [Ikeda et al., 2011] was designed explicitly for gathering provenance on MapReduce-based tasks on Hadoop. RAMP adopts Hadoop API for gathering provenance data and stores them by using HDFS external files. Therefore, specific tools like Hive [Thusoo et al., 2010] or Pig [Olston et al., 2008] must be used for provenance querying.

Titian [Interlandi et al., 2015] provides provenance support aimed at debugging Spark code. It extends the RDD abstraction through programming models, which allows users to trace backward and forward data. The tool maintains data lineage utilizing a newly designed RDD, called LineageRDD, which enables data debugging at runtime focused on fault-tolerance recovery on interactive scenarios. Additionally, unlike RAMP or Newt, Titian enables users to apply new transformations on data instead of just "replaying" the running of a scientific workflow.

BigDebug [Gulzar et al., 2016] follows a distinct provenance approach and provides early access to data through simulation of breakpoints and on-demand watchpoints. The tool is built on top of Titian by taking advantage of data lineage on RDDs for data debugging. It enables the retrieval of intermediate data from either break or watchpoints without actually stopping the overall Spark execution.

Whenever workflows invoke black-box applications that read or write raw files, all solutions mentioned above are unable to gather, store, and query the produced contents because they were not designed for the handling of black-box routines that interchange data and transformations between raw files and RDDs. Moreover, they neither consider nor store the content of produced files, which prevents runtime and *post-mortem* querying of a workflow execution. Such management requires the selection, extraction, and loading of raw files' data elements, i.e., data items within a raw data file, into the main memory, which is not a trivial task. Therefore, in this chapter, we go deeper into the SAMbA approach (Section 5.3) [Guedes et al., 2018] approach to handle all types of provenance data in an integrated fashion. In particular, SAMbA follows the guidelines proposed by de Oliveira et al. [2015] in order to provide domain data analytics regarding the execution of black-box programs in Spark workflows.

5.1.3 EARLY WORK ON SCHEDULING AND DATA PLACEMENT STRATEGIES IN DISC FRAMEWORKS

Although parameter fine tuning and provenance management are critical issues in DISC frameworks such as Spark, the scheduling of tasks and transformations plays a fundamental role in workflow execution. Typically, data-intensive workflows have been designed to execute in HPC environments based on a shared-disk model. However, using a shared-disk model may incur costly data transfers that may jeopardize the workflow execution. Thus, scheduling algorithms should consider data locality when scheduling jobs to the distributed environment. Also, similar to the approaches presented in Chapter 3 and 4, the scheduling strategy could also consider several objectives such as reducing the execution time and financial costs involved in execution.

Spark default scheduler executes jobs in FIFO way. It is worth noticing that when we use the term "jobs," we are referring to internal Spark jobs within a Spark application or workflow. Although many authors use the term "job" for Spark applications, they are two very different constructs. Jobs in Spark are classified into stages, and the first job gets priority on all available resources. Then, the second job gets priority, and so forth. Figure 5.1 presents what we mean by jobs and stages in this chapter.

In most scenarios, Spark runs in multi-user and multi-job mode, where there may be a large number of reuse of jobs. The reuse of some calculations in Spark jobs may dramatically reduce job execution time. Based on that, Tang et al. [2016] propose a novel scheduling algorithm for job reusing. The algorithm proposed by Tang et al. [2016] is based on the original Spark pool

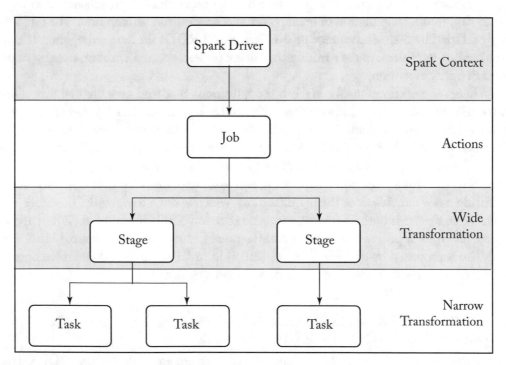

Figure 5.1: Classification of Spark jobs.

scheduling algorithm. The fairness of the original scheduling algorithm is maintained with the benefit of reusing jobs computations.

Li et al. [2018] propose an energy-efficient scheduling algorithm for Apache Spark that aims at reducing energy consumption while satisfying deadline constraints. Li et al. [2018] formulated the scheduling problem as an integer program problem. The proposed task scheduling algorithm trades off execution time and energy consumption. Although the proposed algorithms consume less energy on average than FIFO under deadlines, they do not consider data locality.

Chen and Wang [2015] propose an entropy-based scheduling strategy for efficiently executing Spark applications. Chen and Wang [2015] used entropy (a measure of the degree of disorder in a system) to estimate the reliability of job scheduling in a cloud cluster. The main idea of the proposed scheduler is that it relies on the new resource entropy metric and schedules tasks according to the resource ranking with the help of the new metric to provide QoS (Quality of Service) guarantees for Spark jobs.

Ying et al. [2015] propose a scheduling algorithm that aims at minimizing energy consumption (which is formulated as a minimization problem), which considers data locality for batch and interactive MapReduce applications and workflows. Ying et al. [2015] propose an approach that has a MapReduce scheduler that uses a Markov Decision Process model to design the allocation algorithm. The proposed locality-aware scheduler is designed for guaranteeing the throughput during the transient overload caused by insufficient servers for task allocation. Maroulis et al. [2017] propose a framework that orchestrates the execution of Spark applications, which tunes the CPU frequencies of the machines that are part of the commodity cluster in order to minimize energy consumption and satisfy application's performance requirements.

Cheng et al. [2017] propose a resource-scheduling middleware named iKayak, which aims at improving the resource usage and workflow performance in multi-tenant Spark-on-YARN clusters. As defined by Cheng et al. [2017], iKayak relies on three key mechanisms: reservation-aware executor placement to avoid long waiting for resource reservation, dependency-aware resource adjustment to exploit under-utilized resources occupied by reduce tasks, and cross-platform locality-aware task assignment to coordinate locality competition between Spark and MapReduce applications.

In this chapter, we go deeper into the TARDIS approach (Section 5.4.1) [Gaspar et al., 2017] to provide optimal workflows scheduling in DISC environments using Apache Spark.

5.1.4   CHAPTER GOALS AND CONTRIBUTIONS

In this chapter we consider workflow management in DISC environments, e.g., a shared-nothing cluster formed of commodity machines. The main contents of this chapter are:

1. SpaCE [Oliveira et al., 2019] approach that fine tunes spark parameters. SpaCE focuses on generating decision trees to extract useful rules (i.e., patterns) from this model

that can be applied to configure parameters of future executions of the Spark-based workflow;

2. SAMbA [Guedes et al., 2018] approach to handle all types of provenance data in an integrated fashion. SAMbA provides domain data analytics regarding the execution of black-box programs in Spark workflows; and

3. TARDIS [Gaspar et al., 2017] approach to providing optimal workflows scheduling in DISC environments using Apache Spark.

All of the aforementioned approaches are designed for Apache Spark but can be adapted to different DISC frameworks.

5.2   FINE TUNING OF SPARK PARAMETERS

In this chapter, the two main features of Spark that are considered for tuning are CPU and memory. Although I/O also impact the performance of Spark workflows, it is not considered in the following explanations. In this chapter we assume that Spark is executing on a commodity cluster where network latency does not impact the subjected workflow performance. Thus, only Spark configuration parameters related to CPU and memory are evaluated, as presented below:

- Number of executors: defines the total number of executors (processes) that are created to execute a Spark workflow.

- Number of cores per executor: defines the number of concurrent tasks that an executor can perform.

- Amount of memory per executor: defines the maximum amount of memory available for each executor.

If the scientist does not specify these parameters in the workflow execution, then Spark uses default values, i.e., the values specified in the framework or by the system administrator. Another option that can be employed to adjust the parameters is the use of values that are recommended in tutorials made by advanced Spark developers [Spark, 2012, Tutorial, 2017], called rules-of-thumb. However, the results discussed in Herodotou [2012] and Wang et al. [2016], show that the Spark workflow execution using default parameter values and/or rules-of-thumb do not produce an efficient execution when compared to the solutions proposed in Herodotou [2012] and Wang et al. [2016]. A "correct" parameter setting can effectively improve the performance of Spark-based workflows in shared-nothing commodity clusters.

In this section, we discuss in details the Spark Configuration Engine (SpaCE) [Oliveira et al., 2019]. SpACE aims at optimizing the execution of Spark-based workflows in DISC environments through fine tuning of Spark parameters. SpaCE follows a "black box" optimization model, i.e., it is not intrusive. This way, the parameter setting is just based on the actual observations of the performance of the workflow when executing in a particular DISC environment with specific parameter values.

5.2.1 PROBLEM DEFINITION

In this section, we formally define the parameter setting problem, regarding relevant aspects related to the workflow structure, input data, configuration parameters, and the DISC environment. We extend the workflow formalism defined in Chapter 2. Let us formalize the DISC environment $R = \{r_1, \ldots, r_k\}$ to be the set of commodity machines in the DISC environment available for dedicated execution of the Spark workflow. In this chapter, we assume that all machines resources in the DISC environment are homogeneous, although this formalism does not restrict machines to be homogeneous.

Therefore, given a workflow W, an input dataset I, and a set of computational resources R, let $S(W, I, R) = \{pv_1, pv_2, \ldots, pv_m\}$ be the set of parameter values defined for the execution of the workflow W. Each parameter value pv_i represents one of the aforementioned parameters: number of cores per executor, amount of memory per executor, parameters related to data partitioning, parameters related to the computational resources, and so on, as discussed as following.

In order to execute the workflow, different parameter values should be specified. Regarding the Spark framework standard parameters, there are over 180 parameters that need to be configured. However, here, only a subset of these parameters (10 parameters) is considered for fine tuning. The other parameters are set with default values. These parameters are directly related to the key issues of a DISC environment such as CPU and amount of RAM. Finally, as reported by Wang et al. [2016], users often face performance problems caused by wrongly setting such parameters. The first column of Table 5.1 presents the subset of parameters considered most relevant concerning the workflow performance, while the second column shows their meaning. It must be pointed out that the parameter *EN* has its maximum value defined according to *EM* and *CM*.

Table 5.1: Relevant parameters for Spark tuning

Variable	Meaning
EN	Number of Spark Executors
EC	Number of Cores per Executor
EM	Amount of memory per Executor
DS	Dataset Size
CN	Number of Machines
CC	Number of Cores per Machine
CM	Amount of Memory per Machine

Thus, given a workflow W and its input dataset I to be executed on a DISC environment R, the goal of SpaCE is to find the set of parameter setting values $S^*(W, I, R)$ so that the execution time (ET) of W is minimized. More formally, $\exists \, S^*(W, I, R)$ as presented in Equation (5.1):

$$E_T(W, I, R, S^*(W, I, R)) = \min_{\forall S(W, I, R)} E_T(W, I, R, S(W, I, R)), \qquad (5.1)$$

where $E_T(W, I, R, S(W, I, R))$ is the execution time of the workflow W consuming the data set I and executing on the resources in R with the set of parameters values $S(W, I, R)$. It is important to highlight that the value $S^*(W, I, R)$ is obtained by using the predictive model (explained below). In the context of this chapter, the $S^*(W, I, R)$ is obtained by transversing a decision tree generated by SpaCE.

5.2.2   SPACE: A SPARK FINE-TUNING ENGINE

In order to execute the Spark workflow with a minimum possible execution time, one must find the right parameter setting values $S^*(W, I, R)$, which is not a simple task. There is a high number of parameter combinations to be evaluated. Therefore, this chapter discusses a solution to this problem, named SpaCE, as previously proposed by Oliveira et al. [2019]. SpaCE has the following enumerated steps, which are presented in Figure 5.2.

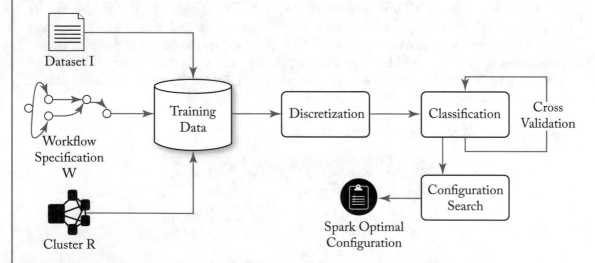

Figure 5.2: SpaCE: engine for performance optimization of Spark Workflows on commodity and shared-nothing clusters.

1. The training data is obtained from the actual execution of the workflow W on its input data I in the DISC environment with resources R varying the values of the parameters.

2. The training data are submitted to the Equal-Frequency discretization method in order to divide the execution time into three intervals with the same amount of elements: *Low*, *Mid*, and *High*.

3. Considering the discretized data, a decision tree is generated by Algorithm C4.5 from Ruggieri [2004], which consequently produces the predictive model.

4. The predictive model obtained is submitted to the 10-fold Cross-Validation method.

5. We extract the set of rules which defines the parameters configuration values that lead to efficient performance, i.e., rules classified as *Low* according to the decision tree;

In order to integrate the proposed approach with Spark and the DISC environment and the needs of the user, the model visualized in Figure 5.2 is proposed. Each instance or scenario is composed of the relevant characteristics of the input workflow: the environment characteristics; the input dataset; and the desired performance class. In the work of Oliveira et al. [2019], the performance is related to the execution time and, therefore, it can be classified in the following *Execution Groups*: *High, Mid,* and *Low*, as previously defined. Next, a search is performed on the provenance database for querying existing configuration rules that lead to the specified performance class or group. If there is more than one possible rule, the parameters and values related to each of them are presented to the user, who must choose one of the rules in order to execute the respective workflow. If there are no rules for a given execution scenario, the training, discretization, classification, and validation are applied for this new scenario and the rules are stored on the provenance base. Finally, a rule that leads to the desired performance group is then selected to execute the workflow in the Spark cluster using the values and parameters specified on it.

5.3   PROVENANCE MANAGEMENT IN APACHE SPARK

In this section, we discuss SAMbA[3] [Guedes et al., 2018], an Apache Spark extension that manages three provenance types (i.e., prospective, retrospective, and domain data) as discussed by de Oliveira et al. [2015]. The main idea behind SAMbA is to wrap both RDD structure and domain-specific content at runtime so that *(i)* RDD-enclosure-consumed and produced scientific data are stored by SAMbA in a structured way, and *(ii)* stored provenance data can be queried at runtime and/or after the execution of the workflow. Figure 5.3 details the Spark components

---

[3]Further details are available at: https://uffescience.github.io/SAMbA/.

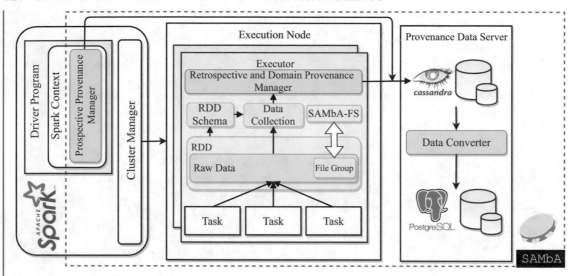

Figure 5.3: SAMbA architecture.

employed in the execution of a regular scientific workflow; the complementary part of Figure 5.3 presents the symbiotic architecture of SAMbA coupled to Spark.

SAMbA works as follows. The Spark Context connects to the Cluster Manager for setting the parallel execution of the workflow. Following, Spark creates executors, which are tasks that effectively execute both *(i)* workflow computations (activities) and *(ii)* the storage of processing data within the DISC environment nodes (shared-nothing environment). Then, each of the executors executes the application that was defined by the workflow specification. The Spark Context monitors the execution of each executor in all execution nodes.

Since the executor is responsible for executing the scientific applications, an essential part of SAMbA design is placed upon each Spark Executor. Figure 5.3 shows that SAMbA deploys a new component within the executor, the Retrospective And Domain Provenance Manager) and also defines a single component that collaborates with Apache Cluster Manager (Prospective Provenance Manager). Both components are essential for collecting and storing prospective and retrospective provenance alongside domain data related to the RDD content. All provenance data is stored in the Provenance Data Server. Provenance data are stepwise stored into the high throughput DBMS Cassandra. Additionally, SAMbA provides a Data Converter component to extract provenance data from Cassandra into relational-based DBMS PostgreSQL. Such conversion enables to perform high-level queries based on either Cassandra CQL or PostgreSQL SQL.

5.3.1 RETROSPECTIVE AND DOMAIN PROVENANCE MANAGER

Figure 5.3 shows how Retrospective and Domain Provenance Manager interacts with system abstraction Data Element, which, in turn, is related to the RDD Schema abstraction. The rationale that motivates the use of the RDD Schema abstraction is that the storage of all domain data elements consumed and produced by the workflow is impractical. Therefore, scientists executing the workflow are able to define their attribute of interest to be extracted and inserted in the provenance database by implementing the RDD Schema abstraction. The RDD Schema is an interface composed of two methods: `getFieldsNames()` and `splitData()`. Both methods have to be implemented for each particular workflow. The method `getFieldsNames()` returns the list of attribute names that are marked as of user interest. Likewise, method `splitData()` enables the extraction of attributes of interest within produced data files. The method returns a list of arrays, with every array associated with a single data value.

The Data Collections are essentially an enveloped version of data within the RDD partitions. Each Data Collection contains a set of values for a specific attribute in the RDD Schema (i.e., Data Element). Figure 5.4 presents the SAMbA pipeline for collecting of Data Collections and Data Elements. SAMbA envelops the Data Instances of RDD partitions into Data Collections composed of the instances' content and their dependencies, which identify the previous instances that point to the current one. Such an "envelope" strategy enables keeping track of data lineage, i.e., provenance data.

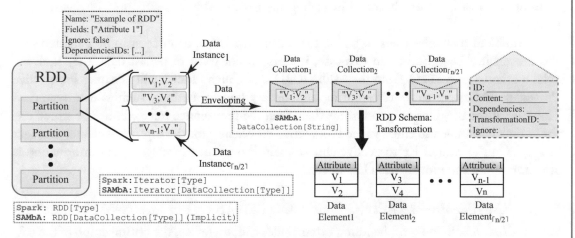

Figure 5.4: SAMbA management of domain data for native and black-box transformations.

Data Elements are tagged with the Collection unique identifier, which is employed for provenance data storage and querying. Therefore, the list of dependencies of a Data Collection is registered in terms of a sequence of unique identifiers, and the entire lineage of data transformations is represented as a sequential list. SAMbA provides default versions of RDD Schemas when users do not do the specification of this component. Default RDD Schemas contain the

RDD attributes that vary according to the RDD type. For instance, if a PairRDD is used, then the RDD Schema contains two attributes, namely key and value, which are employed for the creation of Data Collections composed of key-value pairs. Likewise, a standard RDD has only one attribute we call value. In this case, the values are manipulated as strings, which are collected from the .toString() methods of primitive Java data types. The last default RDD Schema of SAMbA is designed for the cases where RDDs include data produced by black-box and external programs. In this case, domain data are kept in main memory because SAMbA optimizes I/O operations by using its SAMbA-FS component (explained following). Therefore, SAMbA may seamlessly apply the splitData() over data produced by black-box programs as in the case of native Apache Spark transformations. The default RDD Schema in this scenario includes three attributes (file size, path, and name) that essentially describe the output files produced by the black-box application invoked in the task. Such information is collected from the File Group abstraction of the SAMbA-FS component. Accordingly, only attributes of interest are stored in the Provenance Data Server.

5.3.2   PROSPECTIVE PROVENANCE MANAGER

The Prospective Provenance Manager gathers data related to transformations that are applied to Data Collection during the workflow execution. Although it is not mandatory, users may label each transformation to add more semantics for provenance queries to be further performed. The naming of transformations is coded by calling the native method setName() of Spark RDD structure.

SAMbA also enables users to define their transformations of interest to be persisted into the Provenance Data Server. In this case, if users do not want to persist data, they shall invoke method ignoreIT() from the SAMbA RDD class. Such functionality enables Prospective Provenance Manager to avoid capturing unnecessary transformations, such as data type cast. However, if the user sets to ignore some data, then the provenance trace will not be stored entirely. Finally, SAMbA also employs the Prospective Provenance for the capture of cluster manager tasks. As in the case of Retrospective and Domain Provenance Manager, such information is also stored into the Provenance Data Server.

5.3.3   SAMBA-FS–MAPPING FILE CONTENTS INTO MAIN-MEMORY

SAMbA relies on SAMbA-FS for handling external files and, therefore, the optimization of the collection of domain data on Spark. The keeping of file contents in main-memory enables workflows not only to benefit from Spark processing but also enables SAMbA to keep track of file modifications and become aware of results produced during the execution of a transformation. SAMbA-FS central abstraction is the File Group, which includes the specification of data types from files and maps them to in-memory RDDs.

A File Group has three parameters: a set of byte arrays that represent the files' content, a HashMap for representing extra information within a File Group, e.g., file name, and the list of files themselves. An RDD can be created for a File Group by using the `FileGroupTemplate` interface that supports data loading from files into main memory. Two exclusive SAMbA operators are defined for a File Group RDD, namely `runCommand()` and `runScientificApplication()`. The former is used for the execution of single native OS commands, while the latter aims at executing a sequence of commands whose instructions may contain third-party program invocations. Accordingly, SAMbA mounts the associated `File Group` to a temporary directory by using OS calls and binds the directory content into in-memory data.

The last optimization aspect addressed by SAMbA is the storage of outputs from black-box transformations in an external repository of versioned files. Therefore, besides capturing domain data by RDD Schema-matching data kept in main memory by SAMbA-FS, users may choose to persist all transformation data into files after the execution of the workflow. In this case, outputs of black-box transformations also become available for raw data querying.

5.3.4 PROVENANCE DATA SERVER

SAMbA stores both provenance and domain data in an external DBMS during the execution of Spark-based workflows. SAMbA provides runtime data analytics by storing provenance data in a queriable database. The overall idea is providing users with the status of the experiment without waiting for lengthy trials to finish. In our approach, we set the Provenance Data Server to use the DBMS Cassandra for the storage of provenance data. The columnar schema of SAMbA for DBMS Cassandra is as follows.

```
DROP KEYSPACE IF EXISTS samba;
CREATE KEYSPACE samba WITH REPLICATION
= { 'class' : 'SimpleStrategy', 'replication_factor' : 3 };

CREATE TABLE samba."Execution" (
    id uuid,
    "ApplicationName" text,
    "EndTime" timestamp,
    "StartTime" timestamp,
    PRIMARY KEY (id)
);

CREATE TABLE samba."TransformationGroup" (
    "executionID" uuid,
    id uuid,
  "initTasksIDS" SET<uuid>,
  "intermediaryTasksIDS"  SET<uuid>,
    "finishTaskID" uuid,
```

```
    PRIMARY KEY (("executionID"), id)
);

CREATE TABLE samba."Task" (
    "executionID" uuid,
    id uuid,
    description text,
    "transformationType" text,
    "usingDefaultSchema" boolean,
    "schemaFields" LIST<text>,
  "hasDataInRepository" boolean,
    PRIMARY KEY (("executionID"), id)
);

CREATE TABLE samba."DataElement" (
    "executionID" uuid,
    id uuid,
    values LIST<frozen<LIST<text>>>,
    PRIMARY KEY (("executionID"), id)
);


CREATE TABLE samba."FileGroupReference" (
    "executionID" uuid,
    id uuid,// DataElement ID
    "folderPath" text,
    PRIMARY KEY (("executionID"), id)
);

CREATE TABLE samba."DependenciesOfTask" (
    "executionID" uuid,
    target uuid,
    source SET<uuid>,
    PRIMARY KEY (("executionID"), target)
);

CREATE TABLE samba."DependenciesOfDataElement" (
    "executionID" uuid,
```

```
    task uuid,
    source SET<uuid>,
    target uuid,
    PRIMARY KEY (("executionID"), task, target)
);


TRUNCATE samba."DataElement";
TRUNCATE samba."DependenciesOfDataElement";
TRUNCATE samba."Execution";
TRUNCATE samba."Task";
TRUNCATE samba."DependenciesOfTask";
TRUNCATE samba."TransformationGroup";
```

Although DBMS Cassandra was the suitable choice in comparison to other DBMSs regarding data ingestion, i.e., the loading of a large volume of provenance data produced by workflows in a very short time, its querying language Cassandra CQL is semantically limited in comparison to enriched SQL languages, e.g., PL-SQL, supported by relational DBMSs. We address this trade-off by providing a `Data Converter` component on SAMbA's architecture (Figure 5.3). Such a component generates an equivalent PostgreSQL relational schema regarding our Cassandra schema. Accordingly, users may also perform *post-mortem* data analyses with enriched SQL statements on relational DBMSs.

5.3.5   EVALUATION OF SAMBA

SAMbA was evaluated for the capture-and-query of provenance regarding a real-case scenario of a bioinformatics Spark-based version of a fragment of the workflow SciEvol. The fragment is mostly composed of a set of external programs for the construction and evaluation of phylogenetic trees used by drug discovery strategies. In our experiments, we inspect inputs from consolidated protozoan genomes databases and infer phylogenetic relationships of potential drug target enzymes found within such genomes. Overall execution parses 197 input data files and generates 4,531 raw data files. The workflow itself is composed of four activities, where each one is carried out by the following bioinformatics black-box programs: (a) `Mafft`, (b) `ReadSeq`, (c) `ModelGenerator`, and (d) `RAxML`, respectively. All these applications access data through files.

Since SciEvol depends on black-box applications for executing fundamental transformations, SAMbARDD Schema contains the attributes of interest from external files to be extracted and stored. Figure 5.5 shows an example of an RDD Schema for the management of files related to ReadSeq program. In this example, three domain data attributes—FILE_NAME, NUM_ALIGNS, and LENGTH—are selected to be represented as SAMbAData Elements values. Accordingly, Retrospective and Domain Provenance Manager becomes capable of reading the RDD contents and persist such data of interest into the Provenance Data Server.

```
//Schema Implementation for ReadSeq
class ReadSeqSchema extends SingleLineSchema[FileGroup] {

  override def getFieldsNames(): Array[String]
        = Array("FILE_NAME", "NUM_ALIGNS", "LENGTH")
}
```

Figure 5.5: A fragment of a SAMbA RDD Schema.

Next, the user sets the SAMbA-FS File Group abstractions for keeping raw files content into main memory. Figure 5.6 presents an example of a File Group on SAMbA, in which the files listed in inputFastaList.txt are loaded into an Apache Spark RDD. After the setting of RDD Schemas and File Groups, SAMbA runs the fragment of the SciEvol workflow by invoking third-party programs through the runScientificApplication() routine, which enables external applications to run in a managed flow.

```
// SciEvol experiment using Spark
val fileGroup  = new SparkContext(
    new SparkConf().setMaster("local[4]").setAppName("SciEvol")
    .setScriptDir("/workflows/scievol/scripts")
).fileGroup(parserInputFile("inputFastaList.txt"): _*)//File Group
```

Figure 5.6: A fragment of a SAMbA-FS File Group.

In our first experiment, we measured the time spent by SAMbA for capturing provenance data types in SciEvol. All workflow executions were performed on LoboC[4] cluster by consuming the same input dataset. Experiments used 48 processing cores of LoboC cluster, where 44 cores were employed for the workflow execution and the remaining 4 cores were put in charge of provenance persistence into DBMS Cassandra.

The performance of SAMbA was compared to two other approaches: *(i)* SciCumulus SWfMS [de Oliveira et al., 2010] with parallel functionalities, which does not provide in-memory processing; and *(ii)* Native Apache Spark, which was employed without any SAMbA extensions.

Figure 5.7 presents the average elapsed time (standard deviation was less than .5s in all cases) for the execution of SciEvol on SciCumulus, native Apache Spark, and SAMbA with four distinct settings: *(i)* both provenance and versioning (Git) support disabled; *(ii)* provenance

---

[4]Cluster specification: https://www.nacad.ufrj.br/en/recursos/sgiicex.

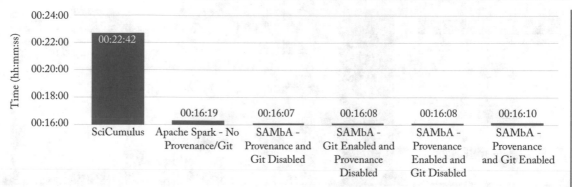

Figure 5.7: Average elapsed time of a fragment of SciEvol workflow executing on SciCumulus, native Apache Spark and SAMbA.

disabled and versioning (Git) enabled; *(iii)* provenance enable versioning (Git) disabled; and *(iv)* both provenance and versioning (Git) enabled.

Results show SAMbA outperformed both SciCumulus and native Apache Spark for all configurations. In particular, SciCumulus was nearly 40% slower than full-set SAMbA (since it writes and reads all data to and from the disk), whereas Apache Spark without provenance support was about 1% slower than SAMbA. Such behavior is due to the SAMbA-FS optimization that avoids I/O operations on disk as much as possible. Accordingly, SAMbA with SAMbA-FS was able to execute the workflow, capture and store provenance data into DBMS Cassandra, and external files and still outperform native Spark execution. Therefore, SAMbA was able to efficiently manage the files' contents regarding black-box transformations at expense of a little overhead, as well as persist extracted and structured information (the Data Elements) into external DBMSs.

In the second experiment, the analytical capabilities were evaluated. SAMbA provides three dynamic reports for evaluation of workflows at runtime. Reports are available through a web interface, which shows formated provenance data from DBMS Cassandra in a structured fashion and enables user interaction. SAMbA online data analytics cover the following aspects:

1. retrospective provenance: Presents the start and end time (whenever available) of a given workflow execution;

2. prospective provenance: Presents the transformation graph of a given workflow execution; and

3. domain data: Presents information about domain data associated with every activity of the workflow.

Figure 5.8a presents an excerpt of the web interface that contains the transformation graph for a user-selected execution of SciEvol—Prospective provenance. This graph includes the

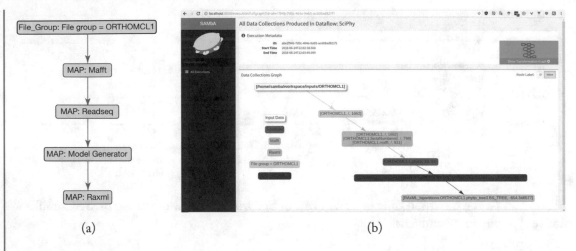

Figure 5.8: Dataflow transformations graph for an input set on `SciEvol`. (a) Transformation flow of a fragment of `SciEvol` execution. (b) Web interface for dataflow visualization of an input set on `SciEvol`.

name of the transformation (activity) and its type, i.e., Map, Reduce, and so on. Users may expand each transformation based on the Prospective provenance to access the repository of domain data (raw files) produced by a `SciEvol` specific execution. Figure 5.8b shows the Retrospective provenance (top-right) and the transformation flow in detail for a given input set (bottom-right), where users can expand and explore domain data associated with each node of the graph—Domain Data. Users may also navigate through the workflow regarding specific input sets for the investigation of every transformation as well as visualize their results.

By clicking on a transformation node in the graph, a new page is dynamically loaded with Prospective provenance. In the interface, users may verify the Data Collection involved in the transformation. Consumed and produced Data Collections are initially collapsed on the interface, as illustrated in the blue and white rectangles of Figure 5.9a. The report also shows the Data Elements in a table format for each user-selected Data Collection (Figure 5.9b). Additionally, if the transformation is carried out by a black-box program, the output values are stored on external files that can be accessed through a directory hierarchy—Figure 5.9c.

5.4   SCHEDULING SPARK WORKFLOWS IN DISC ENVIRONMENTS

Spark-based Workflow scheduling in DISC environments is the process of allocating particular tasks to commodity machines to be executed concurrently. The workflow Activation (i.e., task in the Spark context) scheduling is a well-known NP-complete problem even in simple scenarios, as discussed and proved by Liu and Layland [1973]. Although there are many approaches for

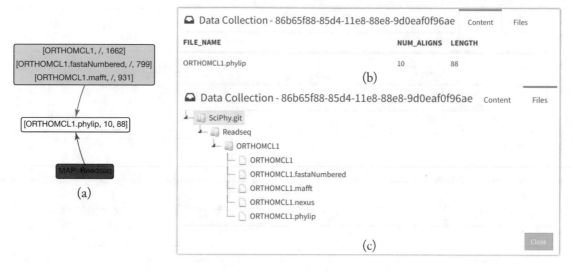

Figure 5.9: Data collections and transformations. (a) Partial transformation dataflow regarding the `ReadSeq` application. (b) `RDD Schema`-matching of consumed data elements. (c) Output files of the transformation executed by the black-box program.

scheduling Spark tasks in DISC environments [Chen and Wang, 2015, Cheng et al., 2017, Li et al., 2018, Maroulis et al., 2017, Nayanar and Upadhyay, 2017, Tang et al., 2016], in this section, we focus on the TARDIS (Task Analyzer Regarding Data In Spark) approach [Gaspar et al., 2017], which aims at providing the optimal workflow execution over a shared-nothing commodity cluster.

5.4.1 TARDIS ARCHITECTURE

TARDIS is composed of two main layers: the master layer and worker layer. The master layer is in charge of allocating files in the machines of the DISC environment and collecting and storing provenance data in the provenance database. The components in the master layer connect to an existing Spark cluster and submit jobs (tasks) to it. The Spark workers behave as TARDIS slave nodes. The main components of the master layer and the worker layer are depicted in Figure 5.10 and discussed below.

1. Job parsing: TARDIS receives the specification of the workflow in TARDIS language (explained following). TARDIS parses the specification file;

2. Job reformulation: The workflow previously specified is translated to a set of Spark activities. Some extra activities can be added in order to perform the correct execution of the workflow (i.e., to transfer data among nodes).

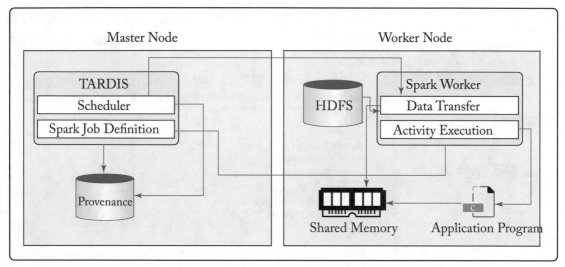

Figure 5.10: **TARDIS** architecture.

3. Scheduling: It is responsible for deciding which nodes the input files of activities should be consumed.

4. Data placement: Whenever the required files for an activity execution are not available in local shared memory, worker nodes download them from other nodes or, if locally available, copy them from local disk.

5. Activity execution: Finally, activities are executed by running external software over in-memory files.

TARDIS scheduler firstly defines the file allocation plan and distributes the input files in their respective machines in the DISC environment once the execution of activities begins. Each job to be executed has to download the necessary files to its execution.

This transfer is performed using an HTTP server. All input files I are loaded into RDDs and then other machines can download the required files. These downloaded files are moved to a shared memory file system, and then the Activity Execution (AE) module starts the actual execution of the scientific application that is part of the workflow. The AE module identifies the file allocated to its machine and sends it as input to its associated black-box program. At the end of execution, the master layer collects the outcomes and stores them in a local folder. The provenance database is currently an SQLite database and only records retrospective provenance data.

In order to specify the workflow for the TARDIS, the user has to generate a workflow definition file in TARDIS language. TARDIS language is similar to a regular Python script that calls previously defined methods. Activities in TARDIS can be defined as maps, partial reduces, and reduces.

A map activity is an activity that consumes a single file as input (loaded to RDD) and produces a single file as outcome. If a user wants to define a map activity that reverses the content of a file, one should use the following call in TARDIS specification file:

```
reverseRDD = tardis.map activity("reverse",
"tac @!input > @!input.rev", filesRDD, "*.txt").
```

Figure 5.11: Defining a map activity in TARDIS.

Partial and final reduce activities consume multiple files as input and produce a single file as outcome. In the workflow algebra defined by Ogasawara et al. [2013], it is equivalent to a Reduce operation. For example, if the user needs to concatenate several files into a single file, the following command should be executed:

```
concatenatedRDD = tardis.partial reduce activity("cat", "cat @!input >
all@!output", filesRDD, ("*.txt", "*.jpg")).
```

Figure 5.12: Defining a reduce activity in TARDIS.

5.4.2 TARDIS DATA PLACEMENT AND SCHEDULING

Data Placement

As previously discussed, TARDIS allocates the input files in the several machines that are part of the DISC environment so black-box applications can read these files locally, thus avoiding costly data transfers. Gaspar et al. [2017] proposes four different data placement algorithms for TARDIS. The general idea is to map each input file $i \in I$ to a machine in the DISC environment $r \in R$.

Several metadata such as file size, its transfer cost, and content have to be taken into account when allocating these files in the DISC environment. The transfer cost usually varies if the nodes are not in the same network. The Scheduler also considers the ideal workload of each machine to perform load balancing. This ideal workload is given by the ratio of the computing capability of the respective machine in relation to the general computing capability of the commodity cluster. Let c_i be the computing capability of machine r_j. $\sum r_j$ is the sum of the capabilities of the entire commodity cluster. When the user executes the workflow W, the partition $p_i \in I$ is allocated to machine r_j; the ideal size of p_i is given by Equation (5.2). [Gaspar et al., 2017] propose four different file allocation algorithms: only local, greedy allocation, locals first, and lazy allocation. They are presented below.

$$ideal\_size(p_i) = \frac{c_i \times size(I)}{\sum c_j}.$$ (5.2)

Only Local algorithm aims at minimizing the data transfer during the execution of workflows. The main idea is to maximize data locality, i.e., to consume "near stored" data. It allocates each file to the same machine where the tasks that consume the file will be executed and where the file was previously produced. Algorithm 5.9 describes the only local allocation. The `rank` is a unique number that identifies the machine in the DISC environment. The function `machine`(i_i) returns the `rank` of the machine that produced i_i. `alloc`(i_i, r_j) allocates file i_i in the machine r_j.

Algorithm 5.9 Only Local Algorithm

1: **for** $i_i \in I$ **do**
2:    **for** $r_j \in R$ **do**
3:       **if** $machine(i_i) = r_j.rank$ **then**
4:          $alloc(i_i, r_j)$
5:       **end if**
6:    **end for**
7: **end for**

Greedy Allocation algorithm allocates the biggest files to the nodes with the highest capability. The algorithm proceeds as follows. After sorting the machines and the files in descending order, it allocates the biggest files to the machine with the highest capability that can still fit this file. If the file cannot fit any machine, the host with the biggest capability, which has fewer tasks than it should, will receive the task even if this makes it have more tasks than what is required. Algorithm 5.10 describes the Greedy Allocation algorithm. The variable *isAllocated*(i_i) defines if file i_i is already allocated to a machine. Function *size*(i_i) returns the file size, and *availableSize*(r_j) returns the available size in machine r_j. *idealSize*(r_j) returns the ideal size of the partition of machine r_j and *currentSize*(r_j) its current size.

Locals First algorithm aims at reducing both the skew and the data transfer among the machines in the commodity cluster. The algorithm allocates data to the machine where data were produced while this machine has enough disk space. In the scenario where the machine does not have available disk space, the remaining data are allocated to the closest machine with disk space available. This is performed by ordering the machines concerning the transfer cost to where the data file is currently stored. Algorithm 5.11 describes the Locals First algorithm.

Lazy Allocation algorithm allocates all data to the machine where data were produced. This is the same behavior as Algorithm 5.9. However, this algorithm redistributes the overflow

---

Algorithm 5.10 Greedy Allocation Algorithm

1: sort R by capability into descending order
2: sort I by size into descending order
3: **for** $i_i \in I$ **do**
4:     $isAllocated(i_i) \leftarrow False$
5:     **for** $r_j \in R$ **do**
6:         **if** $size(i_i) \leq availableSize(r_j)$ **then**
7:             $alloc(i_i, r_j)$
8:             $isAllocated(i_i) \leftarrow True$
9:             *Break*
10:         **end if**
11:     **end for**
12:     **if** $\neg isAllocated(i_i)$ **then**
13:         **for** $r_j \in R$ **do**
14:             **if** $idealSize(r_j) > currentSize(r_j)$ **then**
15:                 $alloc(i_i, r_j)$
16:                 *Break*
17:             **end if**
18:         **end for**
19:     **end if**
20: **end for**

---

data to other machines. Lazy Allocation algorithm orders the files in an overflow node by their size and continuously removes files until the disk usage is close to its ideal size. Then each removed file is allocated to the closest machine with available disk space. Algorithm 5.12 describes Lazy Allocation.

Task Scheduling

After allocating the several $i_i \in I$ in each machine $r_j \in R$, TARDIS can start scheduling the tasks. The scheduling process in TARDIS is performed in four steps. The chosen data placement algorithm produces a file allocation table that is consumed as input during scheduling. TARDIS create an RDD with $n \times f$ integer values, where n represents the number of machines in the DISC environment and f the number of input files to be processed. It means that f slots are reserved for each of the n machines. Each one of the f slots is a placeholder for possible files at each machine. Each placeholder has an individual ID. When the `parallelize` method is invoked with the parameter n, Spark creates n partitions of the allocation table and sends them to the cluster.

Algorithm 5.11 Locals First Algorithm

1: **for** $i_i \in I$ **do**
2:   **for** $r_j \in R$ **do**
3:    **if** $(machine(i_i) = r_j.rank) \wedge (size(i_i) \leq availableSize(r_j))$ **then**
4:     $alloc(i_i, r_j)$
5:     $R \leftarrow \{R - r_j\}$
6:    **end if**
7:   **end for**
8: **end for**
9: **for** $i_i \in I$ **do**
10:   order nodes by transfer costs from $machine(i_i)$ into ascending order
11:   **for** $r_j \in R$ **do**
12:    **if** $availableSize(r_j) \geq 0$ **then**
13:     $alloc(i_i, r_j)$
14:     *Break*
15:    **end if**
16:   **end for**
17: **end for**

TARDIS does not guarantee that each RDD receives a partition with f elements. TARDIS is responsible for post-check if a number of elements allocated to each machine are greater than or equal to the number of files that should be allocated to that specific machine. If this condition is not guaranteed, TARDIS restarts the scheduling and now creates an RDD with $m \times n \times f$ integers. The value of m is increased until the check mentioned above is guaranteed. This way, the master node now has two tables, a file allocation table, generated by the chosen data placement algorithm and an ID allocation, generated by the previous step. By joining both tables, TARDIS generates (ID, i_i) pairs, associating different IDs of one machine to the files it stores. This new table is then broadcast to all machines in the DISC environment.

After broadcasting the table to all machines, TARDIS executes a map over this RDD with a TARDIS method that is executed over each element of this array. This method copies to memory the files associated with the ID. This map returns a pointer to the file allocated in memory. Finally, a Spark filter transformation with a TARDIS routine is executed over the RDD to remove the elements flagged with zero. Thus, in this step TARDIS has the RDD partitioned according to the TARDIS scheduling algorithm.

Evaluation

TARDIS data placement and scheduling algorithms were evaluated by Gaspar et al. [2017] using Montage workflow (detailed in Chapter 1). The Montage was executed in a cluster running

Algorithm 5.12 Lazy Allocation Algorithm

1: **for** $i_i \in I$ **do**
2:    **for** $r_j \in R$ **do**
3:       **if** $machine(i_i) = r_j.rank$ **then**
4:          $alloc(i_i, r_j)$
5:       **end if**
6:    **end for**
7: **end for**
8: **for** $r_j \in R$ **do**
9:    **if** $availableSize(r_j) \leq 0$ **then**
10:       sort $files(r_j)$ by size in ascending order
11:       **while** $overflow(r_j)$ **do**
12:          $i_l \leftarrow files(r_j)[0]$
13:          $dealloc(i_l, r_j)$
14:          $R_{order} \leftarrow$ sort $\{R - r_j\}$ by transfer cost from r_j
15:          **for** $r_{order} \in R_{order}$ **do**
16:             **if** $availableSize(r_{order}) \geq 0$ **then**
17:                $alloc(i_l, r_{order})$
18:                *Break*
19:             **end if**
20:          **end for**
21:       **end while**
22:    **end if**
23: **end for**

Linux (CentOS distribution). Each machine in this cluster has two Intel(R) Xeon(R) CPU E5-2630 v3 running at 2.40 GHz with 8 physical cores each with 94 GB. TARDIS performed better than the SWfMS Swift/K for the execution of Montage workflow when the number of machines was greater than one. With six nodes, the best algorithm is TARDIS with Locals First allocation. Swift/K does not assure data locality. Thus, it presents performance losses. However, it performs better than TARDIS when running in only one machine.

5.5 CONCLUSION

In this chapter, we discussed in detail how to execute a workflow in a DISC environment using SpaCE, SAMbA, and TARDIS. SpaCE aims at fine tuning the Spark parameters, which is a hard task to accomplish. SAMbA aims at capturing and storing provenance data that are fundamental for reproducibility. Finally, TARDIS can be coupled to Spark to provide optimal scheduling of tasks in spark workflows. Although these three approaches were proposed to be isolated from each other, they are complementary and can be used together to manage the execution of workflows in DISC environments.

CHAPTER 6

Conclusion

Many scientific experiments (biology, astronomy, etc.) take advantage of workflows to model data operations such as loading input data, data processing, data analysis, and aggregating output data. This book presents a broad and deep view of data-intensive workflow management solutions deployed in different distributed environments. Each environment introduces specific data management challenges.

We first presented all background necessary to understand existing distributed and parallel execution approaches of data-intensive scientific workflows. Next, we introduced the key concepts, challenges, and solutions to execute data-intensive workflows in a single-site cloud. Most solutions require dynamic scheduling to handle data and activation scheduling, and virtual machines allocation. We presented in details how to provision virtual machines in this environment, and how to execute a workflow while reducing execution time and financial cost.

Next, we focused on multi-site cloud architectures, addressing the fundamental concepts and solutions to deploy data-intensive scientific workflows in a distributed multi-site cloud architecture. The goal was to discuss how to efficiently parallelize and schedule the tasks and activities of a workflow in a multi-site cloud, where each site has its virtual cluster, data, and programs. This requires complex scheduling solutions, involving fine- and coarse-grain scheduling, taking into account data transfer costs among the sites.

Finally, we also considered Data-Intensive Scalable Computing (DISC) environments (e.g., Apache Spark and Hadoop) as an alternative to executing scientific workflows. The main advantage of DISC is that it supports and grants efficient in-memory data management, enabling you to easily speed up big data processing, which is quite common in several application scenarios.

DISC challenges are driven by the goals of the scientific experiment: volume of data processed combined with environment. Many possibilities exist for future work. For instance, taking into account DISC environments, we can envision the use of machine learning techniques to tune the scheduling algorithms or as a support for data placement. Going beyond, the trend is to study intermediate results to steer computation in a human-in-the-loop manner [Spampinato et al., 2015]. Using machine learning may require new models for scientific workflow execution (scheduling, provenance, etc.) and introduces new challenges.

Bibliography

Microsoft Azure Cloud. http://www.windowsazure.com/en-us/ 96

Computing capacity for a CPU. http://en.community.dell.com/techcenter/high-perf ormance-computing/w/wiki/2329 46

Apache Hadoop. http://hadoop.apache.org/ 68, 103

OMA genome database. http://omabrowser.org/All/eukaryotes.cdna.fa.gz 58, 96

Sequence identifier. http://omabrowser.org/All/oma-groups.txt.gz 58, 96

Alice Collaboration. http://aliceinfo.cern.ch/general/index.html 65

Azure Speed Test. http://www.azurespeed.com/ 72

Giraffa. https://code.google.com/a/apache-extras.org/p/giraffa/ 76

HDFS. http://hadoop.apache.org/docs/r1.2.1/hdfs_design.html 33

Lustre—OpenSFS. http://lustre.org/ 76

Amazon cloud. http://aws.amazon.com/, 2015. 41

Somayeh Abdi, Latif Pourkarimi, Mahmood Ahmadi, and Farzad Zargari. Cost minimization for deadline-constrained bag-of-tasks applications in federated hybrid clouds. *Future Generation Computer Systems*, 71, pages 113–128, 2017. DOI: 10.1016/j.future.2017.01.036 68

Mohamed Abouelhoda, Shadi Issa, and Moustafa Ghanem. Tavaxy: Integrating taverna and galaxy workflows with cloud computing support. *BMC Bioinformatics*, 13(1), p. 77, 2012. DOI: 10.1186/1471-2105-13-77 1, 17

Enis Afgan, Dannon Baker, Nathan Coraor, Brad Chapman, Anton Nekrutenko, and James Taylor. Galaxy cloudman: Delivering cloud compute clusters. *BMC Bioinformatics*, 11(12), p. S4, 2010. DOI: 10.1186/1471-2105-11-s12-s4 34

Enis Afgan, Dannon Baker, Bérénice Batut, Marius van den Beek, Dave Bouvier, Martin Ech, John Chilton, Dave Clements, Nate Coraor, Björn A Grüning, Aysam Guerler, Jennifer Hillman-Jackson, Saskia Hiltemann, Vahid Jalili, Helena Rasche, Nicola Soranzo, Jeremy

Goecks, James Taylor, Anton Nekrutenko, and Daniel Blankenberg. The galaxy platform for accessible, reproducible and collaborative biomedical analyses: 2018 update. *Nucleic Acids Research*, 46(W1), 2018. DOI: 10.1093/nar/gkw343 1, 17

Issam Al-Azzoni and Douglas G. Down. Dynamic scheduling for heterogeneous desktop grids. In *IEEE/ACM International Conference on Grid Computing*, pages 136–143, 2008. DOI: 10.1109/grid.2008.4662792 4

Ayoub Alsarhan. An optimal virtual machines provision in cloud market. In *Proc. of the 9th International Conference on Machine Learning and Computing, (ICMLC)*, pages 394–397, New York, ACM, 2017. DOI: 10.1145/3055635.3056567 40

Ilkay Altintas, Chad Berkley, Efrat Jaeger, Matthew Jones, Bertram Ludaescher, and Steve Mock. Kepler: Towards a grid-enabled system for scientific workflows. *The Workflow in Grid Systems Workshop in GGF10-The 10th Global Grid Forum*, 2004. xv, 1, 15, 17, 25

Ilkay Altintas, Oscar Barney, and Efrat Jaeger-Frank. Provenance collection support in the kepler scientific workflow system. In *International Conference on Provenance and Annotation of Data*, pages 118–132, 2006. DOI: 10.1007/11890850_14 18

Cosimo Anglano and Massimo Canonico. Scheduling algorithms for multiple bag-of-task applications on desktop grids: A knowledge-free approach. In *IEEE International Symposium on Parallel and Distributed Processing (IPDPS)*, pages 1–8, 2008. DOI: 10.1109/ipdps.2008.4536445 25

Hamid Arabnejad, Jorge G. Barbosa, and Radu Prodan. Low-time complexity budget-deadline constrained workflow scheduling on heterogeneous resources. *Future Generation Computer Systems*, 55, pages 29–40, 2016. DOI: 10.1016/j.future.2015.07.021 41, 42, 44, 83

Konstantine Arkoudas, Karen Zee, Viktor Kuncak, and Martin Rinard. Verifying a file system implementation. In *6th International Conference on Formal Engineering Methods (ICFEM)*, vol. 3308, pages 373–390, 2004. DOI: 10.1007/978-3-540-30482-1_32 33

Michael Armbrust, Tathagata Das, Aaron Davidson, Ali Ghodsi, Andrew Or, Josh Rosen, Ion Stoica, Patrick Wendell, Reynold Xin, and Matei Zaharia. Scaling spark in the real world: Performance and usability. *Proc. of the VLDB Endowment*, 8(12), pages 1840–1843, 2015. DOI: 10.14778/2824032.2824080 37, 106

M. Asch, Terry Moore, Rosa M. Badia, Micah Beck, Peter H. Beckman, T. Bidot, François Bodin, Franck Cappello, Alok N. Choudhary, Bronis R. de Supinski, Ewa Deelman, Jack J. Dongarra, Anshu Dubey, Geoffrey C. Fox, H. Fu, Sergi Girona, William Gropp, Michael A. Heroux, Yutaka Ishikawa, Katarzyna Keahey, David E. Keyes, Bill Kramer, J.-F. Lavignon, Y. Lu, Satoshi Matsuoka, Bernd Mohr, Daniel A. Reed, S. Requena, Joel H. Saltz, Thomas C.

Schulthess, Rick L. Stevens, D. Martin Swany, Alexander S. Szalay, William M. Tang, G. Varoquaux, J.-P. Vilotte, Robert W. Wisniewski, Z. Xu, and I Zacharov. Big data and extreme-scale computing. *International Journal of High Performance Computing Applications IJHPCA*, 32(4), pages 435–479, 2018. DOI: 10.1177/1094342018778123 35

Adam Barker and Jano van Hemert. Scientific workflow: A survey and research directions. In *7th International Conference on Parallel Processing and Applied Mathematics*, pages 746–753, 2008. DOI: 10.1007/978-3-540-68111-3_78 14

Seyed-Mehdi-Reza Beheshti, Boualem Benatallah, Sherif Sakr, Daniela Grigori, Hamid Reza Motahari-Nezhad, Moshe Chai Barukh, Ahmed Gater, and Seung Hwan Ryu. *Process Analytics—Concepts and Techniques for Querying and Analyzing Process Data*. Springer, 2016. 65

Sergey Blagodurov, Alexandra Fedorova, Evgeny Vinnik, Tyler Dwyer, and Fabien Hermenier. Multi-objective job placement in clusters. In *Proc. of the International Conference for High Performance Computing, Networking, Storage and Analysis, SC*, pages 66:1–66:12, 2015. DOI: 10.1145/2807591.2807636 83

James Blythe, Sonal Jain, Ewa Deelman, Yolanda Gil, Karan Vahi, Anirban Mandal, and Ken Kennedy. Task scheduling strategies for workflow-based applications in grids. In *5th IEEE International Symposium on Cluster Computing and the Grid (CCGrid)*, pages 759–767, 2005. DOI: 10.1109/ccgrid.2005.1558639 25

Cristina Boeres, Idalmis Milián Sardiña, and Lúcia Maria de A. Drummond. An efficient weighted bi-objective scheduling algorithm for heterogeneous systems. *Parallel Computing*, 37(8), pages 349–364, 2011. DOI: 10.1016/j.parco.2010.10.003 41, 42, 44

Carlyna Bondiombouy and Patrick Valduriez. Query processing in multistore systems: An overview. *International Journal of Cloud Computing IJCC*, 5(4), pages 309–346, 2016. DOI: 10.1504/ijcc.2016.10001884 35

Luc Bouganim, Françoise Fabret, C. Mohan, and Patrick Valduriez. Dynamic query scheduling in data integration systems. In *International Conference on Data Engineering (ICDE)*, pages 425–434, 2000. DOI: 10.1109/icde.2000.839442 19

Sarah Cohen Boulakia, Jiuqiang Chen, Paolo Missier, Carole A. Goble, Alan R. Williams, and Christine Froidevaux. Distilling structure in taverna scientific workflows: A refactoring approach. *BMC Bioinformatics*, 15(S-1), p. S12, 2014. DOI: 10.1186/1471-2105-15-s1-s12 18

Scott A. Brandt, Ethan L. Miller, Darrell D. E. Long, and Lan Xue. Efficient metadata management in large distributed storage systems. In *IEEE NASA Goddard Conference on Mass*

Storage Systems and Technologies, pages 290–298, 2003. DOI: 10.1109/mass.2003.1194865 76

Randal E. Bryant. Data-intensive scalable computing for scientific applications. *Computing in Science Engineering*, 13(6), pages 25–33, 2011. DOI: 10.1109/mcse.2011.73 xv, 2, 35

Lucian Busoniu, Bart De Schutter, and Robert Babuska. Approximate dynamic programming and reinforcement learning. In *Interactive Collaborative Information Systems*, pages 3–44, 2010. DOI: 10.1007/978-3-642-11688-9_1 43

Marc Bux and Ulf Leser. Parallelization in scientific workflow management systems. *The Computing Research Repository (CoRR)*, 2013. 11, 21, 24, 25

Steven P. Callahan, Juliana Freire, Emanuele Santos, Carlos Eduardo Scheidegger, Cláudio T. Silva, and Huy T. Vo. Vistrails: Visualization meets data management. In *ACM SIGMOD International Conference on Management of Data*, pages 745–747, 2006. DOI: 10.1145/1142473.1142574 xv, 1, 17

Bryan Carpenter, Vladimir Getov, Glenn Judd, Anthony Skjellum, and Geoffrey C. Fox. MPJ: MPI-like message passing for Java. *Concurrency and Computation: Practice and Experience*, 12(11), pages 1019–1038, 2000. DOI: 10.1002/1096-9128(200009)12:11<1019::aid-cpe518>3.0.co;2-g 29

Abhishek Chandra. Applications-aware virtual machine provisioning. In *Proc. of the 7th International Workshop on Virtualization Technologies in Distributed Computing, (VTDC)*, pages 1–2, New York, ACM, 2013. DOI: 10.1145/2465829.2465837 40

Huankai Chen and Frank Z. Wang. Spark on entropy: A reliable amp; efficient scheduler for low-latency parallel jobs in heterogeneous cloud. In *IEEE Local Computer Networks Conference Workshops (LCN Workshops)*, pages 708–713, 2015. DOI: 10.1109/lcnw.2015.7365918 109, 123

Weiwei Chen and Ewa Deelman. Integration of workflow partitioning and resource provisioning. In *IEEE/ACM International Symposium on Cluster Computing and the Grid (CCGRID)*, pages 764–768, 2012a. DOI: 10.1109/ccgrid.2012.57 88

Weiwei Chen and Ewa Deelman. Partitioning and scheduling workflows across multiple sites with storage constraints. In *9th International Conference on Parallel Processing and Applied Mathematics—Volume Part II*, vol. 7204, pages 11–20, 2012b. DOI: 10.1007/978-3-642-31500-8_2 19, 72

Weiwei Chen, Rafael Ferreira da Silva, Ewa Deelman, and Rizos Sakellariou. Balanced task clustering in scientific workflows. In *IEEE International Conference on e-Science*, pages 188–195, 2013. DOI: 10.1109/escience.2013.40 24, 72

Dazhao Cheng, Xiaobo Zhou, Palden Lama, Jun Wu, and Changjun Jiang. Cross-platform resource scheduling for spark and mapreduce on yarn. *IEEE Transactions on Computers*, 66(8), pages 1341–1353, 2017. DOI: 10.1109/tc.2017.2669964 109, 123

Yeongho Choi and Yujin Lim. A cost-efficient mechanism for dynamic VM provisioning in cloud computing. In *Proc. of the Conference on Research in Adaptive and Convergent Systems, (RACS)*, pages 344–349, New York, ACM, 2014. DOI: 10.1145/2663761.2664217 40

Mosharaf Chowdhury, Matei Zaharia, Justin Ma, Michael I. Jordan, and Ion Stoica. Managing data transfers in computer clusters with orchestra. *ACM SIGCOMM Conference on Applications, Technologies, Architectures, and Protocols for Computer Communications*, 41(4), pages 98–109, 2011. DOI: 10.1145/2043164.2018448 32

Laura Clarke, Susan Fairley, Xiangqun Zheng Bradley, Ian Streeter, Emily Perry, Ernesto Lowy, Anne-Marie Tassé, and Paul Flicek. The international genome sample resource (IGSR): A worldwide collection of genome variation incorporating the 1000 genomes project data. *Nucleic Acids Research*, 45(Database-Issue), pages D854–D859, 2017. DOI: 10.1093/nar/gkw829 65

Workflow Management Coalition. Workflow management coalition terminology and glossary, 1999. 14, 17

Peter F. Corbett and Dror G. Feitelson. The vesta parallel file system. *ACM Transactions on Computer Systems (TOCS)*, 14(3), pages 225–264, 1996. DOI: 10.1145/233557.233558 76

Flavio Costa, Daniel de Oliveira, Kary A. C. S. Ocaña, Eduardo S. Ogasawara, Jonas Dias, and Marta Mattoso. Handling failures in parallel scientific workflows using clouds. In *Supercomputing (SC) Companion: High Performance Computing, Networking Storage and Analysis*, pages 129–139, 2012. DOI: 10.1109/sc.companion.2012.28 19

Flavio Costa, Vítor Silva Sousa, Daniel de Oliveira, Kary A. C. S. Ocaña, Eduardo S. Ogasawara, Jonas Dias, and Marta Mattoso. Capturing and querying workflow runtime provenance with prov: A practical approach. In *EDBT/ICDT Workshops*, pages 282–289, 2013. DOI: 10.1145/2457317.2457365 11, 17, 18, 29

Daniel Crawl, Jianwu Wang, and Ilkay Altintas. Provenance for MapReduce-based data-intensive workflows. In *6th Workshop on Workflows in Support of Large-scale Science*, pages 21–30, 2011. DOI: 10.1145/2110497.2110501 18

Terence Critchlow and George Chin Jr. Supercomputing and scientific workflows gaps and requirements. In *World Congress on Services*, pages 208–211, 2011. DOI: 10.1109/services.2011.32 32, 35

Lisandro D. Dalcin, Rodrigo R. Paz, Pablo A. Kler, and Alejandro Cosimo. Parallel distributed computing using Python. *Advances in Water Resources*, 34(9), pages 1124–1139, 2011. DOI: 10.1016/j.advwatres.2011.04.013 103

João Carlos de A. R. Gonçalves, Daniel de Oliveira, Kary A. C. S. Ocaña, Eduardo S. Ogasawara, and Marta Mattoso. Using domain-specific data to enhance scientific workflow steering queries. In *Provenance and Annotation of Data and Processes*, vol. 7525, pages 152–167, 2012. DOI: 10.1007/978-3-642-34222-6_12 11, 18

Rafaelli de C. Coutinho, Lúcia Maria de A. Drummond, Yuri Frota, Daniel de Oliveira, and Kary A. C. S. Ocaña. Evaluating grasp-based cloud dimensioning for comparative genomics: A practical approach. In *IEEE International Conference on Cluster Computing (CLUSTER)*, pages 371–379, 2014. DOI: 10.1109/cluster.2014.6968789 2, 39, 40, 46, 48, 52, 59

Daniel de Oliveira, Eduardo S. Ogasawara, Fernanda Araujo Baião, and Marta Mattoso. Scicumulus: A lightweight cloud middleware to explore many task computing paradigm in scientific workflows. In *3rd International Conference on Cloud Computing (CLOUD)*, pages 378–385, 2010. DOI: 10.1109/cloud.2010.64 xv, 1, 11, 17, 25, 30, 31, 34, 76, 85, 120

Daniel de Oliveira, Kary A. C. S. Ocaña, Fernanda Araujo Baião, and Marta Mattoso. A provenance-based adaptive scheduling heuristic for parallel scientific workflows in clouds. *Journal of Grid Computing*, 10(3), pages 521–552, 2012a. DOI: 10.1007/s10723-012-9227-2 xv, 1, 11, 34, 39, 41, 44, 53

Daniel de Oliveira, Eduardo S. Ogasawara, Kary A. C. S. Ocaña, Fernanda Araujo Baião, and Marta Mattoso. An adaptive parallel execution strategy for cloud-based scientific workflows. *Concurrency and Computation: Practice and Experience*, 24(13), pages 1531–1550, 2012b. DOI: 10.1002/cpe.1880 24, 30, 34, 39, 41, 43, 44, 53, 83, 88, 91, 103

Daniel de Oliveira, Vitor Viana, Eduardo Ogasawara, Kary Ocaña, and Marta Mattoso. Dimensioning the virtual cluster for parallel scientific workflows in clouds. In *ScienceCloud'13, Proceedings of the 4th ACM HPDC Workshop on Scientific Cloud Computing*, pages 5–12, 2013a. DOI: 10.1145/2465848.2465852 48

Daniel de Oliveira, Vitor Viana, Eduardo S. Ogasawara, Kary A. C. S. Ocaña, and Marta Mattoso. Dimensioning the virtual cluster for parallel scientific workflows in clouds. In *4th ACM Workshop on Scientific Cloud Computing*, pages 5–12, 2013b. DOI: 10.1145/2465848.2465852 34, 40

Daniel de Oliveira, Vítor Silva Sousa, and Marta Mattoso. How much domain data should be in provenance databases? In *7th USENIX Workshop on the Theory and Practice of Provenance*, pages 8–14, Edinburgh, Scotland, UK, July 8–9, 2015. 107, 113

Wellington Moreira de Oliveira, Daniel de Oliveira, and Vanessa Braganholo. Provenance analytics for workflow-based computational experiments: A survey. *ACM Computing Surveys*, 51(3), pages 53:1–53:25, 2018. DOI: 10.1145/3184900 1

Jeffrey Dean and Sanjay Ghemawat. MapReduce: Simplified data processing on large clusters. In *6th Symposium on Operating System Design and Implementation (OSDI)*, pages 137–150, 2004. DOI: 10.1145/1327452.1327492 81, 82

Jeffrey Dean and Sanjay Ghemawat. MapReduce: Simplified data processing on large clusters. *Communication of the ACM*, 51(1), pages 107–113, 2008. DOI: 10.1145/1327452.1327492 2

Ewa Deelman, Gurmeet Singh, Mei-Hui Su, James Blythe, Yolanda Gil, Carl Kesselman, Gaurang Mehta, Karan Vahi, G. Bruce Berriman, John Good, Anastasia C. Laity, Joseph C. Jacob, and Daniel S. Katz. Pegasus: A framework for mapping complex scientific workflows onto distributed systems. *Scientific Programming*, 13(3), pages 219–237, 2005. DOI: 10.1155/2005/128026 11, 15, 18, 32, 76, 103

Ewa Deelman, Scott Callaghan, Edward Field, Hunter Francoeur, Robert Graves, Nitin Gupta, Vipin Gupta, Thomas H. Jordan, Carl Kesselman, Philip Maechling, John Mehringer, Gaurang Mehta, David Okaya, Karan Vahi, and Li Zhao. Managing large-scale workflow execution from resource provisioning to provenance tracking: The cybershake example. In *IEEE International Conference on e-Science and Grid Computing*, pages 14–14, 2006. DOI: 10.1109/e-science.2006.261098 76

Ewa Deelman, Gaurang Mehta, Gurmeet Singh, Mei-Hui Su, and Karan Vahi. Pegasus: Mapping large-scale workflows to distributed resources. In *Workflows for e-Science*, pages 376–394, 2007. DOI: 10.1007/978-1-84628-757-2_23 xv, 1, 25, 71

Ewa Deelman, Gurmeet Singh, Miron Livny, G. Bruce Berriman, and John Good. The cost of doing science on the cloud: The montage example. In *ACM/IEEE Conference on High Performance Computing*, pages 1–12, 2008. 3

Ewa Deelman, Dennis Gannon, Matthew S. Shields, and Ian J. Taylor. Workflows and e-science: An overview of workflow system features and capabilities. *Future Generation Computer Systems*, 25(5), pages 528–540, 2009. DOI: 10.1016/j.future.2008.06.012 1, 15

Ewa Deelman, Gideon Juve, and G. Bruce Berriman. Using clouds for science, is it just kicking the can down the road? In *Cloud Computing and Services Science (CLOSER), 2nd International Conference on Cloud Computing and Services Science*, pages 127–134, 2012. DOI: 10.5220/0003958901270134 34

Ewa Deelman, Karan Vahi, Gideon Juve, Mats Rynge, Scott Callaghan, Philip Maechling, Rajiv Mayani, Weiwei Chen, Rafael Ferreira da Silva, Miron Livny, and R. Kent Wenger. Pegasus, a workflow management system for science automation. *Future Generation Computer Systems*, 2014. DOI: 10.1016/j.future.2014.10.008 1, 11, 25

Ewa Deelman, Karan Vahi, Mats Rynge, Gideon Juve, Rajiv Mayani, and Rafael Ferreira da Silva. Pegasus in the cloud: Science automation through workflow technologies. *IEEE Internet Computing*, 20(1), pages 70–76, 2016. DOI: 10.1109/mic.2016.15 1

Kefeng Deng, Lingmei Kong, Junqiang Song, Kaijun Ren, and Dong Yuan. A weighted k-means clustering based co-scheduling strategy towards efficient execution of scientific workflows in collaborative cloud environments. In *IEEE 9th International Conference on Dependable, Autonomic and Secure Computing (DASC)*, pages 547–554, 2011. DOI: 10.1109/dasc.2011.102 24, 25, 88

Jonas Dias, Eduardo S. Ogasawara, Daniel de Oliveira, Fábio Porto, Patrick Valduriez, and Marta Mattoso. Algebraic dataflows for big data analysis. In *IEEE International Conference on Big Data*, pages 150–155, 2013. DOI: 10.1109/bigdata.2013.6691567 28

Jonas Dias, Gabriel Guerra, Fernando Rochinha, Alvaro L. G. A. Coutinho, Patrick Valduriez, and Marta Mattoso. Data-centric iteration in dynamic workflows. *Future Generation Computer Systems*, 46, pages 114–126, 2015. DOI: 10.1016/j.future.2014.10.021 17

Rubing Duan, Radu Prodan, and Xiaorong Li. Multi-objective game theoretic scheduling of bag-of-tasks workflows on hybrid clouds. *IEEE Transactions on Cloud Computing*, 2(1), pages 29–42, 2014. DOI: 10.1109/tcc.2014.2303077 79, 83, 84

Juan José Durillo, Vlad Nae, and Radu Prodan. Multi-objective workflow scheduling: An analysis of the energy efficiency and makespan tradeoff. In *IEEE/ACM International Symposium on Cluster, Cloud, and Grid Computing (CCGrid)*, pages 203–210, 2013. DOI: 10.1109/ccgrid.2013.62 41, 42, 44

Juan Jose Durillo, Radu Prodan, and Jorge G. Barbosa. Pareto tradeoff scheduling of workflows on federated commercial clouds. *Simulation Modelling Practice and Theory*, 58, pages 95–111, 2015. DOI: 10.1016/j.simpat.2015.07.001 41, 42, 44

Jaliya Ekanayake, Hui Li, Bingjing Zhang, Thilina Gunarathne, Seung-Hee Bae, Judy Qiu, and Geoffrey C. Fox. Twister: A runtime for iterative MapReduce. In *ACM International Symposium on High Performance Distributed Computing*, pages 810–818, 2010. DOI: 10.1145/1851476.1851593 2

Vincent C. Emeakaroha, Michael Maurer, Patrick Stern, Pawel P. Labaj, Ivona Brandic, and David P. Kreil. Managing and optimizing bioinformatics workflows for data analysis in clouds. *Journal of Grid Computing*, 11(3), pages 407–428, 2013. DOI: 10.1007/s10723-013-9260-9 40, 48

Kobra Etminani and M. Naghibzadeh. A min-min max-min selective algorithm for grid task scheduling. In *The 3rd IEEE/IFIP International Conference in Central Asia on Internet (ICI)*, pages 1–7, 2007. DOI: 10.1109/canet.2007.4401694 80, 81, 90

Thomas Fahringer, Radu Prodan, Rubing Duan, Francesco Nerieri, Stefan Podlipnig, Jun Qin, Mumtaz Siddiqui, Hong Linh Truong, Alex Villazón, and Marek Wieczorek. Askalon: A grid application development and computing environment. In *6th IEEE/ACM International Conference on Grid Computing*, pages 122–131, 2005. DOI: 10.1109/grid.2005.1542733 1

Thomas Fahringer, Radu Prodan, Rubing Duan, Jüurgen Hofer, Farrukh Nadeem, Francesco Nerieri, Stefan Podlipnig, Jun Qin, Mumtaz Siddiqui, Hong-Linh Truong, Alex Villazon, and Marek Wieczorek. Askalon: A development and grid computing environment for scientific workflows. In *Workflows for e-Science*, pages 450–471, Springer, 2007. DOI: 10.1007/978-1-84628-757-2_27 1, 25, 70

Hamid Reza Faragardi, Saeid Dehnavi, Thomas Nolte, Mehdi Kargahi, and Thomas Fahringer. An energy-aware resource provisioning scheme for real-time applications in a cloud data center. *Software: Practice and Experience*, 48(10), pages 1734–1757, 2018. DOI: 10.1002/spe.2592 40

Hamid Mohammadi Fard, Thomas Fahringer, and Radu Prodan. Budget-constrained resource provisioning for scientific applications in clouds. In *IEEE 5th International Conference on Cloud Computing Technology and Science (CloudCom)*, vol. 1, pages 315–322, 2013a. DOI: 10.1109/cloudcom.2013.48 34

Hamid Mohammadi Fard, Radu Prodan, and Thomas Fahringer. A truthful dynamic workflow scheduling mechanism for commercial multicloud environments. *IEEE Transactions on Parallel Distribution Systems*, 24(6), pages 1203–1212, 2013b. DOI: 10.1109/TPDS.2012.257. 41, 43, 44

Hamid Mohammadi Fard, Radu Prodan, and Thomas Fahringer. Multi-objective list scheduling of workflow applications in distributed computing infrastructures. *Journal of Parallel and Distributed Computing*, 74(3), pages 2152–2165, 2014a. DOI: 10.1016/j.jpdc.2013.12.004 25, 83

Hamid Mohammadi Fard, Radu Prodan, and Thomas Fahringer. Multi-objective list scheduling of workflow applications in distributed computing infrastructures. *Journal of Parallel Distributed Computing*, 74(3), pages 2152–2165, 2014b. DOI: 0.1016/j.jpdc.2013.12.004 41, 43, 44

Joel Felsenstein. Phylip—phylogeny inference package (version 3.2). *Cladistics*, 5, pages 164–166, 1989. 5

I. Foster, Y. Zhao, I. Raicu, and S. Lu. Cloud computing and grid computing 360-degree compared. In *Grid Computing Environments Workshop*, pages 1–10, 2008. DOI: 10.1109/gce.2008.4738445 32, 33

Ian Foster and Carl Kesselman. Computational grids. In *International Conference Vector and Parallel Processing VECPAR*, pages 3–37, 2000. DOI: 10.1007/3-540-44942-6_2 2

Ian Foster and Carl Kesselman. *The Grid 2: Blueprint for a New Computing Infrastructure.* Morgan Kaufmann Publishers Inc., 2003. 32

Geoffrey C. Fox, Judy Qiu, Shantenu Jha, Saliya Ekanayake, and Supun Kamburugamuve. Big data, simulations and HPC convergence. In *Big Data Benchmarking—International Workshop, WBDB*, pages 3–17, 2015. DOI: 10.1007/978-3-319-49748-8_1 35

Alexandre P. Francisco, Marta Nascimento, and Cátia Vaz. Dynamic phylogenetic inference for sequence-based typing data. In *ACM International Conference on Bioinformatics, Computational Biology, and Health Informatics*, pages 604–604, 2017. DOI: 10.1145/3107411.3108214 1

Juliana Freire, David Koop, Emanuele Santos, and Cláudio T. Silva. Provenance for computational tasks: A survey. *Computing in Science and Engineering*, 10(3), pages 11–21, 2008a. DOI: 10.1109/mcse.2008.79 72

Juliana Freire, David Koop, Emanuele Santos, and Cláudio T. Silva. Provenance for computational tasks: A survey. *Computing in Science and Engineering*, pages 20–30, 2008b. DOI: 10.1109/mcse.2008.79 2, 11, 72

K. Ganga and Service Karthik. A fault tolerant approach in scientific workflow systems based on cloud computing. In *International Conference on Pattern Recognition, Informatics and Mobile Engineering (PRIME)*, pages 387–390, 2013. DOI: 10.1109/icprime.2013.6496507 19

Daniel Gaspar, Fábio Porto, Reza Akbarinia, and Esther Pacitti. TARDIS: Optimal execution of scientific workflows in apache spark. In *Big Data Analytics and Knowledge Discovery—19th International Conference, (DaWaK) Proceedings*, pages 74–87, Lyon, France, August 28–31, 2017. DOI: 10.1007/978-3-319-64283-3_6 104, 109, 110, 123, 125, 128

Ashish Gehani, Minyoung Kim, and Tanu Malik. Efficient querying of distributed provenance stores. In *ACM International Symposium on High Performance Distributed Computing (HPDC)*, pages 613–621, 2010. DOI: 10.1145/1851476.1851567 76

Yolanda Gil, Jihie Kim, Varun Ratnakar, and Ewa Deelman. Wings for pegasus: A semantic approach to creating very large scientific workflows. In *OWLED Workshop on OWL: Experiences and Directions*, vol. 216, 2006. 17

Jeremy Goecks, Anton Nekrutenko, and James Taylor. Galaxy: A comprehensive approach for supporting accessible, reproducible, and transparent computational research in the life sciences. *Genome Biology*, 11(8), pages 1–13, 2010. DOI: 10.1186/gb-2010-11-8-r86 17, 18

Luis Miguel Vaquero Gonzalez, Luis Rodero-Merino, Juan Caceres, and Maik A. Lindner. A break in the clouds: Towards a cloud definition. *Computer Communication Review*, 39(1), pages 50–55, 2009. DOI: 10.1145/1496091.1496100 2, 39

Katharina Görlach, Mirko Sonntag, Dimka Karastoyanova, Frank Leymann, and Michael Reiter. Conventional workflow technology for scientific simulation. In *Guide to e-Science*, pages 323–352, 2011. DOI: 10.1007/978-0-85729-439-5_12 15

Yi Gu, Chase Qishi Wu, Xin Liu, and Dantong Yu. Distributed throughput optimization for large-scale scientific workflows under fault-tolerance constraint, *International Journal of Grid Computing*, 11(3), pages 361–379, 2013. DOI: 10.1007/s10723-013-9266-3 25, 103

Thaylon Guedes, Vitor Silva, Marta Mattoso, Marcos Bedo, and Daniel Oliveira. A practical roadmap for provenance capture and data analysis in spark-based scientific workflows. In *Proc. of the Workflows in Support of Large-Scale Science Workshop (WORKS), in Conjunction with IEEE/ACM SuperComputing, (WORKS)*, 2018. DOI: 10.1109/works.2018.00009 104, 105, 107, 110, 113

Muhammad Ali Gulzar, Matteo Interlandi, Seunghyun Yoo, Sai Deep Tetali, Tyson Condie, Todd Millstein, and Miryung Kim. BigDebug: Debugging Primitives for Interactive Big Data Processing in Spark. In *Proc. of the 38th International Conference on Software Engineering*, pages 784–795, ACM, 2016. DOI: 10.1145/2884781.2884813 106, 107

Dan Gunter, Ewa Deelman, Taghrid Samak, Christopher X. Brooks, Monte Goode, Gideon Juve, Gaurang Mehta, Priscilla Moraes, Fabio Silva, D. Martin Swany, and Karan Vahi. Online workflow management and performance analysis with stampede. In *7th International Conference on Network and Service Management (CNSM)*, pages 1–10, 2011. 17

Jiawei Han, Micheline Kamber, and Jian Pei. *Data Mining: Concepts and Techniques*, 3rd ed., Morgan Kaufmann Publishers Inc., San Francisco, CA, 2011. 106

Andrew Harrison, Ian J. Taylor, Ian Wang, and Matthew S. Shields. WS-RF workflow in triana. *International Journal of High Performance Computing Applications (IJHPCA)*, 22(3), pages 268–283, 2008. DOI: 10.1177/1094342007086226 1

Mihael Hategan, Justin M. Wozniak, and Ketan Maheshwari. Coasters: Uniform resource provisioning and access for clouds and grids. In *4th IEEE International Conference on Utility and Cloud Computing*, pages 114–121, 2011. DOI: 10.1109/ucc.2011.25 34

Herodotos Herodotou. Automatic tuning of data-intensive analytical workloads. Ph.D. thesis, Duke University, Durham, NC, 2012. http://hdl.handle.net/10161/5415 105, 110

Herodotos Herodotou and Shivnath Babu. Profiling, what-if analysis, and cost-based optimization of MapReduce programs. *PVLDB*, 4(11), pages 1111–1122, 2011. http://dblp.uni-trier.de/db/journals/pvldb/pvldb4.html#HerodotouB11 105

Herodotos Herodotou, Fei Dong, and Shivnath Babu. MapReduce programming and cost-based optimization? Crossing this chasm with starfish. *PVLDB*, 2011. 105

Herodotos Herodotou, Harold Lim, Gang Luo, Nedyalko Borisov, Liang Dong, Fatma Bilgen Cetin, and Shivnath Babu. Starfish: A self-tuning system for big data analytics. In *CIDR*, pages 261–272, 2011. www.cidrdb.org http://dblp.uni-trier.de/db/conf/cidr/cidr2011.html#HerodotouLLBDCB11 105, 106

Tony Hey. The cloud computing revolution. In *Proc. of the 11th Annual International Conference on Digital Government Research, Public Administration Online: Challenges and Opportunities, DG.O*, p. 2, Puebla, Mexico, May 17–20, 2010. http://dl.acm.org/citation.cfm?id=1809877 2

Tony Hey, Stewart Tansley, and Kristin M. Tolle, Eds. *The 4th Paradigm: Data-Intensive Scientific Discovery*. Microsoft Research, 2009. http://research.microsoft.com/en-us/collaboration/fourthparadigm/ DOI: 10.1109/jproc.2011.2155130 1

Tony Hey, Dennis Gannon, and Jim Pinkelman. The future of data-intensive science. *IEEE Computer*, 45(5), pages 81–82, 2012. DOI: 10.1109/MC.2012.181 1, 35, 103

Felipe Horta, Jonas Dias, Kary A. C. S. Ocaña, Daniel de Oliveira, Eduardo S. Ogasawara, and Marta Mattoso. Abstract: Using provenance to visualize data from large-scale experiments. In *Supercomputing (SC): High Performance Computing, Networking Storage and Analysis*, pages 1418–1419, 2012. DOI: 10.1109/sc.companion.2012.228 11, 17

Jen-Wei Hsieh, Tei-Wei Kuo, and Li-Pin Chang. Efficient identification of hot data for flash memory storage systems. *ACM Transactions on Storage (TOS)*, 2(1), pages 22–40, 2006. DOI: 10.1145/1138041.1138043 74

Alastair C. Hume, Yahya Al-Hazmi, Bartosz Belter, Konrad Campowsky, Luis M. Carril, Gino Carrozzo, Vegard Engen, David García-Pérez, Jordi Jofre Ponsatí, Roland Kübert, Yongzheng Liang, Cyril Rohr, and Gregory van Seghbroeck. Bonfire: A multi-cloud test facility for internet of services experimentation. In *Testbeds and Research Infrastructure. Development of Networks and Communities*, vol. 44, pages 81–96, 2012. DOI: 10.1007/978-3-642-35576-9_11 70

Robert Ikeda, Hyunjung Park, and Jennifer Widom. Provenance for generalized map and reduce workflow. pages 1–11, 2011. 106, 107

Matteo Interlandi, Kshitij Shah, Sai Deep Tetali, Muhammad Ali Gulzar, Seunghyun Yoo, Miryung Kim, Todd Millstein, and Tyson Condie. Titian: Data provenance support in spark. *Proc. of the VLDB Endowment*, 9(3), pages 216–227, 2015. DOI: 10.14778/2850583.2850595 106, 107

Takashi Iwamoto, Wolfgang Banzhaf, and Kazuo Kyuma. Topological aspects of genetic algorithms. In *Proc. of the 5th International Conference on Genetic Algorithms*, page 638, Urbana-Champaign, IL, June 1993. 40

Kevin Jackson. *OpenStack Cloud Computing Cookbook*. Packt Publishing, 2012. 42

Joseph C. Jacob, Daniel S. Katz, G. Bruce Berriman, John Good, Anastasia C. Laity, Ewa Deelman, Carl Kesselman, Gurmeet Singh, Mei-Hui Su, Thomas A. Prince, and Roy Williams. Montage: A grid portal and software toolkit for science-grade astronomical image mosaicking. *International Journal of Computational Science and Engineering*, 4(2), pages 73–87, 2009. DOI: 10.1504/ijcse.2009.026999 1, 2, 3

Matthias Janetschek, Radu Prodan, and Shajulin Benedict. A workflow runtime environment for manycore parallel architectures. *Future Generation Computer Systems*, 75, pages 330–347, 2017. DOI: 10.1016/j.future.2017.02.029 41, 42, 44

Luiz M. R. Gadelha Jr., Michael Wilde, Marta Mattoso, and Ian T. Foster. Provenance traces of the swift parallel scripting system. In *EDBT/ICDT Workshops*, pages 325–326, 2013. DOI: 10.1145/2457317.2457374 18

Gideon Juve and Ewa Deelman. Scientific workflows in the cloud. In *Grids, Clouds and Virtualization*, pages 71–91, Springer, 2011a. DOI: 10.1007/978-0-85729-049-6_4 34

Gideon Juve and Ewa Deelman. Wrangler: Virtual cluster provisioning for the cloud. In *20th International Symposium on High Performance Distributed Computing*, pages 277–278, 2011b. DOI: 10.1145/1996130.1996173 34

Gideon Juve, Ann L. Chervenak, Ewa Deelman, Shishir Bharathi, Gaurang Mehta, and Karan Vahi. Characterizing and profiling scientific workflows. *Future Generation Computer Systems (FGCS)*, 29(3), pages 682–692, 2013a. DOI: 10.1016/j.future.2012.08.015 76

Gideon Juve, Mats Rynge, Ewa Deelman, Jens-S. Vöckler, and G. Bruce Berriman. Comparing futuregrid, amazon ec2, and open science grid for scientific workflows. *Computing in Science Engineering*, 15(4), pages 20–29, 2013b. DOI: 10.1109/mcse.2013.44 33, 34

Peter Kacsuk. P-grade portal family for grid infrastructures. *Concurrency and Computation: Practice and Experience*, 23(3), pages 235–245, 2011. DOI: 10.1002/cpe.1654 21

Péter Kacsuk, Zoltán Farkas, Miklos Kozlovszky, Gabor Hermann, Ákos Balaskó, Krisztián Karóczkai, and Istvan Marton. WS-PGRADE/gUSE generic DCI gateway framework for a large variety of user communities. *Journal of Grid Computing*, 10(4), pages 601–630, 2012. DOI: 10.1007/s10723-012-9240-5 xv, 11, 25

Alex N. Kalos and Tim Rey. Data mining in the chemical industry. In *ACM SIGKDD International Conference on Knowledge Discovery in Data Mining*, pages 763–769, 2005. DOI: 10.1145/1081870.1081970 2

Beatriz S. Kanzki, Victor Dupuy, Cedric Urvoy, Fodil Belghait, Alain April, Francois Harvey, François-Christophe Marois-Blanchet, Michael S. Phillips, Johanne Tremblay, and Pavel Hamet. GOAT: Genetic output analysis tool: An open source GWAS and genomic region visualization tool. In *International Conference on Digital Health Conference*, pages 55–59, 2016. DOI: 10.1145/2896338.2897729 1, 2, 35, 103

George Karypis and Vipin Kumar. Multilevel algorithms for multi-constraint graph partitioning. In *ACM/IEEE Conference on Supercomputing*, pages 1–13, 1998. DOI: 10.1109/sc.1998.10018 87

Jihie Kim, Ewa Deelman, Yolanda Gil, Gaurang Mehta, and Varun Ratnakar. Provenance trails in the wings-pegasus system. *Concurrency and Computation: Practice and Experience*, 20, pages 587–597, 2008. DOI: 10.1002/cpe.1228 18

Sunyoung Kwon and Sungroh Yoon. Deepcci: End-to-end deep learning for chemical-chemical interaction prediction. In *ACM International Conference on Bioinformatics, Computational Biology, and Health Informatics*, pages 203–212, 2017. DOI: 10.1145/3107411.3107451 2

Palden Lama and Xiaobo Zhou. Aroma: Automated resource allocation and configuration of MapReduce environment in the cloud. In *Proc. of the 9th International Conference on Autonomic Computing, (ICAC)*, pages 63–72, New York, ACM, 2012. DOI: 10.1145/2371536.2371547 105

James Larus. The cloud will change everything. *SIGPLAN Notices*, 46(3), pages 1–2, 2011. DOI: 10.1145/2248487.1950367 2

Andrew W. Leung, Minglong Shao, Timothy Bisson, Shankar Pasupathy, and Ethan L. Miller. Spyglass: Fast, scalable metadata search for large-scale storage systems. In *USENIX Conference on File and Storage Technologies (FAST)*, pages 153–166, 2009. 76

Justin J. Levandoski, Per-Åke Larson, and Radu Stoica. Identifying hot and cold data in main-memory databases. In *International Conference on Data Engineering (ICDE)*, pages 26–37, 2013. DOI: 10.1109/icde.2013.6544811 74

Hongjian Li, Huochen Wang, Anping Xiong, Jun Lai, and Wenhong Tian.   Comparative analysis of energy-efficient scheduling algorithms for big data applications. *IEEE Access*, 6, pages 40073–40084, 2018. DOI: 10.1109/access.2018.2855720 109, 123

Chee Sun Liew, Malcolm P. Atkinson, Michelle Galea, Tan Fong Ang, Paul Martin, and Jano I. van Hemert. Scientific workflows: Moving across paradigms. *ACM Computing Surveys*, 49(4), pages 66:1–66:39, 2017. DOI: 10.1145/3012429 15, 17, 18, 65

Cui Lin, Shiyong Lu, Xubo Fei, Artem Chebotko, Darshan Pai, Zhaoqiang Lai, Farshad Fo-touhi, and Jing Hua. A reference architecture for scientific workflow management systems and the view SOA solution. *IEEE Transactions on Services Computing*, 2(1), pages 79–92, 2009. DOI: 10.1109/tsc.2009.4 1

C. L. Liu and James W. Layland.   Scheduling algorithms for multiprogramming in a hard-real-time environment. *Journal of the ACM (JACM)*, 20(1), pages 46–61, 1973. DOI: 10.1145/321738.321743 41, 122

Ji Liu, Esther Pacitti, Patrick Valduriez, and Marta Mattoso. Parallelization of scientific work-flows in the cloud. *Research Report RR-8565*, 2014a. 52

Ji Liu, Vítor Silva Sousa, Esther Pacitti, Patrick Valduriez, and Marta Mattoso. Scientific work-flow partitioning in multisite cloud. In *Parallel Processing Workshops—Euro-Par 2014 International Workshops*, pages 105–116, 2014b. DOI: 10.1007/978-3-319-14325-5_10 19, 85, 87, 88, 91

Ji Liu, Esther Pacitti, Patrick Valduriez, and Marta Mattoso. A survey of data-intensive scien-tific workflow management. *Journal of Grid Computing*, 13(4), pages 457–493, 2015. DOI: 10.1007/s10723-015-9329-8 13, 15, 41

Ji Liu, Esther Pacitti, Patrick Valduriez, Daniel de Oliveira, and Marta Mattoso. Multi-objective scheduling of scientific workflows in multisite clouds. *Future Generation Computer Systems*, 63, pages 76–95, 2016a. DOI: 10.1016/j.future.2016.04.014 39, 40, 57, 71, 103

Ji Liu, Esther Pacitti, Patrick Valduriez, Daniel de Oliveira, and Marta Mattoso. Multi-objective scheduling of scientific workflows in multisite clouds. *Future Generation Computer Systems (FGCS)*, 63, pages 76–95, 2016b. DOI: 10.1016/j.future.2016.04.014 85, 88, 91, 96, 97

Ji Liu, Esther Pacitti, Patrick Valduriez, and Marta Mattoso. Scientific workflow scheduling with provenance data in a multisite cloud. *Transactions on Large-Scale Data- and Knowledge-Centered Systems (TLDKS)*, 33, pages 80–112, 2016c. DOI: 10.1007/978-3-319-61982-8_19 75, 80, 81, 83

Ji Liu, Luis Morales, Esther Pacitti, Alexandru Costan, Patrick Valduriez, Gabriel Antoniu, and Marta Mattoso. Efficient scheduling of scientific workflows using hot metadata in a multisite cloud. *IEEE Transactions on Knowledge and Data Engineering (TKDE)*, 2018a. DOI: 10.1109/tkde.2018.2867857 72, 74, 76, 77, 84

Ji Liu, Esther Pacitti, and Patrick Valduriez. A survey of scheduling frameworks in big data systems. *International Journal of Cloud Computing (IJCC)*, 7(2), pages 103–128, 2018b. DOI: 10.1504/ijcc.2018.10014859 18, 81

Dionysios Logothetis, Soumyarupa De, and Kenneth Yocum. Scalable lineage capture for debugging DISC analytics. In *Proc. of the 4th Annual Symposium on Cloud Computing*, pages 17–32, ACM, 2013. DOI: 10.1145/2523616.2523619 106, 107

Qinqin Long, Winfried Kurth, Christophe Pradal, Vincent Migault, and Benoît Pallas. An architecture for the integration of different functional and structural plant models. In *Proc. of the 7th International Conference on Informatics, Environment, Energy and Applications, (IEEA)*, pages 107–113, New York, ACM, 2018. 1

Yuan Luo and Beth Plale. Hierarchical MapReduce programming model and scheduling algorithms. In *IEEE/ACM International Symposium on Cluster, Cloud and Grid Computing (CCgrid)*, pages 769–774, 2012. DOI: 10.1109/ccgrid.2012.132 70

Muthucumaru Maheswaran, Shoukat Ali, Howard Jay Siegel, Debra A. Hensgen, and Richard F. Freund. Dynamic matching and scheduling of a class of independent tasks onto heterogeneous computing systems. In *8th Heterogeneous Computing Workshop*, page 30, 1999. DOI: 10.1109/HCW.1999.765094 25, 80, 90

Shamita Malik and Dolly Sharma. Detecting history of species using mining of motifs in phylogenetic networks. In *International Conference on Information and Communication Technology for Competitive Strategies*, pages 80:1–80:5, 2014. DOI: 10.1145/2677855.2677935 1, 2

Tanu Malik, Ligia Nistor, and Ashish Gehani. Tracking and sketching distributed data provenance. In *International Conference on e-Science*, pages 190–197, 2010. DOI: 10.1109/escience.2010.51 76

R. T. Marler and J. S. Arora. Survey of multi-objective optimization methods for engineering. *Structural and Multidisciplinary Optimization*, 26(6), pages 369–395, 2004. DOI: 10.1007/s00158-003-0368-6 83

Stathis Maroulis, Nikos Zacheilas, and Vana Kalogeraki. A framework for efficient energy scheduling of spark workloads. In *IEEE International Conference on Distributed Computing Systems (ICDCS)*, pages 2614–2615, 2017. DOI: 10.1109/icdcs.2017.179 109, 123

Simone L. Martins, Celso C. Ribeiro, and Maurício C. de Souza. A parallel GRASP for the Steiner problem in graphs. In *Solving Irregularly Structured Problems in Parallel, 5th International Symposium, IRREGULAR Proceedings*, pages 285–297, Berkeley, CA, August 9–11, 1998. DOI: 10.1007/BFb0018547 40

Vidal Martins, Esther Pacitti, Manal El Dick, and Ricardo Jiménez-Peris. Scalable and topology-aware reconciliation on P2P networks. *Distributed and Parallel Databases*, 24(1–3), pages 1–43, 2008. DOI: 10.1007/s10619-008-7029-0 68

Marta Mattoso, Cláudia Werner, Guilherme Horta Travassos, Vanessa Braganholo, Eduardo S. Ogasawara, Daniel de Oliveira, Sérgio Manuel Serra da Cruz, Wallace Martinho, and Leonardo Murta. Towards supporting the life cycle of large scale scientific experiments. In *International Journal of Business Process Integration and Management*, vol. 5, pages 79–82, 2010. DOI: 10.1504/ijbpim.2010.033176 1, 7, 8, 15

Marta Mattoso, Jonas Dias, Kary A.C.S. Ocaña, Eduardo Ogasawara, Flavio Costa, Felipe Horta, Vítor Silva, and Daniel de Oliveira. Dynamic steering of HPC scientific workflows: A survey. *Future Generation Computer Systems*, (0), 2014. DOI: 10.1016/j.future.2014.11.017 17, 18

Nimrod Megiddo and Dharmendra S. Modha. ARC: A self-tuning, low overhead replacement cache. In *USENIX Conference on File and Storage Technologies (FAST)*, 2003. 74

Ethan L. Miller and Randy H. Katz. RAMA: An easy-to-use, high-performance parallel file system. *Parallel Computing*, 23(4), pages 419–446. DOI: 10.1016/s0167-8191(97)00008-2 76

Paolo Missier, Stian Soiland-Reyes, Stuart Owen, Wei Tan, Aleksandra Nenadic, Ian Dunlop, Alan R. Williams, Tom Oinn, and Carole A. Goble. Taverna, reloaded. In *International Conference on Scientific and Statistical Database Management*, pages 471–481, 2010. DOI: 10.1007/978-3-642-13818-8_33 1

Hamid Mushtaq, Frank Liu, Carlos Costa, Gang Liu, Peter Hofstee, and Zaid Al-Ars. SparkGA: A spark framework for cost effective, fast and accurate DNA analysis at scale. In *ACM International Conference on Bioinformatics, Computational Biology, and Health Informatics*, pages 148–157, 2017. DOI: 10.1145/3107411.3107438 1, 2, 35, 103

Aparna S. Nayanar and Bhargavi R. Upadhyay. A study of scheduler performance analysis in spark enabled GPU cluster. In *International Conference on Smart Technologies for Smart Nation (SmartTechCon)*, pages 1282–1285, 2017. DOI: 10.1109/smarttechcon.2017.8358573 123

Duy Nguyen and Nam Thoai. EBC: Application-level migration on multi-site cloud. In *International Conference on Systems and Informatics (ICSAI)*, pages 876–880, 2012. DOI: 10.1109/icsai.2012.6223147 68

Lincolin Nhapi, Arun Kumar Yadav, and Ram Shringar Rao. Virtual machine provisioning for cloud scenarios: A survey of approaches and challenges. In *Proc. of the 2nd International Conference on Information and Communication Technology for Competitive Strategies, (ICTCS)*, pages 114:1–114:6, New York, ACM, 2016. 40

Kary A. C. S. Ocaña, Daniel de Oliveira, Jonas Dias, Eduardo S. Ogasawara, and Marta Mattoso. Optimizing phylogenetic analysis using SciHmm cloud-based scientific workflow. In *IEEE 7th International Conference on E-Science (e-Science)*, pages 62–69, December 2011a. DOI: 10.1109/escience.2011.17 2

Kary A. C. S. Ocaña, Daniel de Oliveira, Eduardo S. Ogasawara, Alberto M. R. Dávila, Alexandre A. B. Lima, and Marta Mattoso. Sciphy: A cloud-based workflow for phylogenetic analysis of drug targets in protozoan genomes. In *Advances in Bioinformatics and Computational Biology—6th Brazilian Symposium on Bioinformatics BSB*, pages 66–70, 2011b. DOI: 10.1007/978-3-642-22825-4_9 1, 2

Kary A. C. S. Ocaña, Daniel de Oliveira, Jonas Dias, Eduardo S. Ogasawara, and Marta Mattoso. Discovering drug targets for neglected diseases using a pharmacophylogenomic cloud workflow. In *IEEE 8th International Conference on E-Science (e-Science)*, pages 1–8, 2012a. DOI: 10.1109/escience.2012.6404431 2

Kary A. C. S. Ocaña, Daniel de Oliveira, Felipe Horta, Jonas Dias, Eduardo S. Ogasawara, and Marta Mattoso. Exploring molecular evolution reconstruction using a parallel cloud based scientific workflow. In *Advances in Bioinformatics and Computational Biology*, vol. 7409, pages 179–191, 2012b. DOI: 10.1007/978-3-642-31927-3_16 2, 5, 44

Kary A. C. S. Ocaña, Marcelo Galheigo, Carla Osthoff, Luiz Gadelha, Antônio Tadeu A. Gomes, Daniel de Oliveira, Fabio Porto, and Ana Tereza Vasconcelos. Towards a science gateway for bioinformatics: Experiences in brazilian system of high performance computing. In *Workshop on Clusters, Clouds and Grids for Life Sciences 2019*, pages 1–8, ACM, 2019. xv

Eduardo S. Ogasawara, Daniel de Oliveira, Patrick Valduriez, Jonas Dias, Fábio Porto, and Marta Mattoso. An algebraic approach for data-centric scientific workflows. *Proc. of the VLDB Endowment (PVLDB)*, 4(12), pages 1328–1339, 2011. 13, 18, 19, 76

Eduardo S. Ogasawara, Jonas Dias, Vítor Silva Sousa, Fernando Seabra Chirigati, Daniel de Oliveira, Fábio Porto, Patrick Valduriez, and Marta Mattoso. Chiron: A parallel engine for algebraic scientific workflows. *Concurrency and Computation: Practice and Experience*, 25(16), pages 2327–2341, 2013. DOI: 10.1002/cpe.3032 xv, 1, 11, 15, 17, 18, 25, 27, 29, 30, 32, 57, 73, 85, 125

Thomas M. Oinn, Matthew Addis, Justin Ferris, Darren Marvin, Martin Senger, R. Mark Greenwood, Tim Carver, Kevin Glover, Matthew R. Pocock, Anil Wipat, and Peter Li. Taverna: A tool for the composition and enactment of bioinformatics workflows. *Bioinformatics*, 20(17), pages 3045–3054, 2004. DOI: 10.1093/bioinformatics/bth361 17

Douglas Oliveira, Fábio Porto, Cristina Boeres, and Daniel de Oliveira. Towards optimizing the execution of spark scientific workflows using machine learning-based parameter tuning (submitted). *Concurrency and Computation: Practice and Experience*, 4(12), 2019. 104, 109, 110, 112, 113

Christopher Olston, Benjamin Reed, Utkarsh Srivastava, Ravi Kumar, and Andrew Tomkins. Pig Latin: A not-so-foreign language for data processing. In *Proc. of the ACM SIG-MOD International Conference on Management of Data*, pages 1099–1110, 2008. DOI: 10.1145/1376616.1376726 107

Alexandru Iulian Orhean, Florin Pop, and Ioan Raicu. New scheduling approach using reinforcement learning for heterogeneous distributed systems. *Journal of Parallel Distributed Computer*, 117, pages 292–302, 2018. 41, 43, 44

Simon Ostermann, Radu Prodan, and Thomas Fahringer. Extending grids with cloud resource management for scientific computing. In *10th IEEE/ACM International Conference on Grid Computing*, pages 42–49, 2009. DOI: 10.1109/grid.2009.5353075 34, 70

Simon Ostermann, Kassian Plankensteiner, Radu Prodan, and Thomas Fahringer. Groudsim: An event-based simulation framework for computational grids and clouds. In *European Conference on Parallel Processing (Euro-Par) Workshops*, pages 305–313, 2011. DOI: 10.1007/978-3-642-21878-1_38 34

M. Tamer Özsu and Patrick Valduriez. *Principles of Distributed Database Systems*, Springer, 2011. DOI: 10.1007/978-1-4419-8834-8 18, 27, 28, 72

Esther Pacitti and Patrick Valduriez. Zenith: Scientific data management on a large scale. *ERCIM News*, (89), 2012. 68

Dimitra Panagiotou, Efthymios Oikonomou, and Angelos Rouskas. Energy-efficient virtual machine provisioning mechanism in cloud computing environments. In *Proc. of the 19th Panhellenic Conference on Informatics, (PCI)*, pages 197–202, New York, ACM, 2015. 40

Cesare Pautasso and Gustavo Alonso. Parallel computing patterns for grid workflows. In *Workshop on Workflows in Support of Large-Scale Science*, pages 1–10, 2006. DOI: 10.1109/works.2006.5282349 21

James Perry, Lorna Smith, A. N. Jackson, R. D. Kenway, B. Joo, Chris M. Maynard, Arthur S. Trew, D. Byrne, G. Beckett, C. T. H. Davies, S. Downing, A. C. Irving, Craig McNeile, Z. Sroczynski, C. R. Allton, W. Armour, and J. M. Flynn. QCDgrid: A grid resource for quantum chromodynamics. *Journal of Grid Computing*, 3(1), pages 113–130, 2005. 65 DOI: 10.1007/s10723-005-9005-5

João Felipe Pimentel, Leonardo Murta, Vanessa Braganholo, and Juliana Freire. noWorkflow: A tool for collecting, analyzing, and managing provenance from python scripts. *PVLDB*, 10(12), pages 1841–1844, 2017. http://www.vldb.org/pvldb/vol10/p1841-pimentel.pdf DOI: 10.14778/3137765.3137789 1, 103

Luis Pineda-Morales, Alexandru Costan, and Gabriel Antoniu. Towards multi-site metadata management for geographically distributed cloud workflows. In *IEEE International Conference on Cluster Computing*, pages 294–303, 2015. DOI: 10.1109/cluster.2015.49 76, 77

Luis Pineda-Morales, Ji Liu, Alexandru Costan, Esther Pacitti, Gabriel Antoniu, Patrick Valduriez, and Marta Mattoso. Managing hot metadata for scientific workflows on multisite clouds. In *IEEE International Conference on Big Data*, pages 390–397, 2016. DOI: 10.1109/bigdata.2016.7840628 77

Michael L. Pinedo. *Scheduling: Theory, Algorithms, and Systems*, 3rd ed., Springer Publishing Company, Incorporated, 2008. 4

Adrian Popescu, Andrey Balmin, Vuk Ercegovac, and Anastasia Ailamaki. Predict: Towards predicting the runtime of large scale iterative analytics. *PVLDB*, 6(14), pages 1678–1689, 2013. http://dblp.uni-trier.de/db/journals/pvldb/pvldb6.html#Popescu BEA13 DOI: 10.14778/2556549.2556553 105

Christophe Pradal, Christian Fournier, Patrick Valduriez, and Sarah Cohen-Boulakia. Openalea: Scientific workflows combining data analysis and simulation. In *Proc. of the 27th International Conference on Scientific and Statistical Database Management, (SSDBM)*, pages 11:1–11:6, New York, ACM, 2015. 1

Kenneth W. Preslan, Andrew P. Barry, Jonathan Brassow, Grant Erickson, Erling Nygaard, Christopher Sabol, Steven R. Soltis, David Teigland, and Matthew T. O'Keefe. A 64-bit, shared disk file system for Linux. In *16th IEEE Symposium on Mass Storage Systems*, pages 22–41, 1999. DOI: 10.1109/mass.1999.829973 33

Jun Qin, Francisco Hernandez, Erik Elmroth, and Thomas Fahringer. Towards workflow sharing and reusein the askalon grid environment. In *Cracow Grid Workshops (CGW)*, pages 111–119, 2008. 18

Xiao Qin and Hong Jiang. A dynamic and reliability-driven scheduling algorithm for parallel real-time jobs executing on heterogeneous clusters. *Journal of Parallel and Distributed Computing*, 65(8), pages 885–900, 2005. http://www.sciencedirect.com/science/article/pii/S0743731505000213 DOI: 10.1016/j.jpdc.2005.02.003 41, 42, 44

Babak Bashari Rad, Tinankoria Diaby, and Muhammad Ehsan Rana. Cloud computing adoption: A short review of issues and challenges. In *International Conference on E-commerce, E-Business and E-Government*, pages 51–55, 2017. DOI: 10.1145/3108421.3108426 2

Ioan Raicu, Yong Zhao, Ian T. Foster, and Alexander S. Szalay. Data diffusion: Dynamic resource provision and data-aware scheduling for data intensive applications. *The Computing Research Repository (CoRR)*, abs/0808.3535, 2008. 1

Mauricio G. C. Resende and Celso C. Ribeiro. Biased ranom-key genetic algorithms: An advanced tutorial. In *Genetic and Evolutionary Computation Conference, GECCO Companion Material Proceedings*, pages 483–514, Denver, CO, July 20–24, 2016. 40

Romain Reuillon, Mathieu Leclaire, and Jonathan Passerat-Palmbach. Model exploration using openmole a workflow engine for large scale distributed design of experiments and parameter tuning. In *International Conference on High Performance Computing Simulation (HPCS)*, pages 1–8, 2015. DOI: 10.1109/hpcsim.2015.7237015 1

Maria Alejandra Rodriguez and Rajkumar Buyya. A responsive knapsack-based algorithm for resource provisioning and scheduling of scientific workflows in clouds. In *International Conference on Parallel Processing (ICPP)*, 2015. DOI: 10.1109/icpp.2015.93 92, 93

S. Ruggieri. YADT: Yet another decision tree builder. In *16th IEEE International Conference on Tools with Artificial Intelligence*, pages 260–265, November 2004. 113 DOI: 10.1109/ictai.2004.123

Nick Russell, Wil M. P. van van der Aalst, and Arthur H. M. ter Hofstede. *Workflow Patterns: The Definitive Guide*. The MIT Press, 2016. DOI: 10.7551/mitpress/8085.001.0001 14

Iman Sadooghi, Jesus Hernandez Martin, Tonglin Li, Kevin Brandstatter, Ketan Maheshwari, Tiago Pais Pitta De Lacerda Ruivo, Gabriele Garzoglio, Steven Timm, Yong Zhao, and Ioan Raicu. Understanding the performance and potential of cloud computing for scientific applications. *IEEE Transactions on Cloud Computing*, 5(2), pages 358–371, 2017. DOI: 10.1109/tcc.2015.2404821 33

Russel Sandberg, David Golgberg, Sieve Kleiman, Dan Walsh, and Bob Lyon. Innovations in internetworking. *Chapter Design and Implementation of the Sun Network Filesystem*, pages 379–390, 1988. 33

Olaf Schenk and Klaus Gärtner. Two-level dynamic scheduling in PARDISO: Improved scalability on shared memory multiprocessing systems. *Parallel Computing*, 28(2), pages 187–197, 2002. DOI: 10.1016/s0167-8191(01)00135-1 79, 80

Frank B. Schmuck and Roger L. Haskin. GPFS: A shared-disk file system for large computing clusters. In *1st USENIX Conference on File and Storage Technologies*, 2002. 33

Srinath Shankar and David J. DeWitt. Data driven workflow planning in cluster management systems. In *International Symposium on High-Performance Distributed Computing (HPDC)*, pages 127–136, 2007. DOI: 10.1145/1272366.1272383 20

Zhiming Shen, Sethuraman Subbiah, Xiaohui Gu, and John Wilkes. Cloudscale: elastic resource scaling for multi-tenant cloud systems. In *ACM Symposium on Cloud Computing in Conjunction with SOSP*, page 5, 2011. DOI: 10.1145/2038916.2038921 40, 48

Arie Shoshani and Doron Rotem. *Scientific Data Management: Challenges, Technology, and Deployment*, 1st ed., Chapman & Hall/CRC, 2009. 3
DOI: 10.1201/9781420069815

Konstantin Shvachko, Hairong Kuang, Sanjay Radia, and Robert Chansler. The hadoop distributed file system. In *IEEE Symposium on Mass Storage Systems and Technologies (MSST)*, pages 1–10, 2010. DOI: 10.1109/msst.2010.5496972 68

Gurmeet Singh, Mei-Hui Su, Karan Vahi, Ewa Deelman, G. Bruce Berriman, John Good, Daniel S. Katz, and Gaurang Mehta. Workflow task clustering for best effort systems with Pegasus. In *15th ACM Mardi Gras Conference: From Lightweight Mash-ups to Lambda Grids: Understanding the Spectrum of Distributed Computing Requirements, Applications, Tools, Infrastructures, Interoperability, and the Incremental Adoption of Key Capabilities*, 9(1), pages 9:1–9:8, 2008. DOI: 10.1145/1341811.1341822 4

Sucha Smanchat, Maria Indrawan, Sea Ling, Colin Enticott, and David Abramson. Scheduling multiple parameter sweep workflow instances on the grid. In *5th IEEE International Conference on e-Science*, pages 300–306, 2009. DOI: 10.1109/e-science.2009.49 81

Breannan Smith, Fernando de Goes, and Theodore Kim. Stable neo-hookean flesh simulation. *ACM Transactions on Graphics*, 37(2), pages 12:1–12:15, 2018. DOI: 10.1145/3180491 2

Marc Snir, Steve Otto, Steven Huss-Lederman, David Walker, and Jack Dongarra. *MPI-The Complete Reference, Volume 1: The MPI Core*. MIT Press, 1998. 32

Concetto Spampinato, Simone Palazzo, Francesca Murabito, and Daniela Giordano. Using the eyes to "see" the objects. In *Proc. of the 23rd ACM International Conference on Multimedia, (MM)*, pages 1231–1234, New York, 2015. 131

Apache Spark. http://spark.apache.org/, 2012. 103, 110

Michael Stonebraker and Ugur Çetintemel. "One size fits all": An idea whose time has come and gone. In *International Conference on Data Engineering (ICDE)*, pages 2–11, 2005. DOI: 10.1109/icde.2005.1 76

Michael Stonebraker, Samuel Madden, Daniel J. Abadi, Stavros Harizopoulos, Nabil Hachem, and Pat Helland. The end of an architectural era: Time for a complete rewrite. In *International Conference on Very Large Data Bases (VLDB)*, pages 1150–1160. DOI: 10.1145/3226595.3226637 76

Gang Sun, Dan Liao, Dongcheng Zhao, Zhili Sun, and Victor I. Chang. Towards provisioning hybrid virtual networks in federated cloud data centers. *Future Generation Computer Systems*, 87, pages 457–469, 2018. DOI: 10.1016/j.future.2017.09.065 68

Xian-He Sun and Yong Chen. Reevaluating amdahl's law in the multicore era. *Journal of Parallel and Distributed Computing*, 70(2), pages 183–188, 2010. DOI: 10.1016/j.jpdc.2009.05.002 46, 90

Wei Tan, Ravi K. Madduri, Aleksandra Nenadic, Stian Soiland-Reyes, Dinanath Sulakhe, Ian T. Foster, and Carole A. Goble. Cagrid workflow toolkit: A taverna based workflow tool for cancer grid. *BMC Bioinformatics*, 11, page 542, 2010. DOI: 10.1186/1471-2105-11-542 2

Masahiro Tanaka and Osamu Tatebe. Workflow scheduling to minimize data movement using multi-constraint graph partitioning. In *12th IEEE/ACM International Symposium on Cluster, Cloud and Grid Computing (Ccgrid)*, pages 65–72, 2012. DOI: 10.1109/ccgrid.2012.134 19

Jianchao Tang, Shuqiang Yang, Chao-Qiang Huang, and Zhou Yan. Design and implementation of scheduling pool scheduling algorithm based on reuse of jobs in spark. In *IEEE 1st International Conference on Data Science in Cyberspace (DSC)*, pages 290–295, 2016. DOI: 10.1109/dsc.2016.81 108, 123

Ian Taylor, Matthew Shields, Ian Wang, and Andrew Harrison. The triana workflow environment: Architecture and applications. In *Workflows for e-Science*, pages 320–339, Springer, 2007a. DOI: 10.1007/978-1-84628-757-2_20 25

I. J. Taylor, E. Deelman, D. B. Gannon, and M. Shields. (Eds.) *Workflows for e-Science*, 1st ed., Springer-Verlag London, London, UK, 2007b. DOI: 10.1007/978-1-84628-757-2 3

Gábor Terstyánszky, Tamas Kukla, Tamás Kiss, Péter Kacsuk, Ákos Balaskó, and Zoltán Farkas. Enabling scientific workflow sharing through coarse-grained interoperability. *Future Generation Computer Systems*, 37, pages 46–59, 2014. DOI: 10.1016/j.future.2014.02.016 18, 21

Luan Teylo, Ubiratam de Paula Junior, Yuri Frota, Daniel de Oliveira, and Lúcia Maria de A. Drummond. A hybrid evolutionary algorithm for task scheduling and data assignment of data-intensive scientific workflows on clouds. *Future Generation Computer Systems*, 76, pages 1–17, 2017. 41, 43, 44

Luan Teylo, Lúcia Maria de A. Drummond, Luciana Arantes, and Pierre Sens. A bag-of-tasks scheduler tolerant to temporal failures in clouds. *CoRR*, abs/1810.10279, 2018. http://arxiv.org/abs/1810.10279 41, 43, 44

Ashish Thusoo, Joydeep Sen Sarma, Namit Jain, Zheng Shao, Prasad Chakka, Ning Zhang, Suresh Antony, Hao Liu, and Raghotham Murthy. Hive—A petabyte scale data warehouse using Hadoop. In *International Conference on Data Engineering*, pages 996–1005, March 2010. DOI: 10.1109/icde.2010.5447738 107

Adel Nadjaran Toosi, Rodrigo N. Calheiros, and Rajkumar Buyya. Interconnected cloud computing environments: Challenges, taxonomy, and survey. *ACM Computing Surveys*, 47(1), pages 1–47, 2014. DOI: 10.1145/2593512 68

Haluk Topcuoglu, Salim Hariri, and Min-You Wu. Performance-effective and low-complexity task scheduling for heterogeneous computing. *IEEE Transactions on Parallel and Distributed Systems*, 13(3), pages 260–274, 2002. DOI: 10.1109/71.993206 24, 81

Guilherme Horta Travassos and Márcio de Oliveira Barros. Contributions of in virtuo and in silico experiments for the future of empirical studies in software engineering. In *Workshop on Empirical Software Engineering the Future of Empirical Studies in Software Engineering*, pages 117–130, 2003. 1

Radu Tudoran, Alexandru Costan, Gabriel Antoniu, and Hakan Soncu. TomusBlobs: Towards communication-efficient storage for MapReduce applications in Azure. In *12th IEEE/ACM International Symposium on Cluster, Cloud and Grid Computing (CCGrid)*, pages 427–434, 2012. DOI: 10.1109/ccgrid.2012.104 70

Spark Tutorial. Spark tutorial. https://spark.apache.org/docs/latest/, 2017. 110

Pongsakorn U.-chupala, Putchong Uthayopas, Kohei Ichikawa, Susumu Date, and Hirotake Abe. An implementation of a multi-site virtual cluster cloud. In *10th International Joint Conference on Computer Science and Software Engineering (JCSSE)*, pages 155–159, 2013. DOI: 10.1109/jcsse.2013.6567337 70

Karan Vahi, Ian Harvey, Taghrid Samak, Daniel K. Gunter, Kieran Evans, David H. Rogers, Ian J. Taylor, Monte Goode, Fabio Silva, Eddie Al-Shakarchi, Gaurang Mehta, Andrew Jones, and Ewa Deelman. A general approach to real-time workflow monitoring. In *Supercomputing (SC) Companion: High Performance Computing, Networking, Storage and Analysis (SCC)*, pages 108–118, 2012. DOI: 10.1109/sc.companion.2012.26 17

Wil M. P. van der Aalst, Mathias Weske, and Guido Wirtz. Advanced topics in workflow management: Issues, requirements, and solutions. *Transactions of the SDPS*, 7(3), pages 49–77, 2003. 19

Luis M. Vaquero, Luis Rodero-Merino, Juan Caceres, and Maik Lindner. A break in the clouds: Towards a cloud definition. *SIGCOMM Computer Communication Review*, 39(1), pages 50–55, December 2008. DOI: 10.1145/1496091.1496100 xv, 39

Guolu Wang, Jungang Xu, and Ben He. A novel method for tuning configuration parameters of spark based on machine learning. In *18th IEEE International Conference on High*

Performance Computing and Communications; 14th IEEE International Conference on Smart City; 2nd IEEE International Conference on Data Science and Systems, HPCC/SmartCity/DSS, pages 586–593, Sydney, Australia, December 12–14, 2016.   DOI: 10.1109/HPCC-SmartCity-DSS.2016.0088 105, 106, 110, 111

Jianwu Wang and Ilkay Altintas. Early cloud experiences with the kepler scientific workflow system. In *International Conference on Computational Science (ICCS)*, vol. 9, pages 1630–1634, 2012. DOI: 10.1016/j.procs.2012.04.179 34

Jianwu Wang, Daniel Crawl, and Ilkay Altintas. Kepler + hadoop: A general architecture facilitating data-intensive applications in scientific workflow systems. In *4th Workshop on Workflows in Support of Large-Scale Science*, pages 12:1–12:8, 2009. DOI: 10.1145/1645164.1645176 20, 32, 70

Jianwu Wang, Daniel Crawl, Shweta Purawat, Mai Nguyen, and Ilkay Altintas. Big data provenance: Challenges, state of the art and opportunities. In *IEEE International Conference on Big Data*, pages 2509–2516, October 2015. DOI: 10.1109/bigdata.2015.7364047 104

Jinbao Wang, Sai Wu, Hong Gao, Jianzhong Li, and Beng Chin Ooi. Indexing multi-dimensional data in a cloud system. In *ACM SIGMOD International Conference on Management of Data (SIGMOD)*, pages 591–602, 2010. DOI: 10.1145/1807167.1807232 76

Ke Wang, Xiaobing Zhou, Tonglin Li, Dongfang Zhao, Michael Lang, and Ioan Raicu. Optimizing load balancing and data-locality with data-aware scheduling. In *IEEE International Conference on Big Data*, pages 119–128, Washington, DC, October 27–30, 2014. 41, 44

Kewen Wang and Mohammad Khan. Performance prediction for Apache spark platform. In *HPCC/CSS/ICESS*, pages 166–173, IEEE, 2015. http://dblp.uni-trier.de/db/conf/hpcc/hpcc2015.html#WangK15 DOI: 10.1109/hpcc-css-icess.2015.246 106

P. Watson. A multi-level security model for partioning workflows over federated clouds. *Journal of Cloud Computing*, 1(1), pages 1–15, 2012. xv

Paul Watson, Hugo Hiden, and Simon Woodman. E-science central for CARMEN: Science as a service. *Concurrency and Computation: Practice and Experience*, 22(17), pages 2369–2380, 2010. DOI: 10.1002/cpe.1611 1

Marek Wieczorek, Radu Prodan, and Thomas Fahringer. Scheduling of scientific workflows in the askalon grid environment. *SIGMOD Record*, 34(3), pages 56–62, 2005. DOI: 10.1145/1084805.1084816 81, 90, 91

Philipp Wieder, Joe M. Butler, Wolfgang Theilmann, and Ramin Yahyapour. *Service Level Agreements for Cloud Computing*, Springer, 2011. DOI: 10.1007/978-1-4614-1614-2 32

Michael Wilde, Mihael Hategan, Justin M. Wozniak, Ben Clifford, Daniel S. Katz, and Ian T. Foster. Swift: A language for distributed parallel scripting. *Parallel Computing*, 37(9), pages 633–652, 2011. DOI: 10.1016/j.parco.2011.05.005 17

D. N. Williams, R. Drach, R. Ananthakrishnan, I. T. Foster, D. Fraser, F. Siebenlist, D. E. Bernholdt, M. Chen, J. Schwidder, S. Bharathi, A. L. Chervenak, R. Schuler, M. Su, D. Brown, L. Cinquini, P. Fox, J. Garcia, D. E. Middleton, W. G. Strand, N. Wilhelmi, S. Hankin, R. Schweitzer, P. Jones, A. Shoshani, and A. Sim. The earth system grid: Enabling access to multimodel climate simulation data. *Bulletin of the American Meteorological Society*, 90(2), pages 195–205, 2009. DOI: 10.1175/2008bams2459.1 65

Katherine Wolstencroft, Robert Haines, Donal Fellows, Alan R. Williams, David Withers, Stuart Owen, Stian Soiland-Reyes, Ian Dunlop, Aleksandra Nenadic, Paul Fisher, Jiten Bhagat, Khalid Belhajjame, Finn Bacall, Alex Hardisty, Abraham Nieva de la Hidalga, Maria P. Balcazar Vargas, Shoaib Sufi, and Carole A. Goble. The taverna workflow suite: Designing and executing workflows of web services on the desktop, Web or in the cloud. *Nucleic Acids Research*, 41(Webserver-Issue), pages 557–561, 2013. DOI: 10.1093/nar/gkt328 xv, 1, 18, 25, 34

Justin M. Wozniak, Timothy G. Armstrong, Ketan Maheshwari, Ewing L. Lusk, Daniel S. Katz, Michael Wilde, and Ian T. Foster. Turbine: A distributed-memory dataflow engine for extreme-scale many-task applications. In *1st ACM SIGMOD Workshop on Scalable Workflow Execution Engines and Technologies*, pages 5:1–5:12, 2012. DOI: 10.1145/2443416.2443421 1

Justin M. Wozniak, Timothy G. Armstrong, Michael Wilde, Daniel S. Katz, Ewing L. Lusk, and Ian T. Foster. Swift/t: Scalable data flow programming for many-task applications. In *ACM SIGPLAN Symposium on Principles and Practice of Parallel Programming*, pages 309–310, 2013. DOI: 10.1145/2517327.2442559 xv, 1, 11, 17, 25, 71, 76, 103

Sai Wu, Dawei Jiang, Beng Chin Ooi, and Kun-Lung Wu. Efficient B-tree based indexing for cloud data processing. *Proc. of the VLDB Endowment (PVLDB)*, 3(1–2), pages 1207–1218, 2010. DOI: 10.14778/1920841.1920991 76

Li Xu, Zhibin Zeng, and Xiucai Ye. Multi-objective optimization based virtual resource allocation strategy for cloud computing. In *IEEE/ACIS 11th International Conference on Computer and Information Science*, pages 56–61, 2012. DOI: 10.1109/icis.2012.74 40, 48

Nezih Yigitbasi, Theodore Willke, Guangdeng Liao, and Dick Epema. Towards machine learning-based auto-tuning of MapReduce. In *Modeling, Analysis and Simulation of Computer and Telecommunication Systems (MASCOTS), IEEE 21st International Symposium on*, pages 11–20, 2013. DOI: 10.1109/mascots.2013.9 105

Ustun Yildiz, Adnene Guabtni, and Anne H. H. Ngu. Business versus scientific workflows: A comparative study. In *IEEE Congress on Services, Part I, Services I*, pages 340–343, 2009. DOI: 10.1109/services-i.2009.60 14

Yijun Ying, Robert Birke, Cheng Wang, Lydia Y. Chen, and Natarajan Gautam. Optimizing energy, locality and priority in a MapReduce cluster. In *IEEE International Conference on Autonomic Computing*, pages 21–30, 2015. DOI: 10.1109/icac.2015.30 109

Jia Yu and Rajkumar Buyya. A taxonomy of workflow management systems for grid computing. *Journal of Grid Computing*, 3, pages 171–200, 2005. DOI: 10.1007/s10723-005-9010-8 11, 12, 26, 88

Zhifeng Yu and Weisong Shi. An adaptive rescheduling strategy for grid workflow applications. In *IEEE International Parallel and Distributed Processing Symposium (IPDPS)*, pages 1–8, 2007. DOI: 10.1109/ipdps.2007.370305 25, 81

L. Zadeh. Optimality and non-scalar-valued performance criteria. *IEEE Transactions on Automatic Control*, 8(1), pages 59–60, 1963. DOI: 10.1109/tac.1963.1105511 83

Matei Zaharia, Mosharaf Chowdhury, Michael J. Franklin, Scott Shenker, and Ion Stoica. Spark: Cluster computing with working sets. In *USENIX Workshop on Hot Topics in Cloud Computing (HotCloud)*, page 10, 2010a. 35, 38, 68

Matei Zaharia, Mosharaf Chowdhury, Michael J. Franklin, Scott Shenker, and Ion Stoica. Spark: Cluster computing with working sets. *HotCloud*, 10(1–7), page 95, 2010b. 104

Matei Zaharia, Mosharaf Chowdhury, Tathagata Das, Ankur Dave, Justin Ma, Murphy McCauley, Michael J. Franklin, Scott Shenker, and Ion Stoica. Resilient distributed datasets: A fault-tolerant abstraction for in-memory cluster computing. pages 1–14, 2012a. 104

Matei Zaharia, Mosharaf Chowdhury, Tathagata Das, Ankur Dave, Justin Ma, Murphy McCauly, Michael J. Franklin, Scott Shenker, and Ion Stoica. Resilient distributed datasets: A fault-tolerant abstraction for in-memory cluster computing. pages 1–14, 2012b. 36, 37

Wan Nazmee Wan Zainon and Paul Calder. Visualising phylogenetic trees. In *Australasian User Interface Conference*, vol. 50, pages 145–152, 2006. 1

Qi Zhang, Lu Cheng, and Raouf Boutaba. Cloud computing: State-of-the-art and research challenges. *Journal of Internet Services and Applications*, 1, pages 7–18, 2010. DOI: 10.1007/s13174-010-0007-6 32

Zhao Zhang, Kyle Barbary, Frank Austin Nothaft, Evan Sparks, Oliver Zahn, Michael Franklin, David Patterson, and Saul Perlmutter. Kira: Processing astronomy imagery using big data technology. *IEEE Transactions on Big Data*, pages 1–14, 2018. DOI: 10.1109/tbdata.2016.2599926 2, 35, 103

Dongfang Zhao, Chen Shou, Tanu Maliky, and Ioan Raicu. Distributed data provenance for large-scale data-intensive computing. In *IEEE International Conference on Cluster Computing (CLUSTER)*, pages 1–8, 2013. DOI: 10.1109/cluster.2013.6702685 77

Yong Zhao, Mihael Hategan, Ben Clifford, Ian T. Foster, Gregor von Laszewski, Veronika Nefedova, Ioan Raicu, Tiberiu Stef-Praun, and Michael Wilde. Swift: Fast, reliable, loosely coupled parallel computation. In *IEEE Congress on Services*, pages 199–206, 2007a. DOI: 10.1109/services.2007.63 15, 25, 32, 71

Yong Zhao, Michael Wilde, and Ian Foster. Virtual data language: A typed workflow notation for diversely structured scientific data. In *Workflows for e-Science*, pages 258–275, 2007b. DOI: 10.1007/978-1-84628-757-2_17 71

Yong Zhao, Ioan Raicu, and Ian T. Foster. Scientific workflow systems for 21st century, new bottle or new wine? In *IEEE Congress on Services, Part I, Services I*, pages 467–471, 2008. DOI: 10.1109/services-1.2008.79 20

Authors' Biographies

DANIEL C. M. DE OLIVEIRA

Daniel C. M. de Oliveira obtained his Ph.D. in Systems and Computation Engineering at COPPE/Federal University of Rio de Janeiro, Brazil, in 2012. His current research interests include scientific workflows, provenance, cloud computing, data scalable and intensive computing, high performance computing, and distributed and parallel databases. He serves or served on the program committee of major international and national conferences (VLDB17, IPAW16 and 18, SBBD 15-18, etc.) and is a member of IEEE, ACM, and the Brazilian Computer Society. In 2016, he received the Young Scientist scholarship from the State Agency for Research Financing of Rio de Janeiro, FAPERJ, and the Level 2 research productivity grant from CNPq. He supervised 5 doctoral theses and 13 master's dissertations and coordinated projects funded by CNPq and FAPERJ. He has 2,077 citations in Google Scholar, an h-index of 22 and 96 articles listed in DBLP (`http://dblp.uni-trier.de/pers/hd/o/Oliveira_0001:Daniel_de`).

JI LIU

Ji Liu is at Microsoft Research Inria Joint Centre and Zenith team. The latter is part of INRIA Sophia-Antipolis Mediterranee and LIRMM at Montpellier. His research interests include scientific workflow, big data, Cloud computing, and multisite management. He graduated from the Xidian University in 2011. Then, he obtained his master's degree (diplôme d'ingénieur) from Télécom SudParis in 2013 and Ph.D. in 2016 from University of Montpellier.

ESTHER PACITTI

Esther Pacitti is a professor of computer science at University of Montpellier. She is a senior researcher and co-head of the Zenith team at LIRMM, pursuing research in distributed data management. Previously, she was an assistant professor at University of Nantes (2002–2009) and a member of Atlas INRIA team. She obtained her "Habilitation à Diriger les Recherches" (HDR) degree in 2008 on the topic of data replication on different contexts (data warehouses, clusters and peer-to-peer systems). Since 2004 she has served or is serving as program committee member of major international conferences (VLDB, SIGMOD, CIKM, etc.) and has edited and co-authored several books. She has also published a significant amount of technical papers and journal papers in well-known international conferences and journals.

Printed in the United States
by Baker & Taylor Publisher Services